THE LAST CUP

HOCKEY, LIFE, LORD STANLEY AND THE TORONTO MAPLE LEAFS

BY

LARRY SWATUK

Dedication

*To the memory of
Russell and Winnie Swatuk*

*and to my coach and mentor
Terry Snyder*

1.

'Get the defribrillator!' The words echo around the nearly empty arena. Not my most dignified moment, I must say.

'C'mon Killer, stay with us!'

Killer - a kid's nickname. I mean really, how can that apply to this train wreck of a body, lying back flat on frozen pond, steam rising like a cooling slab of pie. Like a freshly minted corpse laid out for the undertaker. So nice and cool. Though, my skin is starting to itch. This damp cotton underwear starting to cloy, crystallize, and smell! Like somebody died. Somebody died! Now that's funny.

My life in hockey. And so it should end in death, a fitting end, don't you think? Don't we all dream of going out in the act. Doing what we most love to do? Viagra or no Viagra, a shag at my age is anything but dignified. More like two turtles with their shells wrong way round. But hockey - yes! You see, it's the blades. The blades give you dignity, no matter what age or how unfit. The ability to push off and glide, feel the breeze against your face, experience life at a pace far greater than your normal everyday turtle trawl down main street. That's two turtle metaphors in one paragraph: must be the dire situation I'm facing here, given that I'm on my back with no way up.

'Get his helmet off! Let's move. Let's move!' How do I know I'm in an arena where a team sport is being played? People say things twice. So, yes, pick up the pace, boys, pick up the pace! 80 is too the new 40! I'm too young to die! I'm too young to die!

'C'mon Jack, hold still!' That's my dad, he's trying to tighten my skates for me while I try to see around his giant head so I can watch cartoons. Saturday morning: Mighty Mouse, Heckle and Jeckle, The Alvin Show, Captain Kangaroo. Man, it's good to be a kid! Eating a piece of toast, crumbs falling all over my woolen hockey sweater, shoulder pads up around my ears. My dad's slicked down thick black hair smelling sweet as jam. The only problem with this picture is that I have to go to hockey. The pinging of the radiator reminding me that there's a world of cold and snow beyond the frosted windpane.

My dad was my coach. He used to stand on the back of the net next to his best friend, Clem. Clem was our manager, though I think mostly he just liked to hang around with my dad and shoot the breeze. Clem's coming over to shoot the breeze, he'd say to me, the words landing on the top of my head and filtering into my ears as though dropped from a great height. They didn't shoot the breeze at our games, though. Mostly they just laughed and smiled, especially when about half of us would fall over the little wooden boards that divided our game from the next one over. My dad's entire attitude about sport was to have fun. Years later when I'd come home from a game he'd tease me with 'Did you have fun cleaning the ice?' meaning, how many times did you fall down? As a tetchy teenager this used to bug the hell out of me, and, well, that was my dad's goal, to give himself a good chuckle by irritating his over-sensitive son.

'C'mon Killer! Don't be a pussy! Don't wuss out on us like some fairy!' This is guy talk. Men unable to verbally express their true feelings, i.e. that they are worried about their old buddy and hope he doesn't die right here on the spot making everyone feel helpless and emasculated, generally use hyper masculine, homophobic language. It's the verbal version of the man-hug, you know the one, where two guys hug each other then vigorously slap each other's backs twice. Slap Slap! Meaning, I like you a lot, maybe even love you, but I'm not gay.

'C'mon get his gear off.'

'What? Everything?'

'No, you idiot. The top half. These things have to attach directly to the bare skin.'

'Let's move, let's move.'

'Frig... let's get it done. Don't want to miss the start of the Leafs game.'

'C'mon, Doc. Less talk, more action!'

2.

The Toronto Maple Leafs. Or Maple Laffs as we've liked to call them for nigh on what, nearly my whole life. It's been 70 years since they last won a Stanley Cup. Everyone's had a cup or two or ten since the Leafs last did it in 1967. The Chicago Black Hawks under the steady hand of Joel Quenneville won a fistful. Meanwhile, the Leafs never even came close to a Cup final, let alone a win. My nephews ply their trade with the Leafs. Logan, the older one, was drafted by Toronto as a first rounder way back in 2019 out of Rimouski and he's been a first line centreman ever since. An 18 year NHL veteran. A present day Jean Beliveau - long, lean, powerful, intelligent, never injured, a rock - but playing for the Leafs. His younger brother, Andrew, took a different route. Typical goaltender. Like Jim Ralph once said in an interview with himself: 'How did you get to be a goalie, Jim?' 'Well, Jim, like any other goalie I guess. When I was 2 my mother accidentally dropped me on my head, and when I came to, I said "I be goalie!" and the rest is history.' The point being, I guess, that goalies are different kinds of cats. That's our Andrew. Never drafted. Never really liked hockey.

Preferred soccer. Loved to play goal in soccer mainly because of the colorful clobber and clown gloves. But a fierce competitor with a will to win and boundless self-confidence. He was a walk-on goaltender at St. FX and then stuck with the Leafs organization after an invitation to try out after a stellar career with the X-men. Floundered around a bit in St. John's as the second-string, but once he got his chance, following a season-ending knee injury to the number one, he's never looked back. Like his brother he's tough as nails, but unlike his brother, he's got a very short fuse. Enter his crease at your own peril.

Together, these two young boys, as I still like to call them, are clearly on to something this year. There's a sort of chemistry with this crew that's been lacking over the last little while. The addition late last year of Ian Keon and Donny Ellis, brought up for the final 10 games of the regular season from St John's, suggested that the 2036-37 season could be something special. The spitting image of their great grandfathers, these two kids can literally fly! This Leafs team bears a spooky resemblance to that 1967 squad: Ellis and Keon join the spawn of great Leafs past: Jim Pappin's, Marcel Pronovost's, and Shakey Walton's great grandkids also play on this team. And while there's no Frank Mahovlich or Eddie Shack, Bobby Baun or Johnny Bower, there are certainly the same sorts of personalities and capabilities on this edition of the Leafs. Or so it seems to me. Importantly, there's the natural sniper, or, I should say, snipers plural. There's the rookie son of Nazim Kadri, with all of dad's talent but way more desire. You will never see young Naz Jr. wandering around the blue line - his own or the other team's - with one hand on the stick. Like his dad, he played for the London Knights and gave every goalie in the league a sunburn from turning the goal light on. Pure talent, and an excellent complement to Ellis and Keon on 'the kid line'. And there's Frank Chan, first identified by the Leafs Asian scouts as a 12 year old playing club hockey for Chengde City, brought to Canada by his uncle, carefully cultivated through the Metro Toronto system, drafted by Kitchener in the OHL, and ultimately the Leafs, who traded for the opportunity to select him. In junior he filled the net. Leaf scouts said he reminded them of a combination of Josh Ho Sang and Jeff Skinner: balance, speed, uncanny puck sense, and a quick release. As Andrew often remarked, Chan had the sort of shot that, if it caught you on the shoulder it would sting like a mother fucker, which was different from a guy like Horton whose heavy shot, if it caught you in the same place, would make your whole body ache for days. Chan and Kadri were an awesome one-two punch, not to mention great fun to watch.

Can I be frank here? I've never liked the Leafs. Not even after years of watching my nephews play from the comfort of my rinkside seats at the Samsung-Blackberry Centre out in what used to be Milton, but what is now just another piece of the Big Smoke that is the GTA. Having grown up on the Detroit River in Windsor, I was all things Red Wings, and Lions and Tigers and Pistons. But unlike the other teams, most of the Red Wings players were Canadians who lived in Windsor and often stopped by our family roadhouse tavern for a drink and some fish 'n chips. Paul Henderson was one of my dad's best friends, even after he got traded to Toronto. That all changed once Foster Hewitt's 'Henderson scores!' turned him into a national symbol and forced Paul to run off to find the Lord. Not that there's anything wrong with that; it just somehow irreparably damaged the friendship between him and my dad. Plenty of Wings were always hanging around our hotel, and plenty of free tickets came my way over the years. So, I loved the Wings. Funnily enough, though, my dad loved the Leafs. He was a Tronna boy through and through, and carried that Maple Leaf in his heart down to Riverside (which was the name of our town before we got swallowed up by Windsor the year the Leafs last won the Cup and Canada had its first Expo), along with my mother. They got married in 1952, the same year my grandmother took over the mortgage - sight unseen - on a waterfront property in Riverside, Ontario and commandeered her entire family into the hospitality business.

I was born at a good time for a hockey fan but not so good a time for a Red Wings fan. I got to see Bobby Orr's first game ever played against Detroit at the Olympia Stadium. I also got to see the transformation of the game with the switch to 12 teams from the original six. Six additional teams diluted the league's talent pool considerably and gave birth to the 100 point scorer. Lots of goals meant lots of fun for a kid, but plenty of anxiety and lost hairs for coaches and managers around the league. The big trade that brought the Big M to Detroit but sent my dad's buddy Paul to Toronto was all part of that excitement. I once saw Frank Mahovlich score a hat trick on a Sunday night against the Los Angeles Kings, where Eddie Shack had turned up. Frank scored many a hat-trick, but what was interesting about this one was the puck never once touched his stick: one off the back, one off the shin pad, one off the skate blade and bob's your uncle! Bragging rights for the night.

I too scored many a hat-trick, but at my age, they are so difficult to remember. There was one time when... oh, man, I can sort of see it but it's like watching a hockey game played in a thick deep fog. A lot of things are difficult to remember when you hit 80 - like your home address! - but what remains easy is the date when the Leafs last won the Cup! 1967 is forever etched, particularly for Leaf fans, like a deep facial scar: forever visible, often itchy and linked to unwanted memories. Of course, the Wings had their share of unwanted memories such as the 'Darkness Under Harkness' era. That was back when the Broad Street Bullies brawled their way to the Stanley Cup, feeding American bloodlust with an entirely new brand of hockey. My father would roll his eyes and say, 'Yeesh... bring back the era of the straight stick!' Then he'd go on and talk about the Kraut Line in Boston and all of his heroes of bygone eras. Like me, now. But what else is there to do when you're holed up in a hospital bed, plugged and tubed and lubed for who knows what kind of upcoming scientific experiment.

3.

GAME 1

The game was not going well. Already down 3-0 and only midway through the second period. The bench was eerily quiet. The Kid Line - Ellis on right wing, Keon at centre, and Kadri on left - was out there playing tiddly winks, hemmed into their own end by this latest edition of Firewagon hockey Habs style. Where's the grit? Logan thought to himself, as he watched his brother make one acrobatic save after another. Were it not for Andrew, we'd be down by 6 or 7 at least. Game 1 of the Stanley Cup final in Montreal, the year-long number one team, and the old building was rocking. Beads of sweat trickled down the sides of his face. Hockey in June. This is ridiculous, he thought, then caught himself. C'mon man, focus. I've waited my whole life for this moment. Let's not waste this opportunity. Then, a tap on the shoulder, the Coach in his ear.

'Time to step up, Log. Let's get 'er done.'

Over the boards he went, as Ellis chipped the puck down the ice to relieve the pressure and the Kids made a beeline for the bench.

Shakey was the first man in on the D deep in the Montreal zone, Logan lurking shark-like waiting on a loose puck, a lucky bounce, ready to sink his teeth into the play. Montreal's D-man feinted to go behind the net, hoping Walton would take the bait, then curled back up along the far boards with the puck having successfully shaken the forechecker. But not Logan, who took one long stride and pasted his man into the boards, taking the puck from him at the same time. He cycled it back to Walton in the corner who whipped a one-timer into the slot to Wiener who ripped a shot into the short-side top corner. The crowd went silent. Logan felt a sharp shock of adrenaline. That's better. On the board. In the Stanley Cup Finals.

But the game didn't much improve after that. And when horn sounded to signal the end to the game, the Habs had come out on top with a solid 6-2 win.

Later, the media scrum. Captain Cash, 18 year NHL veteran, how did it feel to play in your first Stanley Cup Final game? And why did you and the Leafs suck so badly? That was pretty much the order and tenor of the questions fired time and again at Logan who sat patiently, kitted out in Italy's finest, his thick but slightly greying flow aglisten, calmly answering again and again: this is a dream come true. It may be our only chance. We have to make the most of it. It's a team game. We have to play better, particularly in our own end. We must give 110%. Canned questions; canned answers.

What Logan really felt, though, was that despite the loss this was the absolutely coolest thing that had ever happened to him in his whole life. All those years out on the driveway firing puck after puck after puck. All those years playing one on one against Andrew on their knees in the carpeted basement with their mini sticks. All those hours of travel to and from arenas all through the Maritimes and, as a junior, also in Quebec. All those hours spent in houses and bars and lounges playing table hockey, miming the great hockey announcers: 'He shoots! He scores! Logan Cash scores in overtime to win the Stanley Cup for the Chicago Blackhawks!' Yep, the Hawks. Patrick Kane was his favorite player growing up. He still remembered the time he answered the doorbell at home in Halifax, he must have been about 10 or 11. It was DHL with a package for Logan Cash. Really? He still could feel the excitement rise. Sign here please. So, he signed and in the package was an autographed photograph of Pat Kane: 'To Logan, all the Best, Patrick Kane'. His uncle had organized it through his friend who was the coach of the Hawks at the time, who had retired some years back as the winningest coach in NHL history, whose giant portrait hung from the rafters in Chicago Stadium, Coach Q sporting the world's biggest moustache. The excitement was overwhelming. He could still feel it, that little kid excitedness. Right now. Though he was expected to be the mature team leader, the distinguished veteran to help steady the troops as they went into battle for a shot at their first championship as a team, and the first for the franchise in 70 years! Who wouldn't be little kid excited at the prospects of all that?! But, for the media, for the public, Logan remained poker faced, showing a bit of his real disappointment at the loss and at their poor performance, but betraying nothing else. He would leave all of the emotion to his brother.

Andrew had gone ballistic. Not once, not twice, but three times: once on the ice and twice in the dressing room between periods. Never one to hold back, following Montreal's 6th goal, giving them an insurmountable 6-1 lead late in the second period, Andrew had flipped off his mask and charged his own bench, threatening them all with his goalie stick, like a knight out for a joust.

'What is wrong with you fuckers!? Get your heads out of your asses! Jesus boys, I'm all alone out here! What am I, cannon fodder?!'

Cameras and cell phones were flashing madly all around the arena, video being shot of the crazy goaltender losing his nut. Andrew didn't care. If he did care, he wouldn't have been a goalie, he wouldn't have been a professional hockey player, he wouldn't have been out there for everyone to point their fingers at and to pronounce his fate with a thumbs up or a thumbs down. He was a competitor bar none, and if his teammates weren't up to it, he would make it well known to them regarding his perspective on that. Another long string of metaphors and expletives followed along until he simply ran out of gas. At last he stopped and glared at them one by one, then circled back, retrieved his helmet and mask, flipped his hair back, donned the mask, and resumed his position between the pipes, leaning forward with his hands on the tops of his pads. As if nothing had happened. Or everything. Whatever. Game on!

Things were much worse and far less operatic in the dressing room. At the end of the first period, down 3-1 but outshot 20-5, Andrew quietly placed his stick in the rack, his mask and gloves at his stall, and charged Pronovost and Horton each in turn, trying to punch their lights out.

'First string defence! First string defence! My ass! First string pussies! You fucking assholes!' He was shouting at the top of his lungs. Everyone else sat or stood quietly as he went at Pronovost first, took an awkward swing which was parried away, then turned on Horton, where a wrestling match suddenly began. The rest of the team backed out of the way, letting the two go at it, looking like teenage mutant ninja turtles, with their giant padding which made their heads and hands look so small. Once the garbage can in the middle of the room toppled over, the boys figured it was time to break things up, so in went Shaw and Prince - the second line of defence - to pry their teammates apart.

Between the second and third periods, he was less aggressive, merely smashing his goalie stick into the big metal garbage can, sending it skidding across the room, then bashing it again and again until his $300 goalie stick snapped where the shaft joined the paddle. But it all seemed to work. Or something worked anyway. The

Leafs dominated play in the third period, 'winning' the period 1-0, which as Logan made clear before they went back onto the ice, was their objective: let's play hard, win the period, you never know what can happen, play hard boys, play hard, grind it out, win the battles, at the very least we'll set the tone for game 2.

4.

'Look at 'im! The bionic man!'

'Is it man or machine?! How's she goin' fella?'

The boys. Peach and Hutchie. Both wearing Maple Leaf jerseys. If you wanted an image of 'positive attitude' you'd want a picture of these two old timers. They've been my teammates in one way or another for more than 50 years. Naturally they're the first ones to visit. Only too happy to go charging into difficult situations where many a lesser man fears to tread, fearing, for the most part, an image of their own future. Given the tubes and whatnot, I'm reduced to a sort of blink, nod, my body bloated from all the fluids it has retained.

'Good to see you Killer!' Says Hutchie. 'Thought we'd lost ya there for a while. Don't know what I'd do without my winger.'

I've not been told what happened, and I'm not even sure how I am or what my prognosis is. I sort of feel like I'm in a fishbowl looking out at a slow moving and definitely confusing world. The old brain seems to be functioning well enough, though, if nothing else is.

'You missed the game last night,' says Hutchie. His 22 year old grandson, Donald, is the fourth line centreman for the Leafs. None of grampa's sniper skills, but all of grampa's sheer determination. 'The boys were outclassed. Andrew kept the score respectable.'

'Logan looked good. Logged a lot of icetime. Assisted on the first goal.'

'Young Naz scored the other, but everybody was in the minus column. They'll have to be a lot better moving forward if they hope to win the Cup. The Russkies were unbelievable.'

'Titov potted three. Had a couple helpers too.'

'Andrew was up to his old antics. Hilarious!'

'It's all over the Google. I'm sure he's gone viral.'

Hockey talk. How men communicate. Like the gurgle of a room full of happy babies. I wish I could participate in this conversation, but all I can do is wince and make gurgling sounds of my own. No happy baby this, tho! My throat is as dry as a bone and this friggin tube chafes like a cheap pair of jockeys. Where is the nurse anyway? I'd love to know what the heck is going on.

'We'll get 'em in the next game. The boys looked great in the third period. That should give them confidence, set them up nicely for the rest of the series.'

I'm wondering why Hutch didn't go up to Montreal for the game. It's a question that'll have to go unasked.

'You should be in good enough shape for tomorrow's game. We'll come and watch it with you.'

Ah, there's my answer. All for one, and all that sort of stuff.

5.

'Nurse!' I screamed inside my own head. I pressed the bloody button, the drug button, but there seemed to be no reward. What would Pavlov say about this?! Nurse! Mother fuck this sucks.

I was the Wayne Gretzky of Africa. No, really. It's true. I know I'm cooped up here in a hospital bed, full of drugs and tubes and whatnot. But I'm not hallucinating. At least not at the moment. You see, back before I was an old codger I had a life. I wasn't just the old dude slow-walking the mall. Or the old dude giving another old dude the slip with the world's slowest ever deke to squirt one off the end of my stick into the far corner because yet another old dude is in net and he can't go down. Roller hockey, the inline kind, that's what I played as a member of the Mukwa Leafs during my years in Botswana.

You see, en route to becoming a world famous professional ice hockey player, preferably with the Detroit Red Wings, I got slightly detoured and became an academic. So, in between my various hockey playing forays, I taught for a living, spending a large chunk of my life in Africa. That's where my wife, Mary Adams, is right now. I think.

'Here, try these on. They may be a bit small. They're Lena's.' That's Sandy talking, the mad genius behind the Mukwa Leafs. Lena is his 14 year old daughter and I'm to wear her inline skates. We're in Cape Town 'practising'. I put the word in quotation marks because, well, we're just a rag tag bunch of expatriates come together to contest for the inline championship of South Africa. I should also put 'bunch' in quotation marks too, since we're only five players all told: there's me and fellow Canadians Karl Morrison and Kevin Thomson. Kevin's our goalie. Karl's a totally zen fellow forward who 9 times out of 10 would emerge from a corner scrum both unscathed and with the puck. Together we filled the opponents' nets over the course of that tournament, much to the amazement of everyone including ourselves. On D we had Sandy and Peter Dow, both Americans by birth. Sandy always pretended to be from Canada, often quizzing me about my own life growing up in Windsor, so that he could poach facts for himself. He'd moved to Maun, in the Okavango Delta, in 1968 and over time became a well respected carpenter who worked primarily with Mukwa wood, building all the funky, highly durable furniture for high end camps in the Delta. In the early '90s he got the bright idea to build a rink, out of cement, on his property which bordered the Thamalakane River. Peter lived in Gaborone and was married to Unity Dow, the first woman Supreme Court judge of Botswana. Peter played the whole tournament in his street clothes using a wrong-handed stick. A bit later in the tournament we picked up a fifth player - Mark Barr, a South African strawberry farmer from up near Clanwilliam in the Western Cape. Mark, who like many a player I was later to learn, could skate forward in a straight line but do little else, spared only Sandy, while the rest of us played every minute of every game.

'What about a stick?'

'A stick?' Sandy squinted at me and then looked around as though this was the strangest question anyone had ever asked. We were milling around an unevenly asphalted parking lot waiting our turn at an open air rink that stood on a hill overlooking the newly built Victoria and Albert Waterfront complex. Complete with boards, for the life of me I could not figure out what this rink was doing here. Sandy didn't know and didn't care. 'If they build it, we will come,' he said and smiled conspiratorially.

'Hey, ask that guy over there. Maybe he'll sell you one of his. So I walked over to where a team of men slightly younger than me were putting away their kit.

'Do you know where I can get a stick?' I asked.

'Sticks are very hard to come by around here,' he said.

No introductions. This is guys in action. Straight to the point. No embellishments.

'Would you sell me one of yours?' He had a few laying visibly in the back of his Land Cruiser.

'Sell?' I could see that he was both skittish about selling something hard to come by, but keen to make a killing on a captive buyer. 'Sure. I'll sell you one for 300 rands.' This is 1997, so that would have been around $50 - cheap by today's standards, but quite outlandish for the time and place. What else could I do?

'Deal.'

Poured concrete is murder on wheels - and knees, elbows, wrists, hands, etc. I had never skated on inline wheels before and with my toes cramped up in Lena's skates, I at first hobbled around the rink like a new born foal, the stick providing balance so that I resembled, in all its grace, a three-legged stove.

'How do you stop?' I asked.

'Just turn real quick,' said Sandy. Something more easily said than done. But, rather quickly, I got the hang of things, backward and forward were fine; as a skill, the quick stop was still a long ways off. The sound of the sticks and the hard orange ball banging off the boards brought my Canadianness flooding back to me. I had been in Africa almost continuously for 4 years and thought my hockey playing days were long gone. But on that sunny December day at the southern tip of Africa, those sweet sounds brought me back, had me fall in love with the game, albeit this modified version of it, all over again.

The tournament was being held at the Bellville Velodrome, about a 30 minute drive from downtown Cape Town, and about 40 minutes from where I was staying with my good friends, the Vales, in Muizenberg. Karl and Kevin were staying with Sandy's ex-wife in

Wynberg, while Sandy and his girlfriend, Ruth, were bunking out with Peter somewhere near the venue.

Game 1 was a Friday night and we were due on the floor at 8pm. I spent most of that day trying to sort out some sort of protective gear for myself. In the end, I purchased a skateboarding helmet, knee pads and elbow pads, and cricket batting gloves. It was the best I could do. Which was no worse than the rest of my teammates, who had a bit of this and a bit of that, but we all looked a rag tag bunch. Put it this way, we made the Bad News Bears look like the New York Yankees.

'Sandy, do we have any sweaters?'

'Sweaters?' Again with the squint and look around as though I had asked him about the meaning of life, or whether this was a good place to drill for oil. 'Ya, I've got some t-shirts here.'

He rummaged through his kit bag and produced a small stack of t-shirts that had false tuxedo fronts. On the back he had magic-markered in our numbers: 1 through 6. A very deliberate circle drawn around each number.

'Here,' he said to me. 'You can be number one.'

The arena was packed and had a raucous atmosphere. Not only were there two rinks down on the main floor, but kids of all ages were whizzing around the velodrome, descending from top to bottom in a nano second and stopping on a dime. I watched these kids very closely, trying to pick up any tip available to the naked eye. This was the South African National

Championships of inline hockey and there were clubs from most of the provinces, a few from Namibia and then there was us, the Mukwa Leafs of Botswana. There were divisions all the way up to over-30s and all the way down to under-8s. We were in the over-30 or 'seniors' division, contesting against teams from Gauteng, Western Cape and Eastern Cape province. In the end, we also earned our first international cap as Team Botswana when we played, and handily defeated, the senior South African team in an international friendly.

8pm came and went, as did 9, 10 and 11. Organization obviously wasn't the SA Inline Association's strong suit. By the time we got out on the floor for our first game, which was against Gauteng Province, it was almost midnight. We'd been milling about the rinks for almost 5 hours, anxiously awaiting our turn.

'Will you look at that!' I said nodding my head in the direction of the other team's bench.

'Ya, what about it?' This was Karl. Nothing ever fazed Karl.

'They look like a real team! There's what... 13 guys on the bench. And look at the friggin pads on them.' In truth, they looked like, well, like what an inline team should look like I guess. As opposed to us, the Bad News Bears from the bushes of Botswana. So, it shouldn't have surprised me when they scoffed and mocked us in the warm up. But it did. It pissed me off. Riled me up. We needed a strategy.

'Listen guys, I've been in this set up before. They've got 3 full lines. We've got no spares. Their strategy will be to tire us out, no doubt. So we need a strategy of our own. This is my idea. We try to throw them off their game, rile them up, make them mad at us so they take penalties. I've done this before. Take one for the team sort of thing. If we happen to score first, if I score first, I'm going to ride my stick Tiger Williams style in front of their bench. That will drive them crazy. Then, well, we hang on for the ride. Whattaya think?'

'Coo-ool,' said Sandy.

It couldn't have gone more to plan. I won the opening face off and drew it back to Peter who flipped it high in the air toward the other team's end. I chased it down, got their first and in one swift motion fired it into the net before crashing at full speed into the boards. That would become my main stopping technique over the course of the next few days. So, I whooped it up and yee ha'd my way past the Gauteng bench which pissed them off to no end. They spent the balance of the game trying to kill me.

Let me put it this way: Canadian hockey sense more than makes up for manpower. Karl and I not only out played, but badly out thought our opponents. Sandy and Peter were stellar at the back, basically just keeping their forwards to the outside and Kevin was rock solid in net. Final score, at 110am, Mukwa Leafs 10, Gauteng Lions 1. I scored 6, Karl scored 3 and Peter chipped in with 1 from the blueline - a seeing eye grounder that swirled its way through numerous skates before landing in the net. Having thrashed the vaunted Lions, we not only became the talk of the tournament, but the adopted darlings of underdog lovers everywhere.

The worst part about the win was no beer! It had been steaming hot in that rink. Kind of reminded me of summer hockey, where you'd go to the rink in your shorts, tank top and flip flops, sweat it out for an hour in a foggy musty smelling rink, bracket all of that with a lot of nonsense and trash talk, then repair to the bar, each guy ordering his own pitcher of beer with ice in it, and watch the interminable playoffs for Lord Stanley's Cup. But we hadn't figured on not finishing our game until after the restaurants and bars had closed! What a catastrophe! There is nothing as satisfying as a post-game beer, even at 10 in the morning. It doesn't mean we always drink beer at 10 in the morning. Not always, anyway. Especially now that we've all got one foot in the grave. A beer only means a dozen more trips to the can, for some of us with aching prostates, that's a thought too scary to bear.

Well, it could wait. In the meantime, there were the team pictures to be snapped around the scoreboard. This is an era of film, remember, that means pre-digital cameras. I still have the 6x4 somewhere: the big 10 the big 1 and on either side, me with 6 digits up, Karl with 3, Peter with 1, Sandy with a huge smile and those whacky tinted prescription safety goggles I'm sure he wears while in his workshop at home in Maun, and Kevin lying sideways under the scoreboard, pads stacked, head resting on his hand, looking for all the world like a guy who had a day off, a walk in the park, was out on a lark. The score was huge, to be sure, but we had to fight and claw for it. I can't tell you how many times Karl and I were mugged, one guy getting me in a head lock and trying to pile drive me into the cement floor. We were bruised but not beaten. We would live to play again. In theory our next game was at 2pm, i.e. in 13 hours. With the way things went today, your guess is as good as mine regarding when it would really kick off.

Kevin, Karl and I piled ourselves and our limited amount of gear into the Vale's VW microbus, and we headed off back toward False Bay. A well earned sleep in our very near futures.

Sleep, of course, was hard to come by. Adrenalin coursing wildly through my veins. The post-game rush. I could never sleep after intense sport. If this was Canada, I'd be sitting on the couch drinking beer, eating leftover something or other and channel surfing, depending on the era it could be Carson, Letterman or The Daily Show, and in the world of 24/7 sport, the Blue Jays in 30 on Sportsnet or the loop of overnight information offered up on TSN's Sportsdesk. But this was South Africa in the late 1990s, so it was simply two beers rummaged from the big fridge in the main house drunk out back poolside next to my bedroom in the little granny cottage. A still, star filled night, both too late and too early for the cacophony of dogs that is suburban Africa.

'So? How'd it go?' This was Peter Vale, making himself a coffee - instant with three heaping teaspoons full of cremora. As I watched him scoop this toxic waste into his cup and begin to quietly stir it into the mix, I scratched my head and said 'Ten One.'

'For them?' He said with some surprise.

'For us,' I said. 'You should have seen it. It was a thing of beauty.' I hobbled over to the counter, Peter eyeing me warily but saying nothing. My hips were loudly protesting their role in my inability to configure either a 'very sharp turn', or 'a tight circle'. While the rest of me was mildly protesting the mauling I had undergone at the hands of a mad pride of Gauteng Lions.

'Ten one! Great! What time are the games today?'

'I think 2 and 8. But we didn't get onto the floor last night until almost midnight, so I'm not sure what will happen today. Anyway, I plan to be there around noon. I've gotta fetch Karl and Kevin from Wynberg, so I'll head out around quarter past eleven.' It was currently 830am and I'd had about 5 hours sleep.

'We'll come watch. See how Canadians get things done. By the way, something came in the mail for you yesterday.'

'A Christmas present?' Suddenly I was perked up. 'Where is it?'

'In the front room, on the table.'

Trying to mask both my excitement and my sore ass, I sauntered off toward the living room. Beth and Dan, PV's and Louise's kids, were sitting on the couch trying to out-stare each other. Each wore a determined look, like cranky-faced teddies, cute as buttons really. They ignored me as I walked in, but gave up the game when I picked up the small package, turning it over in my hands.

'What do you think this is, eh?' I said to them.

'Christmas presents!' They said in joyous unison.

Inside was a Christmas card with dashed greetings from my oldest and best friend, Ged, along with, yep, a Hockey News. The kids went back to their own game, and I, leafing through the pages, went back to mine.

6.

The Velodrome parking lot was packed. The facility stood on a rocky outcrop of the Durbanville Hills, a non-descript suburban set-up complete with competing shopping malls and a circuit of gated communities. In amidst this developer's legoland were the remnants of the original settlements, small working class homes, a links style golf course, and off in the distance the old main road leading one way out into the hinterland and the other way, across the N1 highway and on into the Bellville CBD, itself chock a block with service sector enterprise: battery shops, car repair, eyeglass huts, and so on. As I manoevered the microbus into a parking space, I could feel the dark shadow of a groin pull pass across my lap. Better strap myself up, I said out loud, but not meaning to.

'What?' said Kevin.

'Nothing, just a bit sore from last night.'

On the main floor there were two rinks: a smaller one for all teams with players either below 15 years of age, or over 30; and a larger one for the older teens and open divisions. The open division was a mix of hot-shot late teenagers and older players who had played some sort of professional or semi-professional ice or inline hockey and who still wanted to compete at the top level, this usually included the coaches of the club teams. Guys in their 20s who had played Junior in Kamloops or Val d'or, found their way to the Oberliga in Germany or the FFHG Deux in France and eventually to inline hockey in Europe. Imagine playing pro in Barcelona! Who would not want to do that? I had once played Open Division with the Otjiwarango Scorpions in the annual Swakopmund tournament in Namibia. This was before they outlawed playing in more than one division. The Scorpions only had one spare so were happy to take me on. The Mukwa Leafs never had enough players of a certain age and talent to compete in that division. We had lots of under-12s, but as teens these kids all disappeared from Maun as their parents packed them off to boarding schools in South Africa and beyond. The pace was fast in the Open Division and I held my own among what seemed, at times, like a pack of wild dogs. Like I said, Canadian hockey sense takes you a long way among a crowd of energetic but poorly schooled younger players. This is not to criticize the coaches of these clubs - all of them drawn from either Canada or Europe and paid handsome salaries to train the next generation of inline talent. But there's no substitute for having learned your chops on the firemen-flooded park rinks, frozen ponds and lakes of wintry Canada, where you were schooled by older boys who themselves had been at it for their whole lives. And then there was road hockey and tennis court hockey and drive-way hockey. Anywhere there was a flat surface, you would find kids playing hockey. For the rest of the world, a flat surface means soccer, but in Canada it means 'Crosby gets the puck, he dekes one man, now another, he's over the blue line, he shoots, he scores!' spit and snot flying as we narrated our own games, paused to move the nets whenever a car came down the road, learned to use two sticks like chopsticks to fish tennis balls out of the sewers, and roll them around with your shoe to get the wet and stink off them before carrying on. Losing balls and pucks in snow banks on streets and lakes and parks, only to find them all again when the spring thaw came. Like Robertson Davies says, it's bred in the bone.

'Hey!'

'Hey! My ma-aaan!' said Sandy. 'Sleep well?'

'Pretty good, yeh. You?'

'Not bad. Not bad.'

Not wanting to give anything away, eh. The worst thing a hockey player can do is complain about an injury. Got a problem? Keep it to yourself, you wuss. On the other hand, it's ok to demonstrate an ache or pain, which would solicit a knowing, sympathetic 'hey, you ok?' To which you would then just blow it off, like it's nothing. And, well, really, it is nothing; nothing out of the ordinary. It's part of the game, and if something isn't sore, you aren't trying hard enough. Of course, we bring most of this pain upon ourselves. Like playing in a major competition without proper padding and skates that are two sizes too small. That's just asking for it, as the saying goes. But being better than the other team while looking like clowns and fools can only get you into trouble too. Officially this is a non-contact sport. You can't slide on concrete. But that didn't stop the Lions from hacking, slashing, elbowing, headlocking, mauling, and generally bullying us at every turn. Their inability to control their emotions led to their downfall, as the non-stop parade to the penalty box helped us immensely. The Mukwa Leafs learned many lessons from that game: one, we could compete - while we perhaps looked out of place, we actually fit right in; two, winning wasn't going to be easy - we were outnumbered and outweighed by sides that were only too happy to bend the rules; and three, wooden boards and a cement floor could wreak havoc on an unpadded body - some discretion was necessary if a hip or knee replacement wasn't to be in my near future.

Mukwa Leafs? You may ask. Why the hell were we called the Mukwa Leafs? Sandy, our founder, inspirational leader, and Massachusetts-born wanna be Canadian, who turned Mukwa wood into luxury furniture, saw a natural fit between the sources of his livelihood (Mukwa wood), his passion (hockey), and his fantasized citizenship (Canadian - let's be honest, not even Americans want to be American when they're overseas, and not holding a weapon). Combine this with a little bit of marijuana shared among friends under Africa's starry skies and a name is born. We didn't actually start to look like the Toronto Maple Leafs until the early 2000s when Sandy bought a dozen Leaf home jerseys and had 'Mukwa Leafs' stenciled in blue into the centre of the big white Maple Leaf. In the wake of the South African inline championships, we also began to amass all sorts of gear, much of it sourced by me during my occasional return trips to southern Ontario and the Maritimes. I'd come home for a few weeks in the Canadian summer and take up a collection of used sticks and gear from my friends, who always had an extra pair of gloves or elbow pads or shin pads lying around the garage. I would Sherpa all of this stuff back to the bushes where, upon arrival, I felt like Santa on Christmas day! But being properly kitted out was a long way away from day 2 of the SA championships in Belleville.

'Who do we play today?' We were milling around a long bench that served as our 'change room', right in the middle of the hubbub. An under-8 game was underway on our rink and like little kids playing hockey everywhere, wherever the bright orange ball went so skated everyone. They looked like iron filings directed across a white sheet of paper via a magnet held underneath; remember that grade school experiment?! Unlike the Tim Bits kids games held between periods at Junior games, when one of these kids falls on concrete he or she doesn't take out about six others while skidding and twirling slowly down the ice. They just hit and stick.

'Eastern Cape,' said Sandy, which meant absolutely nothing to me. I knew nothing about any of these teams. They all looked the same. The guys were all giants and looked every inch a proper team. Given my 1 game of experience, I could only suspect more of the same.

Today, everything was on schedule. 2 pm and we were on the floor. Sandy had managed to recruit Mark Bahr over night, so we were 5 skaters this time round. Peter Vale stood next to where I was sitting getting ready to go on the rink.

'Watch him, Dan. This is what Canadian hockey players must do before they go on the ice. They must remove their face.'

Dan, being 6, was quite interested in all of this.

'You see, first you take off your eyes and then you remove your teeth.'

I had simply taken off my glasses and deposited them in one shoe, and my dental plate, which I deposited in the other shoe, placing them neatly under the bench. Then I smiled my gap toothed smile, revealing my two missing teeth. Dan thought this was absolutely amazing. Still smiling I popped on my little round skateboarder's helmet, my virtually useless cricket gloves, picked up my over-priced piece of lumber, tapped my shins which were protected by soccer shin pads, and off I went.

The game started poorly. Within five minutes of the start we were down 2-0. These guys were no better than the Gauteng Lions, but we were clearly flat. Quite a crowd had gathered to watch, and all around the boards people were standing two-deep. It had a slightly surreal element to it, maybe because we were all still half asleep.

'C'mon boys, let's play smart. Stop running around chasing the puck. Stay in position and let the play come to you. Hold our shape.'

Then it was 3-0. I could hear Ruth from the bench: 'Fucking hell.' The end of the first of two periods couldn't have come fast enough for us. We were sluggish, wishy washy. We were half of the 7 dwarfs: grumpy, sleepy, dopey and bashful. If it was left to us to get us out of this funk, I think we would have failed. But often times the other team does you a favour. A 3-0 lead is a terrible lead to try to hold on to in a hockey game. You need the 4th goal to really cement your advantage. 2-0 forces you to play with a bit more desperation. As the saying goes, they score one and they're back in the game. So you keep your attention and your work rate up. But 3-0 lead often evaporates because it looks big enough to be insurmountable, so teams often ease off, go to sleep, get lazy. Your prima donna players start floating out near centre wanting to pad their stats. If you are down 3-0 and can get one early enough in the final period, you can often turn the momentum into your favour, and your opponent will find it very hard to get out of their funk and back to the hard work that got them the lead in the first place.

So, up 3-0 against this rag tag squad, the Eastern Capers starting dogging it, guys floating out around centre. And suddenly there was more space for me and Karl to manouevre, to wheel and deal. We got rolling from a set piece. I dropped back to the point with the plan being that Karl would draw the ball back to me and I would let one rip. Sandy would run interference in front of the net and Peter would hold the fort on the far side of the blue line. The rink was hot even though the Velodrome ceiling was hundreds of feet above us. I was leaking sweat like mad. Every time I tilted my head forward a steady stream would pour forth like a dripping faucet. It stung my eyes. I shook my head and caught sight of Peter, Louise and their kids Dan and Beth, as well as Ruth, Lena and Lena's mom, Sandy's ex-wife, Karen Ross, standing about 5 feet away from me shouting encouragement. This often happens in games. You tune out the crowd. It's simply white noise, sometimes so loud you can barely hear a word anyone says on the bench. But at particular moments you will tune in to a voice or a face, hear them or see them clear as day. When this happens it feels like a wake up call. Like you are more aware of your surroundings, like you've just gotten a shot of adrenalin. Everything seems crystal clear at moments like that. It lasts perhaps for only a second or two, and then the white noise closes in around it, but it changes you. Revs you up.

I turned back to the play and just as we had planned it Karl drew the ball cleanly back to me, I gained control, shuffled two steps to my left and let one rip. The ball left my stick like a rocket and flew in a clockwise arc, gaining a height of about 7 feet before dipping wildly back down to enter the net just below the crossbar. The crowd erupted. We had fans. It was game on.

I took the ensuing face-off. As the ref dropped the ball, I angled my stick so that it chipped the ball forward beyond the opposing centre. I sidestepped him and off I went in a mad dash goalward. I deked to my forehand, flipped the ball into the top right corner beyond the reach of the goalie's glove and then crashed wildly into the boards. 3-2. There was no stopping us now.

Like I said, had the Eastern Cape kept their work rate up they would have beaten us handily. We were asleep on our feet for the entire first period. But they didn't. They got cocky. They got sloppy, and we turned the tide. Everything seemed to be happening so fast, but also slow, as in a dream. Play was hectic but I felt as though I was standing apart from it, watching everything unfold in slow motion. Noise and commotion would creep in, but I was mostly in a zen state. You are often at your finest when you are least conscious of what it is you are doing. You are just acting and reacting, a finely tuned machine. We washed over the Eastern Capers like a tsunami, scoring 5 unanswered goals. I scored four in a row in a span of about 4 minutes, and Karl added the capper with about a minute to play. They were left shaking their heads.

The Eastern Cape team was quite different than the Gauteng Lions. They were more disciplined and seemed to play with joy, not anger. For them this was sport, not life or death. I was bloody happy to see the backside of the Gauteng Lions, a surly unlikable crew of expats, probably mostly Canadians too, who swaggered in expecting everything to be handed to them on a plate, but when faced with adversity took you to the woodchopper's ball. Eastern Cape, in contrast, were more than a team. They were family, with each of the Senior player's kids playing in the tournament at all different levels. They were here to compete to the best of their ability, but above all, to enjoy the moments of family and friends. Which, didn't make losing to the Bad News Mukwa Leafs any easier. But, well, we'd take that win - which guaranteed us a spot in the playoffs.

'What a wicked shot!'

'Ya, it was awesome!'

This was Beth and Dan, newest members of my fan club, whose membership had risen to, well, two. Aside from everything else that went on, they were most impressed with my crazy curving slapshot from the blueline that helped get the Mukwa Leafs out of their rut. We don't play with the orange balls in tournaments any more. Only at Mukwa Leaf Gardens in Maun where a puck would lie flat for about 4 feet before hitting a crack, tipping up on its side and veering off sharply into a corner. Pucks were introduced to the Southern African inline game right around the same time that clubs covered their concrete floors with Sport Court, a smooth synthetic surface where the use of very soft wheels also allows you to stop ice hockey style! We'd played with the orange ball for decades in organized ball hockey. Unlike the tennis balls we used as kids, the hard orange ball would sting like a mo-fo if you were game enough to block a shot or too slow to get out of the way. Though a frozen, hairless tennis ball could do some serious damage too. The real beauty of the orange ball was its lightness, so striking it in different ways would impart different spins leading to wildly curving shots as often by accident as by design. Contact from the inside out with a high follow through and you'd get a nice rising hook shot. Contact from the outside in with a low follow through and you'd get a hard low slice. How high, or how low, though, was usually anyone's guess, especially during the heat of a game where you didn't have time to tee it up and think about what you were doing. Act and React.

'Did you mean to do that?!' Asked Dan.

'Of course. I knew exactly where it was going.' Legends are founded on the basis of little white lies.

Four hours between games: not enough time to go back home and sleep (which is what we all wanted to do), and too much time to hang around the rink watching game after game after game. This is the tournament player's dilemma. In adult men's recreational hockey the dilemma is too often resolved by heading to a bar. We all know what the results of that bright idea usually are: a sound beating by those who chose another path. The Mukwa Leafs chose another path: we went across the street to the mall for lunch and a movie. Sitting in the cool dark of the theatre, munching on popcorn and sipping giant cokes, we watched Men in Black, a summer release in the U.S., but hot to the Christmas market in South Africa where everything arrived about 6 months after the fact. Tommy Lee Jones and Will Smith were magic: just the right tonic for aching bones and tired muscles. As the credits rolled and the house lights came up, we rose with a collective groan. Elbows popped, knees creaked, hip joints levered with the grace of a rusty building crane.

'Everyone ok?' asked Coach Sandy.

'Ya. Great. Just great,' we replied cracking wry smiles.

We got back to the rink around 730 only to find our next opponents, the Western Cape pretty boys or whatever they called themselves, already out on the floor taking their warm up. Apparently, we were now ahead of schedule.

'Well, there you are! We thought you'd gotten scared and decided to forfeit. Heh heh heh,' he chuckled. This was the tournament organizer, Hennie, a big strapping Afrikaner who looked the classic farmer but was a property developer in and around Durbanville area. He held a pen and clipboard in his left hand and, armed only with a huge smile, he shook hands with each of us in turn, our hands one by one disappearing into the meat platter of his grip. 'Good to have you with us! All the way from Botswana. And you seem to have developed quite a following already.'

'People love the underdog,' I said.

'Who you calling an underdog?!' said Sandy.

'Well, you've got your hands full tonight, I'm afraid,' said Hennie. 'Western Cape are the reigning champions of SA inline not only at senior level, but across almost all other age categories too.'

There's nothing worse than a partisan organizing committee. We all just hemmed and hawed, went back to sorting through our gear.

'There's always room for a new winner,' said Sandy, as he swopped out his regular eyeglasses for his Hanson brothers safety glass specials.

'Good luck to you, gentlemen. We'll get started as soon as you're ready.'

We all nodded, muttering pleasantries, watching him move across to Western Province's bench where he started chatting amiably with their coach.

'Asshole,' I said, doing up my skates. I cast a glance in Kevin's direction. Kevin was on his knees adjusting his goalie pads, lost in a world of his own. I looked over at Karl who was already dressed and standing, resting Ken Dryden style with his gloved hands on the top of his stick, and his chin on the top of his gloves. He couldn't weigh more than 160 pounds 'soaking wet with rocks in his pockets', as my father used to say. But he was tough as nails and had incredible balance. To knock Karl down took some serious strategizing. I guess he could feel my eyes on him, because he turned his head in my direction, gave a half smile and winked. I knew he was ready.

Meanwhile, the 'veterans' - Sandy, Peter and Mark - each in their late 40s I'd guess, were leaning on the boards chatting about who knows what. Grace under pressure, I wondered, or lemmings to the slaughter? Speaking of 'grace under pressure', I thought to myself, I could use a little Geddy Lee, Neil Peart and Alex Lifeson pick me up right about now.

'Let's go, boys!' said the ref.

'Hey, man. No Rush,' I said.

I could tell from the way we lined up that we were in for it with the Western Province beauties, or whatever they called themselves. We in our sweat soaked, stinking clobber, looking for all the world like something the cats dragged in. They in their sparkling kit, smelling Bounce or FeBreeze or what-have-you fresh as daisies, their NHL-approved helmets sparkling under the lights of the Velodrome's big top. Gloves and pants matching their socks and sweaters. It was enough to make me puke. But it was the smirking arrogance that really got under my skin. Arrogant pricks. You know the type. Talented pretty boys. The kind that drove the hot car and got the cool chicks in high school, a wad of dad's hard-earned dough in their LL Bean pockets. Captain of the football team bullshit. I hated them then, and I hated them now. Only now there were 20 of them, all feeling their oats, prime of life, mid-30s full power assholes. What Bukowski called their 'unoriginal macho energy' on full display. Like I said: puke.

Well, the only thing to do was give it the old college try. Give no quarter. Stand up to their tactics. Outsmart them. Outwork them. Play smart. Take advantage of our opportunities. Stay out of the box. Give 110%. Ah... who am I kidding. We lost. They beat us. But barely. 2-1. It was the usual story. We fell behind 2-0 very early on largely because we were dog tired and no matter how hard those synapses were firing the legs, the hands, were slow to respond. I managed to get one back early in the second half, corralling an ally oop pass from Karl just inside their blue line and snapping one home, top shelf short side. But that was it. A day late and a dollar short. My dad again. He had a saying for every situation. What about a day early and a dollar extra?! Where was that saying? Hiding out with grim reality no doubt.

National championships. 3 games, no spares. All within 22 hours. And we were 2 and 1, so off to the semi-final game against the Eastern Cape, who had handily disposed of the Gauteng Lions, losers of all three of their round robin games. Western Cape Province surfer dudes or whatever they called themselves had gone through unblemished at 3 and oh. Of course they were 'unblemished', fucking pretty boys. What was that sour taste in my mouth anyway, then? We lived to fight on. Defeat the Eastern Cape again and we'd get another crack at Province in the final. Of course, they'd all be getting a lovely night's sleep and only have to play the one game - winner take all - on Sunday. But every defeat leaves a sour taste, particularly one so close as this one. A lucky bounce here, a bad bounce for them, and it would have been a different outcome. If we weren't so friggin tired. At one point, down 2-1 with about 2 minutes left, we tried the ally oop again. Karl lofted a beauty down court but it was just beyond my reach and it had this funny spin on it, so that when it landed it squirted hard away from me toward the corner. There was a defenceman right on me and he squeezed me out of the play toward the far boards. The puck ricocheted harmlessly from the corner to the back of their net where blond asshole number 4 was waiting to collect it and reset the play. I was so tired. I leaned with my stick across the tops of my knees, felt the sweat stream from beneath my helmet onto the cement floor, closed my eyes and took a very deep breath.

'Don't give up, number 1!'

What?

'Don't give up, number 1!'

I perked up as the small voice reached my ears. I stood up straight and stretched my back, turning back into the play that had moved to the far side near centre court. Oh ya, I thought, I'm number 1. I've got my stupid fake tuxedo t-shirt on with my number - 1 - inscribed on the back. For all I know, the cheap magic marker has leaked that ink straight into my back where I'd be number 1 forever. I took a sideways glance over to where the sound had come from. (It was uncool to actually look at the crowd and acknowledge them in any way. Sort of like admiring your own flow in the glass during a warm-up. You would pay big time in the locker room if ever caught doing that.) And I noticed a huge throng of people of all ages all rooting for the Mukwa Leafs. The little engine that could. But sadly, not on this night. It was a loss that would plague me across my next 40 years. Don't ask why. I'm just like that. A lot of guys are like that: you can score a hat trick every night and take that for granted, but forever remember the one that hit the post or was tipped just wide with only seconds to play. That's how I felt. Like it was there for the taking and we had failed on the day.

If there was any consolation to that defeat, it came in two forms: respect and beer. The arrogant pricks of Western Province or whatever they called themselves had prevailed, but narrowly. Typical of many sports teams, they were magnanimous in victory. Full of accolades for the vanquished. Like I said, assholes. Defeat a team like that, or even come close to defeating a team like that, and things would get real ugly real fast. In subsequent years I'd been on the receiving end of many a tag-team mugging, a deliberate slash to mid-calf, a barely disguised slew-foot, designed to take me out of the game. The closer they got to a narrow victory, or - heaven forbid - a defeat, and the more like the Broad Street Bullies did these sorts of teams behave. At least the Philadelphia Flyers of the mid-1970s deliberately decided to play that way game in and game out. Everyone knew it, and everyone expected it. Either 'man up' or pack your bags and go home you cry baby. But this was different. It was not unique to inline hockey in Southern Africa, in fact it was quite common across the beer leagues of the world. Dare to show up the local heroes and you'd pay for it one way or another. That's why in ice hockey you carry an enforcer - to protect the snipers, the danglers, the dipsy doodlers, the guys who can score from the unlikeliest of situations. Karl and I could look after ourselves and each other. But when you are only four or five guys, and three are playing minor roles, and when the dirty stuff is all behind the ref's back, on the sly, on the Q.T., it's almost impossible to openly fight back. In fact, this was a deliberate tactic often trotted out over the course of our three days: hack Karl or hack me and see if you could goad us into a penalty, even a minor scuffle would do - offsetting minors would destroy our chances, while they'd just wheel out version 19 of handsome Charlie. Full marks to us. We kept our heads. In retrospect, I don't know how, or rather, I don't know how I managed since I'm the loose cannon - my nickname is 'Killer' after all - whereas Karl is cool as a cucumber. My dad again, eh. So, bring on the compliments. They come easy to winners.

But better, bring on the beer. It was only 930pm and our next game wasn't until 9 the next morning. A few cold ones were in order.

Driving back to the coast, I had to use two feet on the clutch. I mean, granted the VW microbus was a Clydesdale not a quarter horse, with a dodgy clutch from the start. But my groins were so sore that I could not push down with sufficient power in one leg to actually be able to change gears.

'Oh, man!' I squawked as I lifted my left leg with my right arm, then pushed it , aided by my right foot, in order to depress the clutch. (Cars in South Africa are right hand drive.)

'You, ok?' Said Kevin, riding shotgun on my left. His eyes twinkling with amusement at the state of his teammates.

'Brilliant! Absolutely brilliant!' Nothing an ice bath and a bottle of whisky wouldn't fix. Since neither was available where I was headed, RICE would have to do.

The night was cloudless and filled with stars. It was about midnight and I was sitting naked up to my waist in the Vale's pool. The house was quiet, only the light snoring of old Joe, the pater familias of their brood of border collies, could be heard. The pool water was nice and cold. It would do my groin a world of good. I had significantly calmed down. Time heals all wounds - that's my mother's saying this time round. First spoken when I was dumped by my first girlfriend.

7.

'Time heals all wounds,' she said.

This was my doctor. She'd finally pitched up now that the hard work had all been done by the nurses. The fat plastic tube was gone from down my gullet, and the little oxygen delivery tubes were gone from my nose. I was operating mostly under my own steam now. Though the IV was still delivering its combination of narcotics and vitamins. My throat was scratchy as hell, and I sucked on a weird little water soaked sponge to help bring some relief. Dr Scott-Black - Holly to me, as I'd been around when she was born - was standing by the window chatting seriously with my sister, Lori, who was a long retired nurse. Lori'd been through her own heart troubles some 25 years earlier but now seemed as strong as ever. Hadn't touched a cigarette since, but still loved the odd pint of Newcastle. The fish and chips were harder to give up than the cigarettes, she'd say. She'd driven up to Toronto from Windsor, about a three hour drive - at least it used to be when I was younger. I hadn't been down that way for decades, only once or twice since our mom died and the house got sold. Life just takes you on its twists and turns and before you know it you're 80 years old and smelling funny in a hospital bed. She was wearing jeans, sneakers and a Leaf sweater. I could tell from the number on the sleeve that the sweater most likely had GILMOUR across the back. My sister and my dad loved the Leafs, so loved to gang up on me in the friendly household rivalry. For me it was all water off a duck's back, since Leaf fans had almost nothing to show for their faith. You'll have peace in the Middle East before the Leafs win another Stanley Cup, I would say teasingly. Ah! Gowahn wit cha! My dad would say, waving his hand vaguely in my direction, his head turned toward the action on the TV screen, he and Lori on couch and easy chair enjoying a mid-week ritual. Look at the two of ya, I'd say, living proof that misery loves company.

He'd been dead a long time, but I would often invoke his spirit as Logan, Andrew and the boys took to the ice. Russy would've been proud of you, I'd say. The way you play, you'd give him hope. You give us all hope. I wasn't talking about hope for a Cup, so much as the hope of a future, of some sort of eternal youth to be found in a game played with élan and joie de vivre. Played by young men who not so much believed they'd live forever, but simply didn't consider time's passage. And because the context never changed, because the players were forever young, and because we ourselves were once young too, it was easy to be transported back to a time when that was us. Hockey allowed everyone to step outside of their own cramped and dwindling lives and step into a fountain of youth. Gilmour was long gone, but here was Cash, and Cash reminded us of Beliveau, so as we watched the present day version of the game we could step across the generations, be nostalgic and present at the same time. And the older you got, the more layered and nuanced was the experience, even though it was often somehow beyond your immediate consciousness. You watched the game, you had a few drinks, you argued and laughed, you hoped and were rewarded or not, and then you went home, out into the cold winter's night away from your friend's house where the two of you could be 10 or 35 with family and kids or 75 and waiting to die. But the game was the game was the game.

Boy, I missed my dad. I could feel the hotness of tears rising at the corners of my eyes, so blinked them back, willed them away. Couldn't let my kid sister see me acting the fool. I cleared my throat, as if to speak, but remained silent.

'Did you say something, big brother?' Lori loved to play the 'little sister - big brother' thing even though we were as old as the hills. She and Dr. Holly were both turned toward me now. Holly was a chip off the old block. She had her mother's gentle beauty and kind manner, a manner which I felt was a tactic well used by doctors who wished to disarm difficult or unduly anxious patients. She also had her mother's sharp eyes, eyes that seemed to be able to see the truth, to penetrate beyond the many layers of bullshit and bombast and see what really mattered.

'Hello Jack. Welcome back to the land of the living. I hope you're feeling a bit better, or at least happy to still be with us.' Holly smiled a crooked smile, disarming me instantly.

'Just in time to see my Leafs win the Cup!' Lori chimed in. Chipper and chiding at the same time.

'Go Habs go!' I rasped, immediately wincing from the rawness in my throat. They both chuckled, knowing full well how conflicted I was regarding the outcome of the Final. But really, why is it so hard to switch teams? To switch allegiances? Jerry Seinfeld once said that with all the mercenary behavior of players in sports these days, what we are really doing is rooting for a sweater, for a team's colours. There is really no 'team' beyond its immediate configuration. Rare is the Steve Yzerman who spends his entire playing career with one team and then moves up to the head office. Jarome Iginla once looked to be that sort of player, but once he left CalJack he became a suitcase hockey player, living out of the back of his truck, chasing team after team in the hopes of lifting the Cup. Shoulda stayed in CalJack. The Flames seemed to turn a corner when Iggy left. Sure there were a few more fallow years, but around about 2015 they seemed to click, with one clever acquisition followed by another, a mercenary here, a draft choice that panned out there, and there was the Cup in Calgary in 2018. While Iggy was singing the blues down in Nashville, the whole of Calgary was sporting giant moustaches shouting 'Go Flames Go!' And good for them, their sweaters won. And my sweater was still the red and white of the Motor City, though the motor had long conked out of the city itself. I loved watching my nephews play, was happy whenever they won, but sitting there in my rinkside seats when the Wings were in town just gave me the happiest feeling. In fact, the warm-up was often what I loved most. Just watching the kids wheel around, run through their pre-game activities, not wearing helmets. It was easy to be transported back to the original 6 or original 12 days. Here was Howe, Mahovlich and Delvecchio. Gordie leading the team in scoring during the 1969-70 season despite his advancing years. Jack Unger with his crazy white, kangaroo leather skates. Funny to think of Howe as 'old' then when a player that age today would be half my own age. What I wouldn't give to be that old again. If I had a nickel for every sigh, I'd be a very rich old guy.

So, somehow, the blue and white could never be my team. To tell the truth, I have often tried to have them be my team. When Logan was drafted I swore that I'd be a Leaf fan. I remember having a very serious conversation with his father, Steve, about this. Yes, serious. Allegiance is no laughing matter. If it wasn't, they why do we make it so difficult for people to immigrate to Canada? As with states, so with sports clubs. Steve is a pure laine Habs fan. He's a decade younger than me, so whereas my memories of the Habs begin with Jean Beliveau and the Pocket Rocket, his begin with Ken Dryden and Guy Lafleur. Why is he a Habs fan? Is his dad a Habs fan? No. His dad isn't even interested in sports. Did he grow up in Montreal or in the vicinity of Montreal? No. He grew up on the island of Cape Breton, in a small town called Irish Cove where the television reception was so weak that during the winter there was as much snow on the tube as there was on the ground outside. Who could tell if it was the Habs or Leafs playing anyway? But that's the thing: it was the Habs playing. The CBC carried Montreal games out East. Danny Gallivan and Dick Irvin were as much household names in Sydney or Halifax as Bill Hewitt and Brian McFarlane were in Toronto and Thunder Bay. And the Habs of the late 1970s and early 1980s were as charismatic as a sports team ever was. Their brand of firewagon hockey was infectious, a precursor to the styles played by the Islanders and Oilers that followed them. So, timing and geography. Which was pretty much the same thing with me. We got the Red Wings on local Detroit TV - WKBD Channel 50 - and I got to see Howe and company as my entry point to the game. My first NHL game to see live and in person was during the 1966 Stanley Cup finals between Detroit and Montreal. It was May 1st and my Wings went down to the Habs 2-1 which marked the beginning of the end for Detroit that year. Roger Crozier won the Conn Smythe Award that year, which was small consolation to a 9 year old who loved the Red Wings from the moment he saw their sweaters. Still do, I'm sad to say. I mean, of all the important things to think about and engage with in the world, arguing over sweaters seems pretty stupid. Yet, there was Steve and I quietly discussing a change of allegiance over a pint at the Lower Deck in Halifax.

'So, it's the big time for Logan, eh buddy.'

'Yep,' Steve said quietly, head tilted forward, nodding slowly, two hands on his beer. It was a Thursday afternoon and the bar was packed. I could never figure out the Maritimes. Nobody had work but everybody had money. Not Steve, of course. Steve had both a job and money. If he didn't how else would Logan have been able to make it to 'The Show'? Putting your kids through hockey, especially travel hockey, is a near bankruptable activity. It's an exercise not for the faint of heart. And it's often not even about what the kid wants. It may start out that way, but once your son starts to show potential, the context shifts pretty rapidly from 'having fun' and 'learning to be part of a team' to 'oh my god, I've spawned the next Gretzky!' Parents invest their dreams of glory as well as their hard earned cash in these young boys. The pressure is immense, especially when the boys turn into young men and the Junior draft becomes a consideration. Let's not lie: we all wanted Logan to play in the Q. We all wanted Logan to go all the way. We all often argued with Logan about what he wanted, which, as a young kid, is often about being left alone for one goddamned minute if you please!

Logan had thrown his toys out of the cot on many occasions. Good for him. Unlike his brother, who turned toys out of the cot throwing into performance art, Logan was slow to anger. He was a patient and considerate kid. But, try to push him too far and he'd stand his ground. But, like all kids, he was just a kid, so articulating his interests, issues and concerns was not easy. Which, of course, is often part of the problem.

Parents misreading a series of shrugs peppered with a few muttered 'I don't knows' as insubordination when really it was just a youngsters way of saying 'please, just leave me alone for one goddamned minute!' And, of course, the boys were as thick as thieves. So trying to figure out what was really bothering one by attempting to bribe the other never worked. Somehow it all worked out. I say somehow because I've watched many hockey parents in action and it's never very clear why one kid turns out just fine and another rebels, abandons the sport, or, on occasion, abandons life altogether.

'Everything will work out just fine, knock on wood,' said Steve, rapping the knuckles of his right hand lightly on the top of his head. Logan was a gifted athlete, about that there could be no doubt. He'd sailed through junior with barely a scratch, finished top-10 in scoring in each of his three years, won the Guy Carbonneau trophy as the best defensive forward each of his last two years, and been a nominee for the Michel Brière Memorial Trophy as the League's outstanding player in his final year of Junior with the Océanic. So, being drafted in the first round by the Leafs was not really a surprise, except to his father who had prayed and prayed that the Habs take him.

'You're a Leaf fan now, buddy boy.'

'Bite your tongue!'

'Maybe he'll get traded?'

'Would you trade him?'

'No.'

'Didn't think so. The Leafs won't either. They can't be that stupid.'

'They've done it before.'

That gave us Leaf haters a good chuckle.

'No, but really, Steve, he's going to be a Leaf. What're you going to do? You already know what Christine will do.'

'Ya, she'll have the house painted blue and white before I get home tonight.'

Christine was the classic hockey mom. The only thing more devoted than a hockey mom to her brood is a she-bear. Or maybe it's the other way around. My sister was a hockey mom for more than a decade, her oldest boy, Dan, having gone the normal route through the system, in at 5 and out at 18. I attended a few games with Lori, and they were great fun. I attended many more with Christine and it was much the same, though the difference between the caliber of play in house league and in Triple AAA was like that between someone trying to scratch out the St. Anne's Reel on their fiddle in a Cape Breton kitchen and Itzhak Perlman playing Vivaldi's Four Seasons with the New York Philharmonic. Though at opposite ends of a very wide spectrum, it was still hockey, and hockey mom's loved their hockey rituals. Kid's ferried to the rink, little tyke's skates tightened, quick run to the Tim Horton's, 'make mine a double-double', 'who wants a bagel?' Cow-bells ringing encouragement. Air horns blaring after a goal. 'What, are you blind, ref?!' 'Anyone got a looney for the heater? It's freezing in here.' Mom's all seated and blanketed together. Dad's sitting or standing some distance away. One or two pacing madly like a caged wild animal.

'Whattaya say we give it a try? I'm not kidding. It's only a sweater. Steve Shutt is long gone, my man. Your Habs haven't won a Stanley Cup for almost as long as the Leafs.'

'Whut're you say-yin!' This is Steve affecting his deep Cape Breton Gaelic accent, which always gets a chuckle from all within earshot.

'We don't have to tell anyone. Just try it out. Secretly. Like, whenever the Leafs and Habs are playing, watch the Leafs game. Cheer when they score. Feel sad when they lose.'

'But I'd feel sad all the time, there b'y!'

'Very funny. All's I'm saying is your son is soon to be a Toronto Maple Leaf. Get used to it.'

'Maybe. Until he finds a regular spot in the line-up, though, I'm just going to pray for a trade. I'll start tweeting about that right now. Hashtag HabsGetCash4Cash&FutureConsiderations.'

'Don't forget the two rolls of tape and a broken hockey stick.'

But somehow it doesn't work. I tried and tried to care about the Leafs. I mean, I live in Kitchener, just a 20 minute straight line on the LRT to the arena. I can go behind the scenes anytime I want. Hutchie and Peach and I are always hanging around the locker room, like team mascots. And Ged's son, Eric, is Director of Hockey Operations for the Leafs. We're in deep. But my heart still resists. Even though I can barely name more than a handful of today's Red Wings. So stupid.

'What's stupid?' That's my sister again.

'What?' I mutter, swallowing hard and with difficulty.

'You said something is stupid. You were off in la la land again. Have a nice dream?'

'Terrible dream,' I rasped. 'The Leafs won the Cup.'

She punched me in the arm.

8.

'He'll be just fine,' said Holly.

Lori stood there, brows knitted, arms folded, rocking back and forth in her white sneakers, looking every inch the Head Floor Nurse that she was. She was a no bullshit sort of person. Decades attending to gun shot wounds and drug overdoses at Detroit Metro bestows upon you an ability to see beyond the feel-good crap. Not cynical, just realistic, she's often say of herself.

'It was a serious event, to be sure, but his friends did the right thing and we got him packed in an ice suit straight away. There's no brain damage despite the oxygen deprivation, and we've had a look around in there pretty good. Two stents should do him for now.'

'What does 'for now' mean? You know my brother, he'll be angling to be back on skates before the week's out.'

'Not a chance of that. Not for a good long while. He'll have to go to rehab not the rink to get his heart strength back up. There needs to be strict supervision. I mean, he's 80. And he's an intelligent man. He's always listened to his body, looked after himself, and found his way into my office for the required tests and check-ups, at least after Mary has pestered him enough times. Once he's well enough to leave I'm sure he'll be listening acutely and looking for signs of what is and is not possible.'

'How long does he have to be here?'

'I'd say three more days at least. We need to keep him monitored, and manage his pain while the stents settle in. You know, you've been there before. It's a pretty standard set-up. We see many more just like him every week.'

'Thank god for Canadian healthcare.'

Holly nodded, smiled her crooked smile, and turned to walk away. Lori also nodded, smiled, and turned to come back into Jack's room. No pleasantries necessary. When she poked her head around the opened door, she saw that he was once again fast asleep. He seemed to be resting peacefully, no great gnashing of teeth, crunched up faces, incessant tossing and turning. Just lying quietly on his back. Air in, air out. Chest rises, chest falls. A light flutter behind his closed eyelids. Probably dreaming, she thought to herself. She leaned over him and took a good, long look, kissed his forehead, rubbed his bald head. Sighed. Boy do you ever look like Russ, she said out loud. Then settled back in the chair by the window to read her book, Over the Boards: The Ron Ellis Story by Ron Ellis with Kevin Shea. She'd found it in among an old box of books she thought belonged to her mother. But this had popped up amidst the mountain of paperbacks that was

59

Philippa Gregory. When she saw the book she thought, this is an omen! I must read this book. If I read this book, the Leafs will win the Cup. She was already halfway through and far from seeming a good omen, its frank consideration of the nature of hockey as a business depressed the hell out of her. Not that it wasn't an interesting biography. Ron Ellis was a great hockey player on a great team during a great era. A member of the greatest team of the 20th Century - Team Canada 1972. He took the bad with the good. Rose to meet life's challenges head on. Struggled with depression. Found the Lord. How could such a story not be inspiring? But, where, she thought, were the good hockey novels anyway? Field of Dreams! Now there was a book. W.P. Kinsella. Wasn't he a Canadian? Why did such a gifted Canadian writer write a book like that about baseball anyway? She had plenty of questions, but no answers.

Jack was muttering in his sleep again. Lori left him to it. While her brother was soon to be out of the woods, Ron Ellis had problems of his own.

9.

The sun was long up. It was time to giddy-up. Get the horses moving. But I lay there in my little bed in the granny house at the Vales flipping through The Hockey News, the summer sun streaming in through the slightly parted curtain. They'd produced a list of the 50 greatest players of all time and my man was number 3. How could Mr Hockey be third? Gretzky and Orr were ranked ahead of him. Mario Lemieux was fourth. That's some good company. Maurice Richard was fifth, followed by Doug Harvey, Jean Beliveau, Bobby Hull, Terry Sawchuk and Eddie Shore. Sawchuk was the only goalie in the top 10. There's something about the best players, they've got this sort of grace, a kind of other-worldliness to them. It's hard to put a finger on it, but I knew for certain I didn't have it. Sure, I could fill the net against these jokers, and had played the odd starring role here and there over time. But I lacked that je ne sais quois. Grace. That's the only way I could put it. Even when Gordie or Bobby were in a scrap, pounding the crap out of some guy, there was something about their style, their approach to everything that distinguished them from a mere plodder like Bob

Probert or John Ferguson. Don't get me wrong, I loved those guys. They could play the game. They were enforcers with hockey talent. But they were without grace as was I. This should not be confused for a lack of style or talent. Most of the players in the NHL have style and talent, but only the greatest have that certain something. Sid the kid, in my view, sits on the borderline. There's something about him that keeps him out of the Wayne, Bobby, Gordie and Mario circle. He's rough around the edges. A bull, not a matador. And my second favorite player of all time, too, Marcel Dionne. He was fun to watch, but he was more bricklayer or carpenter than Frank Lloyd Wright or Christopher Wren. A craftsman to be sure; but no visionary.

I had a vision for the day: beat the Eastern Cape and then gain our revenge over Western Province. I may have only been a bricklayer, but today I'd try to be the best damn bricklayer I could possibly be. Better yet, let Kevin be the bricklayer - he's the goalie. Let him build a Buhlin wall, as impregnable as was old Nikolai back in the day. All these mixed up metaphors were beginning to hurt my head. Better to get out of bed and let others argue about who was the best player ever and on what basis did you rest your argument. Just sitting up in bed reminded me that everything hurt. I could feel the groin pull migrating up into my lower abdomen. The bruises on my hips looked like I'd been kicked by a mule. My left forearm was so swollen, I looked a bit like Popeye - the result of a nasty two hander in Game 1. My right elbow was full of water and shaped like a golf ball.

I could feel a bone chip rattling around in there as I squished the fluid around. As I swung myself up and out of the saggy bed, my hamstrings felt as tight as piano wire, my knees creaked, my neck cracked, my back snapped, my knuckles snap crackle popped. Gotta remember to buy some gauze and adhesive tape on the way: tape up everything that aches and, for what can't be taped, take a painkiller. What hadn't suffered, though, was my belief in the Mukwa Leafs, in our ability to get the job done, to bring home the glory, to hoist the Cup or Mug or Stick taped to a base of some sort, or some African carving - whatever it was, it didn't matter. What mattered was bragging rights. That's what we play for, those of us who play to win anyway.

'Are you coming to watch today?' I asked Peter who was in his customary spot at 7am, stirring another mountain of powdered goo into his morning coffee, fresh back from a long run along the Muizenberg beach.

'Not today, boet. The missus and I have to do some Christmas shopping. What time do you play?'

'The semi-final is at 9. We play the Eastern Cape again. That's the team you watched yesterday morning. The finals all go in the afternoon. I don't know when we're to play. I mean, if we win this morning.'

'You'll win. Don't forget to take your face apart before you play!'

'Just like a good Canadian, eh!'

10.

'OK, Sandy, what's the plan?'

We were standing in a little circle on the rink floor in front of our net, getting ready for our little team chant.

'Plan?' Said Sandy, suddenly straightening up and lifting his head high. He looked like a meerkat on the veld trying to get a whiff of a predator, or a female meerkat. 'The plan, boys, is to win. To win big! And, in doing so, to help me score a goal.' We all laughed.

'No joke. Uh-uh,' he said shaking his head vigorously. 'I'm serious. The girlfriend is giving me grief. She said no sex until I score. She said it's a shame that Karl and Jack have to do all the work.'

'Hey, wait a minute now, what are we? Chopped liver?'

'Ya, the game isn't just about scoring goals,' said Kevin, 'it's about stopping the other team from scoring too.'

'Not today it isn't,' said Sandy. 'Today it's about pounding them into the ground and getting me a goal.'

'But that would mean you'd have to go forward,' said Karl, sticking the knife in.

'Don't worry about that, buddy boy. Just be ready to cover me when I do decide to move up.'

'You can be our muscle in front of the net,' I said. 'On powerplays. We'll bank a few in off your head, or your shins. Just be ready to take a bit of lumber across the back.'

'Whatever works,' he said. 'Whatever works. OK, boys, on 3, 'slap that bitch!''

'One - Two - Three!'

And off we went, once again into the fray.

Today was different. It was another day. We had jump. We had zip. We had all taken our meds. Standing around was for hitchhikers and bus riders, for guys trying to wave down a cab, or catch a fish off the end of a dock. Standing around was for bank tellers and barbers, beauticians and T-Ball centre fielders. Standing around was not for hockey players. Today we were clear the track here comes Shack! We were the Big M circling back behind his own net before taking off like a 747 rumbling up the wing. We were Sittler letting one rip from the top of the circle. We were Mats Sundin, head up, through heavy traffic. We were Wendel crash bang in a straight line. We were Bobby Baun giving it his all on one leg. We were Borje Salming blocking shot after shot after shot. And we were Potvin, Palmateer, Bester and Wregget all rolled into one acrobatic package, pads stacked, a lightning quick glove hand snatching away sure goal after sure goal after sure goal.

It was 4-nil after the first half. I had scored a natural hat-trick and Karl added a buzzer beater, a beautiful end-to-ender where he slipped and slid and ducked and weaved between and among the heavy bodied determination of our lumber wielding opponents. Like stick-handling through a series of phone booths, Karl took the ball at the blue line and weaved down low along the left boards, before cutting a sharp angle and accelerating along the goal line and across the front of the net, but rather than carry the ball with him, maybe to try and flip it high glove side, he took his right hand off the stick, let the left hand extend far from his body, and as the goalie crossed the crease with Karl, he dragged the ball in from behind. It's a move we've all tried in pick-up, but rarely has anyone had the nerve to give it a go under pressure in a real game. It's the sort of move that, as often as not, would get you a two-handed chop on the left wrist from a trailing defenceman. But he pulled it off.

'What a move!'

'Awesome!'

'Hey, Lemieux, I bet you can't do that again!'

Fortunately, it was four and not three. Feeling pretty cocky, we took the pedal off the gas a bit, not intentionally, but just because that's what usually happens in a 4-0 game. I took a stupid penalty - there aren't any other kind; though you often hear 'he took a good penalty', he didn't because there aren't. Early in the second half I took a slash to the ankle behind the play and decided that I'd had enough.

'What the fuck is wrong with you, you asshole!' I shouted, stopping and turning back into my attacker.

'Fuck you. What's your problem?' He said, playing ever the innocent. But I'd had enough at that particular moment in time. So, I cross checked him across the upper arm as hard as I could. Right on the bone in the small gap between the shoulder and elbow pad. I knew it would hurt, for days. He crumpled only slightly, not wanting to give anything away, though I could see it in his eyes that I'd hit pay dirt. I'd be lying if I said I didn't like it. I'd taken so much crap over four games that it felt very good, no, it felt magnificent, to give a little back.

'Asshole,' I snarled, ready to drop the gloves. But the ref had seen enough, blown his whistle and called me for cross-checking, which it obviously was. I had no argument.

'What about the slash, ref!' I hollered.

This never works. It never works with sibling rivalry - but mommy he hit me first - and it never works with referees. Better to shut up, take your lumps, cool off, and reorganize. The quick whistle probably saved me from doing something very stupid anyway. The ref had saved me from myself. You don't get a nickname like Killer based on your intelligent play. This way I could simmer down and get my very first rest from play in the entire tournament. It felt good to sit down. For 10 seconds. No sooner had I gone to the box than Eastern Cape had us hemmed in, Karl, Sandy and Peter trying to play a triangular defense. Standing up in the penalty box I shouted encouragement as Kevin made one, two, three saves, before they managed to chip one over his prone form. 4-1.

Released from the sin bin, I skated over to Kevin and tapped him on the pads. 'What, can't you save that fourth rebound?' I said, and smiled.

'What about 'play smart and stay out of the penalty box',' he shot back. He had a point.

The goal gave the Eastern Cape a bit of jump. The game see-sawed until Peter took a hooking penalty - a penalty of exhaustion, not laziness, in this particular case - and they came at us again. About 30 seconds into the penalty, Karl won a draw in our own end, the ball going straight back to Sandy who turned and tried to fire it around the boards and down the court. In this case, it only got as far as the far side blueline (another crime of exhaustion) where the defenseman stopped it and under pressure from me, chipped it back into the corner where their centreman was waiting. He had some room so turned, took a look around and sent a sharp pass into the high slot where the other defenseman had snuck into open space and one timed a low hard one between Karl's legs. 4-2.

'Don't panic boys, it's still a 2 goal lead,' I said.

'Play smart now, c'mon, there's only two minutes to go.'

Yada yada yada. Players and their platitudes. But we were OK. We played smart, didn't panic, and managed to draw one of their players into a penalty with about 50 seconds left. Only so many chops can go unwitnessed before the ref catches on. This didn't stop the entire Eastern Cape bench from howling like a pack of lovelorn wolves from their bench. Oh, such injustice! Such bias! All teams are the same. Had it been the other way around it would have been us howling - but not from the bench, since we had no one other than Mark over there anyway, and Mark was as laid back as they come.

With the face-off to the right of their goaltender, Karl set up to take the draw. The plan was to pull it back to either Peter on the left point or me on the right and for one of us to get a shot on net where Sandy, in theory, would be screening the goalie. It didn't quite go to plan. Karl did win the draw, but it went to the near boards where Peter pinched in and retreated with the ball back to the blue line, drawing the lone forward toward him. As the defender got within a half-step, Peter angled the ball off the boards back to Karl down low. I shouted for him to kill the clock, but instead he must have thought I was calling for a pass which in short order arrived precisely on my stick. I had plenty of room at the point so took a stride in toward the high slot where I wound up and instead of letting one rip I slap passed it to Sandy who was standing calmly at the side of the net, with his stick on the floor. He didn't even move. The pass whizzed along the court floor, hit his stick blade and popped into the back of the open net. 5-2. Game over. High fives, hugs and pats on the back all around.

'Woo hoo!' I shouted. 'Guess who's getting' laid tonight!'

11.

So, we were off to the finals. There's nothing better than a chance to get even with your rivals. I'm not exactly sure how Western Province got to be 'our rivals', or even if they felt we were 'rivals', but it felt that way. They were the reigning champions and we were the pretenders' to the throne. They had beaten us the first time round, but everyone who had played or watched that game knew that it could just as easily have gone the other way. Whatever the case, it was clear we were ready; we were all running on adrenalin and feeling no pain. Sort of.

'Hey, look what I brought,' said Ruth, wheeling over a big blue and white plastic cooler. I half expected to see a 2-4 of Canadian or Blue or - god forbid - Bud Lite when she popped the lid. 'Ice!' She exclaimed.

'Hallelujah!' I said.

'Oh man, give me some of that!'

'Me too!'

There were about six big bags of ice inside, purchased just before game time at the gas station down the street.

'Saint Ruth of Maun!' Said Kevin, breaking up the bagged ice against the cement floor then gingerly nestling his elbow into the cold pack. I took an entire back and placed it between my legs. 'Two groins for the price of one,' I said. We looked like the back room between matches at the WWF.

'What time do we play next?' I asked.

'Don't know,' said Sandy. 'We'll have to check the big board. There'll be about 10 finals today.'

'If it ends later than 3, Kevin and I can't play,' said Karl.

'What?!'

'We've got plane tickets home tonight.'

'What? Why didn't you tell me?' There was a long silence. Sandy seemed totally disoriented. Like he'd been out on a date with Kim Basinger having the time of his life, only to have his shoulder rudely shaken by his college roommate, asking, 'Hey man, who's Kim?'

'We told you, Sandy, long back. It's a direct flight to Heathrow leaving at 540. We'd need to be at the airport no later than 330.'

'We're packed and ready to go,' said Kevin.

Since we all had so little kit, I never thought twice about the contents of their gym bags.

'No showers?' This was kind of a non sequitur that came from Sandy. Like, really, who gave a shit if they showered or not before they flew the 18 hours in the air plus whatever stopover they had in London en route to Toronto. The fact of a shower or no shower did not help us at the moment.

'Let's not panic,' I said. 'Maybe they've got us slotted in first or second. You know, get the old guys out of the way.' Sandy didn't look too hopeful. Tournaments usually went the other way around, with the tykes up first and the Seniors second to last, just ahead of the Open Division. Parents had to get kids home, fed, settled, and to bed.

'Mo-ther fucker,' muttered Sandy. 'OK, let's not panic, where's Hennie?' There was that meerkat act again.

'Can you change the ticket?' I asked.

Karl and Kevin just smirked.

'What?'

'We work for WUSC,' said Karl, who thought the meaning should be obvious, but I didn't get it and said as much.

'N-G-O,' said Karl, waiting for me to clue in.

'Non-governmental organization means 'Cheap ticket',' said Kevin, 'and 'cheap ticket' means you miss your flight at your own peril.'

'And turn over your first-born son as payment for a change.'

'Mo-ther fucker,' I muttered.

Just because we were in a panic, didn't mean that anyone else was. The Sunday morning atmosphere at the Velodrome was positively festive. This was playoff hockey. Lose and go home. Everything on the line. Everyone's nerves were up, parents and kids alike. The young guns playing Open, under-18, under-16 and under-14 were all keen to impress coaches, scouts, girlfriends (or girls in general), parents, friends and fans. There were girls on plenty of teams, but none playing above the under-12 division. At the time, in the late 1990s, there was no woman's or girl's division of any kind. Hockey then and in this part of the world was heavily gendered. Men played, women cheered and minded the children. That mold was quickly broken in the early part of the 21st Century, and I often said that, next to me, the best player on the Mukwa Leafs was Ruth Stewart. Had we had Ruth in the line-up back in 1997, I know we would have beaten Western Province in the round robin. But we didn't, so we didn't.

As far as the finals went, there were actually eight games to be contested, three on the smaller rink and five on the larger rink, with the first matches, the under-8s and the under-14s, set to begin at 2pm. They would be followed, on the hour, by the under-10s and under-12s on the smaller rink, and the under-16s, under-18s, the Seniors (over-30), and the Open on the big rink. If you are doing your math, that means, the Mukwa Leafs were scheduled to face off against Western Province at 5pm. Upon learning this, we were gutted.

When Hennie gave us the news, there was a collective groan.

'What? What's the matter, fellows?' Asked Hennie.

'We can't play at 5,' said Sandy.

'Or 4 or 3,' I added.

'Why not?'Asked Hennie.

'Because two of our players are scheduled to fly back to Canada early this evening and there's no possibility of changing their tickets.'

'Can we shift our final to 2pm?' I asked. 'Go first?'

'Maybe,' said Hennie. 'I don't see why not, if the other team agrees. We could bump the others down by one hour, that's not so bad. The Senior Final is the only game set for 5pm anyway. We could give the under-18s prime-time. I know they would love to play in front of the bigger crowd.'

Suddenly we were full of hope. The gods of hockey were smiling down upon us, or so it seemed. But not so fast. There was the small matter of the opposition.

'Where's Dieter? Is he here anywhere?' Asked Sandy. Dieter Brauch was a Canadian-born German who was the head coach of Western Province. He had played ice hockey in Germany for Rosenheim in the Bundesliga I for many years. He had been recruited by Province on the recommendation of their former coach Rudy Zimmerman, who had been a teammate of Dieter's in the 1990s, before swapping Europe for South Africa.

Since all of Province's teams were in the playoffs, Dieter was bound to be here somewhere.

'Let me give him a call,' said Hennie, pulling out his Nokia 2110.

Dieter pitched up a few minutes later.

'Hello, boys, what's up? How's everyone today? I watched you play this morning. Good stuff. But you're up against a different sort of foe this evening aren't you? Ah, there's no shame in silver! It's something you'll have to get used to anyway; everybody else has.'

Smug bastard.

'Listen, Dieter, how's about we play the final at 2 instead of 5?' That was Sandy, straight to the point.

'Not possible,' he said.

'Why not?' We all began to whine like puppies in a cardboard box. Dieter could feel his power growing. I could almost see him straighten his back, puff up his chest a bit.

'Many of our players are not here. They know the game is at 5, so they've got other things going on.'

'Like what?' I said. It came out sounding a bit more irritated than I'd intended.

'Sleeping, shopping, going to the beach. What does it matter to you anyway what they do before game time?' He had a point.

'How many aren't here? I bet most of them are here watching their kids play?'

Dieter laughed. 'You over estimate the age of my players! They are not yet poppas like you? They are young men. They have lives to live. They are out with their girlfriends.' He gesticulated like he was maestro of an oom-papa band. I could almost hear the wheeze of an accordion. Picture him in his lederhosen.

'Anyway, there are maybe four or five here now. Not enough for a game.' The irony of that statement was not lost on me. By 5pm we'd be down to 3.

Sandy looked crestfallen. Defeated. Tapped-out. 'Well, he said, we'll have to forfeit. We can't play with 3 players and no goalie. So, we're done. Sorry, Hennie, but that's the way it goes. We're done.'

Hennie too looked disappointed. The Senior Final was always a popular warm-up before the main event, the Open Division championship game. For a few moments he was at a loss as to what to do. We had obviously become the people's choice, the fan favorites, the little engine that could, the 20 dollar timex that takes a licking and keeps on ticking, a band of eveready bunnies, the Bad News Bears triumphing against all odds in their half-assed clobber. What's with the guy in his street clothes playing with a wrong-handed stick anyway, you could hear people saying. And the guy in the funky goggles, do you think he's high? But, in the end, it was no Cinderella story, we were no David facing Goliath. Or if we were, then David was underfoot and Goliath was once again champion of all he surveyed.

'Let me get the medals,' said Hennie. 'I'll be right back.'

We milled about, made small talk with Dieter, shuffled our feet, considered our couldas, wouldas and shouldas.

'It is what it is,' said Karl. I fucking hate that phrase, I thought to myself.

'Ya, heh heh,' said Kevin, his voice trailing off.

But, to be fair, these plane tickets were purchased a long time back. And who could have predicted we'd make it to the final? Or that the final would be at 5 and not 2. So many variables. It sort of is what it is, I said to myself, wincing at the thought.

Hennie returned with medals piled high over his left arm. We stood there awkwardly as he made a little speech. Thanks for coming. Great to have a team from Botswana. Well played by all. Congratulations to Western Province once again, etc. He then counted out 20 gold medals for province and handed them across to Dieter, who was smiling and frowning at the same time. Happy to be champion, but unhappy about the back door route to the title. 'Well, we did beat you in the round robin, so we could say this is fair,' he said. We all remained silent, silently fuming that is.

'How many medals do you need, or want, Sandy?'

'Six, no, make it seven. I would like to give one to my daughter.'

'Seven it is.' And he counted them off. Sandy in turn passed them round to each of us. They looked really cool, I must admit, though the colour was off.

'How about a team photo?' Asked Ruth, camera in hand.

'Sure,' we said in unison, donning our medals.

'There's no shame in being runners-up, boys!' said Sandy, and while it was true, it didn't sit well with any of us.

'Smile,' said Ruth. 'Say cheese!'

It was still only 11am and none of us knew what to do. We'd had the legs cut out from under us. The wind taken out of our sails. All that stuff. So, we sat around the cooler drinking beer. Beneath the ice, Saint Ruth had been kind enough to pack a dozen Castle Lagers.

'So, what now? I mean, I know what Kevin and Karl are doing later today. How about you guys?' This was me, mopey and deeply disappointed. I had nowhere to go. I was just heading back down the coast to spend a nice Christmas with Peter, Louise and their family.

'We're going to drive up the coast,' said Ruth. 'Do some camping. Stay a few nights with Mark and his family. Make our way to Swakop. We'll be back in Maun early Jan.'

It sounded fun. 'It sounds fun,' I said, raising a smile.

Just then, Hennie was back.

'Listen, there's talk of putting a senior all-star team together and playing you in an international friendly. Are you up for it?'

'Wh-when?' Asked Sandy, clearing his throat.

'Today. Now. I mean, at 1. We have a free hour before the finals. The game would be officially sanctioned by the SA Inline Association, so everyone would earn their international cap. We would play you as official representatives of Botswana.'

Since no one other than the Mukwa Leafs and a few of their Batswana neighbours - none of whom had a passport - played inline hockey anywhere in the country, we couldn't see how anyone would object.

'We would allow you to pick up two non-South Africans to at least give you some extra players.We'll be on the big surface. What do you say?'

'Well, boys, whattaya say?' Asked Sandy.

'Here's to Team Botswana!' I said, raising my beer can. We clinked cans, said 'here here!', and agreed to play.

We picked up a Canadian and a German from Gauteng province - two of the nasty bastards who tried to kill us in game 1. Oh well, I thought, what goes on the court stays on the court. Enemies yesterday, allies today. So, we were 7 skaters and a goalie. On the big rink we were allowed 5 skaters at a time, unlike the smaller court which had limited us to 4. So two spares. Luxury! Word spread very quickly that there was to be an international friendly played at 1pm and by 1230 a hefty crowd began to gather. The organizing committee managed to rustle up some plain blue, numbered, practice jerseys for us. So there we were in our Botswana blues.

'What number do you want?' Asked Sandy.

'Why, number 1, of course,' I said, and winked at him.

The funny thing about this international game is that ultimately about 2/3 of the South African squad was made up of Western Province players. Everyone wanted to earn their first international cap, so guys were coming out of the woodwork asking to play. But the SA Inline Association was very meticulous in its selection, sitting with the coaches of the other teams and trying to assemble a squad of the most deserving, not the best connected. Obviously, phone calls had gone out to Western Province players that they'd been selected to play in an international friendly. And obviously, they'd been only too happy to drop their sleeping, shopping, or beach going to suit up against us. The bastards.

'You see that, Karl?'

'Ya, the whole fucking team is here.'

'Think they're going to have their cake and eat it too.'

'They better think again.'

'You can say that again,' said Kevin.

'Let's get 'er done,' said Sandy.

'You bet, coach, let's get 'er done.'

It was a cake walk. For us. The big rink made all the difference. They couldn't catch us, or corner us, they couldn't squeeze us out along the boards because their was simply too much room for us. I have to admit, having the two knuckleheads from Gauteng Lions back on D also made a big difference. We moved Sandy up front with us, and he switched off regularly with Mark as he'd been doing all along. At the back, Peter rotated in with the frick and frack from Gauteng. Karl was a marvel that game. And so was Kevin. Perhaps they wanted to give it their best, feeling somehow responsible for our second place finish, though clearly this was not their faults. Sandy scored his second goal of the weekend, so assuring regular sex at least well into the new year. I potted another pair, but it was Karl who really shone during this game, scoring four and setting up everybody else. The final score was Botswana 7, South Africa 1 - you can look it up on the internet, I kid you not. Or, as we all prefer to think of it the Mukwa Leafs 7, Western Province and assorted allstars 1. We so kicked ass.

Following the game, we all went up to the bar for a few beers. This, of course, is where all the arguing and justification began. We weren't really the Mukwa Leafs because we had picked up two excellent players (true). They were really Western Province since only 3 or 4 other players came from the other teams (true). So, in our hearts we were the champions of South African inline hockey for 1997. And in their hearts, it was Western Province that ruled the roost. They had the gold medals to show for it, and we had the silver. There was no arguing with that. But as anyone who plays or watches sports knows, there's always an argument about the true outcome no matter what the final score.

12.

I groaned, opened my eyes, glanced around the room, got my bearings. I could see my sister, fast asleep, in a chair by the window, head tilted on to her shoulder. She'd pay for that posture when she wakes up, I thought to myself. She had a book on her lap, but without my glasses, I couldn't see what it was. Backlit by late afternoon sun she looked rather angelic, and, youthful. Fading light was kind to old folks like us. When our mother was Lori's age she'd had cataracts removed from her eyes. How's your eyesite, mom? I'd ask and she'd respond 'Too good. Now I see things I don't want to see.' Like what? I'd ask. 'Like the old broad in the mirror', and she'd laugh, shoulders moving up and down. Now my sister was the old broad in the chair, looking both angelic and youthful, but, remember, I wasn't wearing my glasses. I cleared my throat, trying to get her attention.

I lived in Africa for a long time, most of it in Botswana - a highly unlikely place to end up for a boy who grew up on the shores of the Detroit River in industrial southern Ontario. I was seven years in Gaborone, the hot, dusty capital city, where during the cool, dry winters you could walk to the yacht club. Yep, a yacht club. On the Gaborone Dam, a reservoir that was rarely more than 40% full at any one time. Though back during the El Nino floods of 2000, the waters overflowed the dam walls and inundated a good chunk of the city. Rainy season was a different story altogether. But why is every flood a disaster? I've been asking this question for about 50 years. Why is no one ever prepared? Every year the rains come, then the floods, and then poor peasants are being helicoptered out of trees. Back in 2000, no one could raise the gate to release the waters downstream. Why? Because it had never been used, never been tested, was 40 years old and rusted shut. Use it or lose it, is that so hard to remember? For days people were canoeing up and down some of the main roads in the older part of the city, called The Village, where I lived. Gabs was a city seemingly permanently under construction. I used to tease my colleagues that the national bird of Botswana should be the yellow building crane. Either that or the warbling car alarm. You couldn't go 100 metres in any direction without hearing a car alarm go off. Robbery? Maybe, but the sound was so common that no one reacted, and after a while you forgot you were even hearing it. Like the dogs that barked all through the night. My first few weeks there were torture. How could anyone get any sleep? It was summer and summer was hot! And in those days air conditioning was an open window and a ceiling fan. And in through the open window every night came the barks and howls of dogs, dogs, dogs. Sleep was a problem. But within a month, like everybody else, I didn't even hear them anymore. Thieves going over your fence? Maybe. But no one paid any attention to the barking dogs.

I often dreamt of Botswana. Weird dreams as dreams tend to be. But this most recent dream, of Mukwa Leaf near glory, was no fantasy. I hadn't thought of Sandy and the gang for quite some time, so the dream raised pleasant memories, even if, no matter how hard I tried to rewrite history, we still fail at the final hurdle. Maybe one day I will write a book about it, just so I can change the ending. Make myself the hero. Don't give up number 1! Headline in the daily paper: number 1 doesn't give up, Mukwa Leafs crowned champions of Africa.

My sister was awake now. Watching me quietly, intently. Like a birder, or a German tourist in a game-viewing hide. All that was missing were the binoculars, pith helmet and many-pocketed khakis. She was rubbing her neck almost absent-mindedly.

'Hello brother,' she croaked, cleared her throat, tried again. 'Feeling better?'

'A bit,' I whispered, scanning the side table for the weird little sponge and a glass of ice. No dice. I'd have to ring for the nurse.

'Holly says you'll be out of here in a few days. Rare is the on-ice heart attack fatality. Figures show only about 10 a year, despite the fact that most of you look ready to die before you get to the ice.'

'Tough as nails, the old ticker,' I said, a bit more confidence in my voice box.

'What were you dreaming about?'

'How do you know I was dreaming?'

'I heard you muttering every now and then.'

'Oh ya, like what?'

'Like, I think I heard you say 'mo-ther fucker',' she smiled.

I chuckled. 'Yep. There's no escape from the past,' I said.

'What do you mean?'

'I was in South Africa, playing inline hockey again.'

'How was the weather?' She said, looking out on a glorious June late-afternoon.

'A lot like ours, actually.' It was the height of the southern summer. Christmas time. Trees and decorations all over the place. Santas of all colours. Everybody in shorts and t-shirts. Cape Town is a very happy place at that time of the year.

'I mean, in the dream, you goof. I was making a joke. I didn't expect a weather report. There's no weather in a dream.'

'Oh,' I said. 'Well, anyway, I dream about Africa a lot.'

'Did you have a farm at the foot of the Ngong hills?'

'Very funny. No, I didn't, but I did have a time share and three cats,' I said, smiling. I pushed the button to summon the nurse. If there was to be conversation, there'd have to be ice.

'Anyway,' said Lori, 'Holly also said no more hockey til you get a passing grade at rehab.'

I remained silent. I was an old fool, but not that kind of old fool. As my dad used to say in reference to his collapsing golf game: 'At least I'm on the right side of the grass!' I'd be a good boy, go to rehab, etc. It was still too early to check out of Hotel Planet Earth. But I'd be back on skates eventually, even if it was later rather than sooner. My old friend and colleague, Ian Macdonald, played til he was 90. Imagine that. And he was good too. Used a straight bladed wooden stick right to the end. He was the first president of York University in Toronto, had served in the Ontario government, been president of Hockey Canada, a Rhodes scholar back before written history, and a member of the commonwealth council of higher education. I met him while on a post-doc at York, but stayed in touch through the commonwealth initiative which brought Ian to Botswana on several occasions. The York faculty had a hockey 'team'. I use italics because it was really a band of gypsies: current and retired faculty, some sons, lots of friends, the coach of the York men's hockey and basketball teams, a few former stars of the women's team, exceedingly mixed skills but everyone played the game with wild intent. I used to get a big kick out of the fact that in order to get to the rink at the Beatrice Ice Gardens, next to York University and across from Tennis Canada, Ian had to circumnavigate a campus ring road named 'Ian

Macdonald Boulevard'. When it came to 'old timer' hockey, Ian was my role model. If Ian had a heart attack on the ice, would he defy doctor's orders and jump straight back into the game at the moment he felt 'good enough'. Not likely. You don't get a road named after you by being stupid. The nurse came in.

'Everything all right here?' That sing-songy voice. Creeped me out. When the grim reaper comes for me, I thought to myself, she will look and sound like this nurse - not the whacked out hooded dude with the scythe. She'd be there to cut me down, no doubt about that, but it would be sing-songy, happy happy, whoops, what the hell, and then off you'd go to never never land. A sneak attack. Women were very good at sneak attacks. Academics call it 'soft power'. Getting you to do things you otherwise would not freely choose to do, even if it was in your best interest. My wife, Mary Adams, was the best at this. You don't get to the top of the UN system using brute force. You use a sing-songy voice.

'Yes, fine, fine,' I said. 'Can I have a cup of ice with that weird little sponge on a stick thing, please?'

'Sure, no problem, coming right your way,' she sing-songed. Then she took a brief look at my chart at the end of the bed, looked up at me, nodded at my sister - two nurses in cahoots! - and went off on her merry way, white nurse shoes making squidging sounds all the way down the hall.

'What are you snarling about over there?' asked Lori, the look in her eyes both quizzical and mirthful.

'There goes the grim reaper,' I said.

'What are you talking about, she's very sweet.'

'Exactly!' I said.

'Oh, really, you talk so much nonsense. You're as bad as dad. You're just tired of being stuck in that bed. You're very lucky to be alive, you know.'

'Gotta know how to pick your friends. You get to be my age and you need to surround yourself with health care professionals, preferably those who can also skate. Make sure there are a few younger fellas playing too. Wouldn't want your buddies to have a heart attack while they're trying to move you. It's all very strategic.'

I was talking more nonsense, and Lori knew it, so didn't bother to engage. But there's a bit of truth to this, even if only through happenstance. Unlike other sports, hockey is played on blades, so the ability to glide unites players across different generations. And the game itself can unite across other common social divides - class, race, gender. If you can skate, and you have ten dollars in your pocket to pay your freight, then you can play. If you're useless and in over your head, you'll find out soon enough. And if your talent level is too high for the current crowd, you either adjust your play so as to fit in, or score at will and be known as 'the dick' who nobody wants to play with, or you move on, ask around, find the proper fit. If you're over 30, chances are there's a doctor in your group, or a dentist, someone to fix your roof or your plumbing, a car salesman, a guy who's great with computers, and a guy like me, a retired academic who's full of self-importance and bloated opinions. Don't like me, or Joe Blow the mechanic who thinks he used to be somebody? You can always dish out the odd chop out on the ice, but you'd better expect one to come your way eventually, probably when you least expect it. And remember, you're going to have to play with this guy week after week, so get used to it, learn to drink beer with him, and leave the on-ice aggression where it belongs, on the ice.

Speaking of ice, the nurse had arrived with my treat. I was definitely getting antsy. My ass was sore, my back itchy. Not to mention the whole bed pan thing which gets real old real fast. I would swop a sponge bath from Sofia Vergara for the ability to get up and go to the toilet on my own any day. Lori could sense my growing discomfort.

'Game 2 tonight!' She said brightly.

'Lambs to the slaughter,' I said, deadpan, hoping I'd be wrong but also hoping to have a little fun with my sister.

'You watch! The way they played in the third period the other night. It'll be a different story tonight.'

'Such hope!' I said, preacher style, lifting my head skyward, the 'p' lightly aspirated. 'Aren't you embarrassed at all?' I asked her.

'Of what?' I could see that I was starting to hit my target, get her going, rile her up. Boy this was going to be fun. Like we were under-10s again! And no mom to twist my ear, tell me to 'leave your sister alone'. I reached up, lightly touched my ear and smiled.

'A grown woman of considerable years still misguided enough to think that the Leafs will win the Cup before she passes on to the next world.'

But Lori wouldn't take the bait. This was an argument as old as the hills. And a form of teasing that had gone stale by, oh, 1987. That was the year when my Wings beat her Leafs in 7 games in the Divisional semi-finals. Worse still, was the fact that Toronto blew a 3-1 series lead, getting outscored 10-2 and shut out twice in the last three games. Boo hoo hoo! I had teased her. Did Tawanna woose? The truth is that neither one of those teams was any good. Sure, Wendel Clark scored 37 goals that year, punched everybody's lights out - except Proby's - and was a lot of fun to watch. But that was about it. How they upset the Blues in round one, well, that was 50 years ago. I killed those brain cells a long time back. And my Wings subsequently got blown out by the Oilers who were en route to the Cup. Gretzky scored 62 goals that season and added 121 assists. Jari Kurri added 54 and 54. Messier flew under the radar with 37 goals and 107 total points. They were in the prime of their careers, all three of them 26 years old at the time. How could anyone be a Leaf fan, or a Wings fan, when a team as beautiful as the 1986-87 Oilers were showcasing their talents? Like I said, it's the sweater. I'd have been an Oilers fan, no problem, if they wore Red Wings jerseys.

Lori rolled her eyes at me, which was code for 'are we really going to go down this road again?' She probably would've added 'you asshole', too if I was honest about it. But 80 and 78 years old or not, it's a big brother little sister thing. Anyway, I let it go.

'Peach and Hutchie are coming to watch the game with me tonight,' I said.

'Where's Ged?' She asked.

'He's in Montreal with Eric, corporate box and all that stuff. I think Steve and Christine are there too. Are you going to stay, watch the game with us?'

'You three old coots? You must be kidding. Besides, I wouldn't want to cramp your style.'

'That's true. We really are too cool for school,' I said moving my head up and down in a way that I thought was maybe cool.

'Anyway, I've made plans. Martha and I are going down to Ryerson Arena - you know, the old Maple Leaf Gardens - to watch it on the big screen. Just us and 19,000 of our closest friends! Leaf fans one and all!' She put her right hand over the big Leaf crest on her sweater, tilted her nose up and looked off in the distance, like she was the Queen Mother of Bloor Street.

'Oh my God! You guys will single-handedly revive the pulp and paper industry in New Brunswick what with all the Kleenex you'll be needing to soak up your tears. Boo hoo hoo! My weefs!'

'We'll see about that,' she said. 'Hey, look at the book that I'm reading.'

13.

Game day. Logan and Andrew were back at the hotel room, just in from the 'optional' morning skate. It's the Stanley Cup Finals - there's nothing really optional about it, unless of course you're nursing a sore groin or dodgy wrist and want to avoid any undo pain and aggravation. Make it worse in a practice and miss a Cup game? No chance. Even if you wanted to skate, the coach would force you to stay put, sleep in, come down for some physio whenever you felt like it. Fortunately for the Leafs, they were all as healthy as anyone could expect them to me. Ten pre-season games, four of them in China, 84 regular season games, and so far 17 playoff games: that's 111 games all told. This means that no matter how much food you jam down your gullet; no matter how many post-game beers you drink, you are going to be about 10 or 15 pounds below the weight you were when you reported to training camp - in 'the best shape of your life'. And here you are on a bright June morning, a mass of aches and pains, bruises here and there, bothered by bits of this and that. In other words, everything was just fine.

The brothers roomed together on the road. Though they had taken very different paths to the NHL and to this very moment in time, though they were in fact very different personalities, rooming together felt just like it did when they were pre-teens. Sure they'd squabble about this and that, maybe even throw the odd punch, get each other in sweat-flying, heart rate -raising headlocks, you know, the usual boy stuff, but they were each other's own best friend. Try to come between them - as had many an unsuspecting young woman - try to divide them up, and you'd pay the price. Get up in Andrew's business and you'd have Logan to answer to. Try to lay a beating on Logan and here came Andrew flying at you like the Iron Sheik. Tribal is what they were. A band of brothers, a tribe of two.

It was 11am and it was mostly down time til puck drop. A team meeting in the hotel at 2 for an hour or so, down to the Bell Centre at 5 for all of the pre-game mumbo jumbo - interviews, stretches, a bit of cycling, Swiss ball shit, skates sharpened, sticks retaped, a little physio, a mix of the necessary and the ritualistic. Visiting team dressing rooms and dressing room areas were still a gong show in the NHL. Cramped and poorly lit, filled with dark passageways, so a walk to an exercise bike would feel like a scene out of The Blair Witch Project. The best thing about playing in Montreal, Logan thought to himself, was, aside from the fact that Montreal was the greatest city in Canada - sorry Toronto! - was that the Marriott was a short walk to the Bell Centre. It also had a great weight room and indoor pool, and since this was Montreal, nobody cared a damn whether you were the famous hockey playing Cash brothers or Jack and Bobby Kennedy. If you weren't a Montreal Canadien, past or present, Celine Dion, or the ghost of Gilles Villeneuve, then you were nobody who mattered - sorry Arcade Fire!

The skate this morning was just fun. Logan and Andrew had a routine on free skate days. Andrew would leave the goalie gear behind, and suit up in a set of spare 'out' gear - remember that lingo, when you were a kid? Who's playing net and who's playing out? And if you were out, you were then either up or back. He and Logan would play keep away in the centre circle for about half an hour. An amazing work out! And if you got too tired, you could call someone else into the circle and swop out with them. Like most of the best goalies, Andrew could both dangle and skate better than almost everyone else on the team. But, also like most goalies, he was too crazy, too much of a loose cannon, to be allowed 'out'. After keep away, they'd place two nets against the boards, facing each other at centre ice and then team up in a 2 on 2, no raisers, and take on all comers. They'd been undefeated the entire season, partly because Andrew was not afraid to throw his body across the net no matter how much zip there was on an oncoming puck. Andrew loved the free skate. Switch it up. Force your brain into new patterns of thinking, create new connections across distant synapses, do it right and deepen that pathway, thicken the myelin. Andrew was a big believer in neuroplasticity. Practice makes perfect. No doubt about that. A century of Soviet bloc training techniques had shown us that. But, at the same time, it wasn't called the 'same old, same old' for nothing.

Funny to think of two grown men, each a multi-million-dollar-a-year player, 'rooming' together on the road. True, about half the teams in the NHL were on capitalism's death door, and true there were only a handful of teams - most of them in Canada - that bankrolled the league's shared revenue structure, but rooming together wasn't about economics, about saving money. Teams spend as much on incidentals as they do on hotel rooms. You know how many thousands of kilometres of tape teams use in a year? Cubic kilometers of Gatorade? OK, that last one's a bit of an exaggeration, but take my word for it, rooming is not about economics, it's about one for all and all for one, it's about the buddy system, it's about the seasoned veteran helping the rookie learn the ropes, it's about two guys that used to hate each other because they played on opposing teams, learning to watch each other's backs, and it's about ensuring that your most valuable commodity - your players - are in the best frame of mind so that when they hit the ice, in Dan Bylsma's immortal words: 'We are able to play the way we play, and willing to do what it takes to play that way'. Ah, hockey platitudes. Gotta love them. I'm not sure I even know what Bylsma means, but what I think he means is that peak performance requires the fewest possible distractions, and on the road the possibility for distraction increases exponentially, and, where young alpha males are concerned, these distractions mostly manifest in skirts and bar stools. I mean, just because you are a gentleman on the ice, a wizened scholar of the game, a flawless talent, a Nureyev of the dangle, doesn't mean you aren't a liquor pig who would sleep with anyone when on the road, or, for the single guys, even at, or especially, at home.

Of course, this wasn't the case with either Andrew or Logan. At least not anymore. Andrew had already logged 13 years in the bigs. Logan had 18 under his belt. Andrew was married with a passel of children. Though such facts hardly stopped Tiger Woods or most of the NBA from such laddish behavior. After all, these guys had money, fame and, many of them, charisma. The hyper masculine attracts the hyper feminine - for every Mars there is a Venus or 10 - so while the boys married their high school sweethearts and treated them like angels (rather than people or equals, which might have been a better approach to long lasting relationships), they shagged whatever came their way on the road, and make no mistake, these girls would line up 3-deep for a chance to catch the eye of some fly guy. Every male hockey locker room suffers a plague of the Madonna-Whore syndrome. And if you don't think that way, the hyper masculine culture will force you into silence, where silence is not necessarily compliance. Take Logan, for example. Logan was still single, but ever cautious, and, like his grandpa Charlie, a true romantic, so though prone to mistake lust for love in the early years, he'd been burned enough to stay out of harm's way. If guys wanted to risk their marriages, and sometimes their health - hello Magic Johnson - or girls wanted to be treated like trash, that was their business. Consenting adults. Not very smart adults, but nonetheless, free to make their own decisions. Anyway, thought Logan, there's a game to be played. Leave the shenanigans to the other 28 teams who were already a ways into the golf season, some of them a long long way.

Andrew and Logan were not roommates to keep each other out of trouble. They were roommates because it was comfortable. Rooming with each other was like donning your favorite sweats and kicking back to play video games, no questions asked. In fact, that's exactly what Logan did. Off with the Leafs garb and on with his maroon colored St Mary's Huskies sweatshirt and basketball shorts. His aunt and uncle had continued to give him these as a Christmas gift but also as a sort of inside joke. Back when he was a young teen, Logan dreamed of playing hockey for SMU, largely because SMU's coach was also his provincial team coach. They got along famously. Which was very important because, even though Steve was entirely supportive of Logan's hockey, he couldn't skate to save his life. Basketball. You shoot up tall and suddenly people are shoving a basketball into your hands, saying 'Look at 'im! He's so tall, he's going to be a basketball player.' Since basketball and hockey are both winter sports in Canadian schools, it was one or the other. Steve really had no choice. So, Logan's dad had been a basketball star. Fans would shout: 'Give the ball to Cash! Steve, drive to the net!' Not really so different from Logan's experiences on a team, as a star, but Steve couldn't help him with technique. Encouragement and positive reinforcement would have to suffice. Steve had gone the usual Cape Breton route for those who make it off the island and into tertiary education. By this I mean, St. Francis Xavier University, on the mainland in nearby Antigonish. Good Catholic boys went to St. FX. Or, rather, good Catholic children went to St. FX. But, as far as Steve was concerned, it didn't matter what your religion was, if you were a smart person interested in success you went to St. FX. Took business. 'Brian Mulroney went there, don't ya know', he'd say, effecting his gaelic brogue, 'and Danny Gallivan too'. He was determined that the boys follow in his footsteps. Logan's uncle Jack and aunt Mary had also attended schools in the Maritimes, neither one being St. FX. Mary, ever the rebel, had gone to Acadia down in the valley in Wolfville. Jack had attended Dalhousie in Halifax, where he earned a PhD in Political Science. He'd also been a bit of a mercenary academic, teaching several courses at SMU. He liked SMU a lot. Steve dismissed this attitude as totally misguided, 'What is there to like about it? He'd say. 'The high school on Robie Street!' He'd wrinkle up his face as though he'd just scented fresh dog poo on the bottom of his shoe. So, one Christmas Logan's aunt and uncle bought him his first SMU jersey, a real beauty, a bright deep maroon hoodie with a giant SMU and the face of a husky knitted into it. Logan rarely took it off over the course of the entire Christmas holiday. This didn't set well with Steve who got that funny look on his face every time he looked over at his son. It got so bad that during the Christmas tournament in Tantallon, Steve took to wearing his old St. FX jacket just to be sure anybody seeing him together with his son wouldn't be so misguided as to believe that the father was a SMU alumnus. So, every couple of years, Jack and Mary would buy a fresh sweatshirt for Logan, who loved the new one he was wearing right now as much as he did the first one nearly 25 years ago.

Logan never did go beyond high school. The road to the NHL was short and straight. Three years in Rimouski had made him bilingual, trilingual if you count Cape Breton English as a language all its own. So that was a plus. And he was naturally intelligent and curious, widely read. Had a good head for business, his father would say. He hadn't travelled much, save for the usual off season few weeks here and there around the northern half of the Western hemisphere. He was a homebody: Halifax and Cape Breton in the summers which meant two months of golf and dry-land training. The rest of it was all hockey all the time. If an escape was needed, he'd trot out his game console, dial up some of his regular mates in China, Burkina Faso and Brazil, and lose himself in a cyber paradise. Which is exactly what he was in the process of doing.

'Not too long, Logan. Gotta get some rest. Don't want you all googly eyed for the game tonight.'

'Yep, don't worry. Just twenty minutes or so'. Which, for Logan, really meant an hour. Andrew didn't press the issue. Buddy system: he'd press when necessary.

Andrew's road to the big time was quite different from his brother's, reflecting their very different personalities: Andrew the Jack Russell; Logan the Great Dane;

Andrew the broadway entertainer only too happy to put on the tap shoes and give it all he's got; Logan the quiet, Hollywood leading man, happy to let the soundtrack tell you how he felt. They were as different as Fred Astair and John Wayne, or Danny Kaye and Clint Eastwood, each a leading man who always got the girl, only Logan didn't have to sing and dance to get her attention. Like many hockey players, Logan was a two sport guy. In his case, it was golf and hockey with a little tennis on the side. Andrew liked them all, and in any given year, he'd swop out hockey for soccer, or soccer for taekwondo, or taekwondo for gymnastics, then all of it for only golf, and eventually, seemingly on a lark, all of it for hockey. This, of course, both puzzled and annoyed his ever supportive parents. From a distance it was easy to see that Andrew chose positions in sports, or types of sports where not only all of the attention but all of the pressure would be on him: in the ring or on the rings, in net or on the parallel bars, Andrew was the last line of defense, where his performance alone would determine the outcome. He and his brother were both scratch golfers, but it was Logan who excelled as a team player, he was captain on every sports team he ever played. Andrew was a team player as long as he could anchor the squad, be the go-to guy in the rubber match. Andrew wins, we all win, all eyes on Andrew. The kid loved pressure, and attention. Like I said, a natural goaltender. Fearless but mercurial. Win and own the world, lose and you betrayed your family.

It had taken Logan a very long time to talk him back from the ledge after Game 1. But he had the required patience, persistence, and experience for it. Andrew was as good as gold today. Game 1 was done and dusted. He was excited for tonight's challenge, especially since his mom and dad would be out there among the 21,000 rabid Habs fans, his dad included! He knew that Steve was permanently conflicted with the whole Leafs-Habs thing, wanted his boys to excel, be happy, stay healthy, but wanted his beloved Habs to win win win. That was good enough for Andrew. To engender conflict in the heart of a lifelong Habs fan was pretty good, it seemed to him. And what did it matter to Andrew anyway, what Steve thought. Andrew was in it to win it for Andrew, and Andrew was in it to win it for his team. The truth is, the jersey really is incidental. Over the course of a career, you played on a number of teams, you either gelled or you didn't, you would lie down in rush hour traffic for each other, or you wouldn't. Teams are unique each and unto themselves. The combination of personalities is sometimes just right, and sometimes lacking that certain something. But you gave it your best and if over the course of a season you gelled, you'd sacrifice your body for each other, the personalities were just right, it was the best journey from start to finish, whether you won it all or not. There's nothing better, thought Andrew, than playing on a team full of guys you really loved. That's how he felt about his family too. He married early, right out of university, got the girl of his dreams - actually, the girl of his best buddy's dreams. In the subsequent 15 years he and Bianca had had 6 kids, 3 boys and 3 girls and to Andrew they were a real team. He'd lie down in traffic for every one of them, and he knew they'd do the same for him. Though some were still barely higher than the bumper on his SUV.

'Five more minutes, Log,' shouted Andrew from the kitchenette of their hotel suite. He was slathering cheez whiz onto a toasted plain bagel. 'You want something to eat?'

'Isn't there a team lunch or something? '

'No. But there'll be fruit and stuff at the meeting.'

'Can you call room service for me?' He said, eyes glued to the TV screen, fingers flying over the console.

'Order me up a t-bone. And a baked potato.' When it came to diet, Logan was old school. If it was good enough for Darryl Sittler, then it's good enough for me, he'd tell anyone who raised an eyebrow at his preferences.

Andrew dialed in, waited for an answer, watched his brother seemingly in a trance at the edge of the bed. Look at him, a 220 pound 6 foot 4 inch little boy, said Andrew to himself, smiling. -Hello, room service, I'd like to place an order.

Steve and Christine had missed Game 1 for the simple reason that they'd been delayed by gale force winds in Halifax. Hurricane season seemed to get longer and more intense every year. They'd gone east to open the cottages, get the raft in the water. Usually the boys' hockey season would have long been over, and they'd have gone out to air out the properties themselves, play a few rounds of golf ahead of the crowds of Germans and Japanese who seemed to take over the island every summer. When Andrew decided to attend St. FX his dad was out of this world. When Andrew decided to take a business degree, his dad was over the moon. When Andrew made the hockey team as a walk-on try out, Steve saw stars but began to wonder what was going on. And when Andrew switched into Fine Arts/Theatre, Steve was back down to earth but not really surprised.

'Who's going to take over the business?' He'd moan, out loud or to himself and on a daily basis.

'Logan will do it after he retires,' said Christine.

That was Steve's hope. But not his only one. He was never one to hedge his bets. That's why he'd taken on the boys' oldest and best childhood friend, Cameron, as an apprentice. Made a deal with Cameron long back that he'd pay for the boy's education - business, St. FX - if he would sign a written contract stating his intention to come aboard as a junior executive upon graduation. Cameron, also one to never hedge his bets, had happily agreed, become a chip off the old block, a little Steven in waiting. Big Steve had spent decades building up his own financial management company. Gone from zero to 60 in 3.5 seconds. Straight to the top. Big success. Worked damn hard at it, too. Wanted to show the boys the value of hard work, not to mention a St. FX education. But here they both were playing pro hockey, for the friggin Toronto Maple Leafs. Steve had been the recipient of many a classic Maritime back-handed compliment. Such as: 'Boys have done well for themselves. Real well. Given that it's the Leafs and all, eh, Steve?' That was Malkie McPhee, older than dirt, and life-president of the Toronto Sucks fan club, Cape Breton County chapter. If I had a loonie for every smart arse remark about my boys playing for the Leafs, I'd have quite a few loonies, thought Steve, smiling to himself. At least Andrew had got the X-ring, which Jack claimed signified membership in a cult. -You're just jealous, Steve often said, hand in the air, like he was posing for a Pond's commercial, admiring the giant ring with a giant X on the ring finger of his basketball player's primary shooting hand. Nobody would have to know he got it for theatre arts. Which, to Steve, was no different than getting a degree in working a loom, and would pay about as well too.

But that needn't have worried Steve, as Andrew went from strength to strength first in the nets for the X-men, then for the Leafs in St. John's, and now for the parent club. And along the way he'd managed to pay his own way, get married, and get Bianca knocked up about every other year, raising a half dozen of the sweetest little gaffers you'd ever lay your eyes on. Christine doted on all of them, but the three girls to her were something special. After all, she'd raised only boys - all that testosterone in one house had sunk many a marriage, and led many a woman down a booze ridden road. But not Christine. She was made of sterner stuff and in the end it had paid off: 3 granddaughters, who had now become old enough to carry on a conversation without burping, farting or punching each other in the arm.

What had driven Andrew back to hockey? If he himself knew, he wasn't saying. He acted as though it was the most natural thing in the world to have done and, in so doing, everyone else acted that way too.

The doorbell rang. It was room service. Logan was famished. -I could eat a horse, he said.

'Remember, this is Quebec, Logan. Careful what you say about horsemeat.'

14.

The phone rang. I opened my eyes, scanned the white ceiling, watched the floaters swim across my vision, took a deep breath and hoisted myself up into a half-sitting position, the IV tugging slightly against the back of my right hand. I looked left, out the window, then down at the phone which was sitting on the little industrial table next to the bed. I could see the sun refracted a thousand times against the glass building across the way. It appeared to be still quite high in the sky, though I could tell by the relative quiet of the world beyond the window that the work day was long over. The phone continued to jangle away. 2037 and hospitals still had these clunky relics in every room. I picked up the big yellow receiver, felt its heft, placed it against my ear. -Hello, I said.

There was a long pause and I could hear some white noise. Long distance. It must be the wife.

'Hello Jack, how are you? It's Mary, Mary Adams, your wife.'

She only called me Jack when she was either concerned for my welfare or irritated with my behavior. I hoped it was the former, not the latter, though I did recognize that I'd put himself in harm's way by continuing to play old timer hockey, or 'geezer hockey' as my sister called it. But what else was there to do? You're 80, yes, I get that. But how to give up something you love, especially when to give it up is to acknowledge the grim reaper out in the yard, pacing around, having a smoke, looking at his - or her - watch? And when, in your heart, you're actually about 35. In the presence of beautiful women or great power I sometimes could be reduced further, to a mere teen, a wee Jackie my boy. Mary was both beautiful and powerful, but also very familiar. I can handle Mary. Sort of.

'Hello my angel,' I said, trying to impart the idea of fitness through the timbre of my voice. 'How are you, and, perhaps more interestingly, where are you?'

'You know I can't tell you that, Jack. Anyway, I'm fine. It's all very hectic and terribly stressful here, I must admit. Belligerence must be a genetic trait among the Netenyahus.'

'They're not called "ya-hoos" for nothing,' I said and chuckled to myself.

Mary was on a peacemaking mission. That much I knew. She'd been tasked by the UN Secretary General, Joanna Tapela - a former student of mine originally from Malawi - to gather the Arabs and the Israelis together somewhere and try to sort them out. She'd left for New York about two weeks ago and now she was who knows where. I could hear a distinctive hoo-hoo hoo-hoo-hoo in the background, the first two tones sounding a bit uncertain, the latter three fired off in rapid succession. Emerald spotted wood dove? It's not that I know my birds, but I'd listened to that song for many many years. Botswana somewhere? A 5-star in Kasane maybe; Some deep delta elite hideaway known only to princes, kings and BraJolena? Then again, those doves are all over the sub-continent.

I met Mary while teaching a summer course at Dalhousie. Following her kinesiology degree at Acadia, she'd been climbing the biomed corporate ladder, had an epiphany following a tour of duty with Medecins sans Frontiers in Haiti, chucked it all in, moved home to the Maritimes from the Big Smoke, and decided to go back to university to become a granola crunching, Birkenstock wearing, student of international development. When I met her she hadn't yet graduated to the Birkenstocks, thankfully never would. If she had, we'd probably never have gotten married. I was living in Maun, working at the university there, a full time member of the Mukwa Leafs, but was in Halifax at the invitation of my old buddy Dave, Doc Holly's dad. We'd done our PhDs together - and by 'together', I mean we started at the same time, with Dave the whiz kid finishing long before a plodder like me. We've remained close friends ever since. In a way he set the stage for Mary and I to meet: invited me to teach; suggested that she take this course as a good way of getting back into the swing of being a student after years in the no holds barred world of corporate cut and thrust.

'What's yur faaahther's name?' I drawled in my best rendition of Cape Breton English. This was shortly after the final grades were in. We were out for a beer at The Old Triangle.

'Cash, as in Johnny,' she began, and then proceeded to tell me a potted history of Irish Cove, which had a current population of about 11. Mary was at least ten years older than the rest of the students, all of whom were either first year grad or 4th year undergrad. But she was almost 15 years younger than me. I knew I would marry her from the moment she thrust her hand in the air and disagreed with me, 'Excuse me, sir, but that's not how it happened when I was in Haiti.' Big bright blue eyes, wild lion's mane of blonde hair, honesty and earnest intent written on her face. Smart and beautiful. A woman who would, in the words of a long ago ex-girlfriend, 'give me a tangle for my tackle'. Indeed. Five minutes after the first intervention: 'Excuse me, sir, but I'm not sure about that. When I was in Costa Rica...' I had to marry her. So I courted her cross-continentally for a year and then got her. He shoots, he scores.

I loved passing through Halifax because it gave me a chance to play some pick up hockey with my old buddies - Lee, Andrew, Warren, Newman - out at Centennial Arena just off Dutch Village road, or in Dartmouth - with Bobby's gang - at the Sportsplex, a few hundred metres from the old Macdonald Bridge. How I got hooked up with these guys is a long story, but the skinny is simply that if you've got talent, word gets around, even if you are from big bad Ontario. Many a morning I would head out to my car only to find a giant dried gob on the driver's side window. Ontario plates invited bad behavior. Being from a working class neighborhood and working class family, I didn't get this. It's about class, boys, not geography. We're in this together, I often argued, usually in the dressing room over a post-game beer. But that didn't stop the local boys from taking runs at me during shinny, test my mettle. An elbow to the chops, a behind the play slew foot before returning to the bench to snicker with their buddies. Even your own teammates not wanting to pass you the puck. Fucking irritating. So, I'd have to stand up for himself, yet again, prove I belonged. That's a funny thing about hockey. New in town? You can find a game but don't expect everyone to welcome you with open arms. There'll always be one or two guys out there, like Peach, who treated you like family: like hockey? Well then, I like you. That is, unless you turn out to be a dick. You know the kind of guy I'm talking about: arrogant, puck hog, overly aggressive, stick man, hates the guys he's playing with, gives them no respect, likes to see his own reflection in the glass, preferably when he has his helmet off, thinks he's still got a shot at the Cup though the only cup he's likely to get his hands on contains a Tim Horton's double double. Yep, that's the guy, whether he has only one of these traits or, more likely, a combination of them, he's a dick. Usually every team has one, no matter what the level. And there's always one or maybe two in shinny hockey, especially the sign-up sheet, municipal rink version of the game. I steered way clear of that sort of hockey. The guys in Halifax were not dicks - at least not all of them.

They were just marking territory, laying out stud piles all around the new thoroughbred in town. In their minds, everyone from Ontario was a thoroughbred, a Mr Fancy Pants, a spoiled rich kid. A guy who reads, plays golf, goes to the theatre, thinks the fall leaves are pretty is suspect at best. Still, he's someone who comes from away, takes what he wants, often times higher education and a wife, and leaves. A fly-by-night sort of guy, a guy not to be trusted. So, want to play hockey with us? Let's see if you can handle it. It could be easier or tougher. Introduced by a friend of a friend and the path might be smoother. Ask to play, knowing no one at all, and you'd be in for a rough ride.

According to the specific criteria of a dick, I didn't qualify. I was always the solid, second line winger, the power forward, the dog on a bone, the team guy who took his lumps while giving the puck to the goal hunter, the tor jäger, who was in truth sometimes a dick. But according to the Maritime version of a dick, well, I sort of did. I'd got both a wife and an education out of the province and moved away. But, I always came back, stayed in touch, and over the last several decades spent every summer on the island with my lovely Cape Breton bride in our cottage, a lightly converted old sawmill on the Bras d'Or. The cottage used to belong to one of Mary's uncles, before that to her grandfather who'd built the mill. The rough, hand-hewn main beams offering testimony to the calloused labour behind its sturdy structure.

'Jack? Jack?' Mary inquired, 'You still with me, Jack?'

'Yes, yes, I'm here dear heart, dear sweet-tart,' I said, drawn back to the present by Mary's voice. 'It's a long and winding road,' I let out a big audible sigh. Put the receiver down on my lap for a second, vigorously rubbed my eyes, quickly snatched it back.

'Yes it is, Jack, for me as well,' I heard her say.

'No, what I mean is, I was just thinking about how we met. The sound of your voice, the meds, it's playing havoc with my, my, lived reality. Like the time my dad was laid up in hospital after his aneurysm. Remember this story? I'm sure I've told you this a hundred times. I visited him in his hospital room and he seemed well enough, until he asked me if I could see the guys playing basketball on the ceiling. That's how I feel. Lucid and out of it, almost at the same time.'

'Well, you just rest up, little baby boy,' she said in her goo-goo mama voice, which always made me laugh, got the old blood circulating. 'Don't go running off to join the circus, OK? Or worse, the Leafs.'

'I'm not going anywhere, at least not while this IV is attached to me,' I said, lifting my arm up as if for her to see. 'Anyway, the boys are coming by to watch the game tonight. Game 2 of the Finals in case you aren't up to speed with Canadian front page news. I know you're in a sort of isolation setting wherever you are.'

'Yes, if you hadn't had a heart attack I wouldn't have been able to call you.'

'I'll be sure to have another so that you can call again.'

'Very funny. And don't you dare! I'll be home to see you soon enough, so please please please listen to your doctor, and behave yourself around the nurses.'

I tried to think of something clever to say, but failed. The daily grind of doing nothing but staying alive in a hospital bed had wiped me out. Nothing said 'mortality' like a heart attack at 80. I pictured Hamlet, handsome guy, great posture, looking a bit like Eric Lindros. Stage left, skull in hand, held high toward the false moonlight. 'Alas, poor Yorick', etc. All those moments of sitting in a dark theatre silently identifying with the protagonist. Now, I'm bloody Yorick. I winced at the thought - at the near fact. How the hell did that happen? We said our good byes and rang off.

15.

'Hey, big fella! How's she goin'?' This was Hutchie. At 80, I most certainly wasn't a 'big fella', but I appreciated the sentiment.

'Good, dear, good,' I replied, mimicking my mother-in-law. This was lost on Hutchie. It was game time and he was all business.

'Go, fight, win,' said Peach, who remained a 'big fella' despite his decades long battle with gravity.

'Where's the beer?' I asked, though, given my condition, I wouldn't have drunk it even if it were a cold bottle of my favorite Sleeman's Honey Brown.

'Wait for it,' said Peach, who propped a man-bag at the edge of the bed. Rummaging around he soon produced a large thermos, tartan patterned it looked to be about a hundred years old.

'What've you got there old buddy? Whisky? Lemonade?'

'Nope,' said Peach. 'Tea!' He seemed very proud of this fact.

'Par-tee!' I said, non-commitally.

Hutchie rearranged the furniture so that the two side-chairs both faced the TV screen, the small round coffee table in between. Peach set the thermos down on the table and took a seat. I could see him making several silent calculations regarding height of the little table (slightly too low for a big guy like him), distance to the bathroom (not so bad even in an emergency, though he would have to pass in front of us perhaps momentarily blocking the screen), size and placement of the TV screen (a nice big flat screen at just about the right height - hospitals seemed to finally get this right after eons of cramming a too-small monitor off into a high far off corner). The volume he would check later. Leaning down, he produced a bag of potato chips from his satchel. -If you're good, there may also be ice cream later, he said, cracking a smile.

Hutchie had commandeered the remote control and was eyeing it carefully. After a few silent seconds, he turned it around, pointed it at the screen and pressed the little red power button. Presto! All systems go. He channel surfed for a bit before settling on the CBC. After years in the sports desert, the CBC had finally regained control of Hockey Night in Canada from the media behemoth that was Rogers, as well as its signature theme song from TSN. TSN had fragmented into a hundred different micro-focal channels: Want all UK darts all the time? You got it! Want mixed martial arts live from Bangkok on Mondays and Wednesdays? You got it! If you're willing to pop out the extra 50 dollars a month, you can have whatever your heart desires. CBC was no different. After all, it was a dog-eat-dog world out there. Grow or die. It was Micro-Economics 101. After several decades of slash and burn tactics used by governments of all stripes, the CBC had emerged a lean, mean neoliberal machine. You want news? Get it somewhere else. You want Ann of Green Gables style heartwarming old timey programming? Get it somewhere else. What to listen to creative, innovative, interesting programming? Listen to CBC radio. Want hockey, only hockey, all hockey all the time? The CBC is your destination of choice: team specific channels; league specific channels; country specific channels; country, team and league specific channels. It was a global money maker and today the CBC was rolling in dough, no longer the whipping boy of Conservative, Liberal and NDP governments alike, it was hands-off the CBC, because that was the lone government venture that resulted in profit. And profit helped keep the navy afloat, the air force airborne and nuclear power plants humming like chin-stroked kittens.

'We've still got about half an hour til puck drop,' said Hutchie.

'Want some tea?' Said Peach.

16.

'Do you know that I'm the same age that Tim Horton was when the Leafs won the Cup in '67,' asked Andrew.

'Yep. And I'm the same age as Dick Gamble,' said Logan.

'Who?'

'Exactly!' Exclaimed Logan, whose point was simply that, man, my best before date is now past. Win now or never win at all.

They were legging it along Rue Sainte Antoine, heading for the Bell Centre. The Kid line was in tow. They were sort of walking in a flying V, Mighty Ducks style.

'My great grandfather won the Conn Smythe that year. Led the team in scoring during the regular season too.' Ian Keon had every stat ever compiled about his great grandpa, the great Dave Keon, at his fingertips.

All heads swivelled in his direction but nobody said anything, their grimaces seeming to say, 'What do you think we are, idiots? Everyone knows the story.' But the kid was clearly excited and had the feeling that he -

they, the whole team - had a date with destiny and this time, destiny would not stand them up.

'Well,' said Andrew, 'now we know who's been reading Kevin Shea. Or was it Damien Cox this time?'

'Ian can read?' Said Naz. 'That's news to me!'

They all had a good laugh.

'Listen boys, it's important to know the past, but not live in it. We are here to make our own history. Be part of a story that people will never forget,' said Logan.

'Ya, a success story,' said Andrew. 'Positive reinforcement, boys. Visualize the win. See the pass completed. See the check finished.'

'See the cheque cashed, not the Cash checked!' Said Naz, looking up at Logan. The boys were in a lighthearted mood. They were full of nervous energy, but the legs were good, the attitudes positive, they'd have jump. They'd give the Montreal Canadiens a run for their money tonight, that's for sure. They were at the Bell Centre, entering through the front door, no bus driving back-entrance for these guys. They were all class.

'Welcome to the show,' said Donny Ellis, who'd been quiet on the walk over.

'Punch that ticket! Let's get 'er done!' And in they went, long strides, shoulders rolling, looking ever so much like Will Smith, Tommy Lee Jones, Josh Brolin: The Men in Black.

17.

'The grandkid looked good the other night, Hutch,' said Peach, always a glass half full sort of guy.

'A lot better toward the end,' said Hutchie ruminatively. 'Seemed to get their legs in the third. The whole line looked flat to me,' he said, perking up. 'Like they were nervous, couldn't get rid of the jitters or something. Papps and the Swede, little Hutchie too, they've gotta play a lot better tonight.'

Forget politics, the state of the world, who was the better Prime Minister - Harper or one of the Trudeaus - the prospects for peace in the Middle East, the reunification of the Koreas, sea level rise: this was way more important in the lives of the average Canadian: who will win the Stanley Cup? And in the lives of the average southern Ontarian: can the Leafs win a Cup before I die? Hockey had always been a second tier spectator sport, relegated to the insulting nomenclature of 'ice hockey' on the world stage, where the rest of the planet considered 'hockey' to be a game played with a short stick and a hard ball on grass. In the US, despite decades of the hard sell, the soft sell, the Wayne

Gretzky sale, cheerleaders looking more suited to a beach volleyball court than a hockey arena, and oodles of 'free stuff' (made in China) handed out at game after game, unless you could promise a fist fight no one beyond the snow belt gave a damn. And this includes California, where every team that ever played in the NHL - save for the California Golden Seals - had at least one of Lord Stanley's Cups to its name. The NFL, the NBA, major league baseball, mixed-martial arts, soccer, even golf - a rich man's game in the eyes of most Americans - eclipsed hockey when it came to attendance figures, media ratings and commercial merchandising. And it wouldn't be long before cricket would be added to that list. Sure, the NHL had made significant strides in Europe and Asia over the last 25 years. But while 10 million fans of Frank Chan translated into a lot of cash through internet merchandising, the facts were that 'Mahjong TV' reeled in 100 million viewers at 3am across a sleepy-eyed China.

As a sport actually played by real people, no sport could compete with 'the world's game': all you needed was a round object and a moderately flat space. Soccer was played everywhere by almost everyone, including an increasing number of Canadians. And, well, well done soccer! It is a beautiful game. But to lose out to basketball in the sweepstakes of participation in sport around the world was simply painful. Particularly for a Canadian boy of a certain, shall we say, vintage. For us kids growing up in Windsor, Ontario, hockey was always number one. Basketball was that other sport you only played when they took the ice out in the summer, and even then, dribbling was optional, travelling mandatory. We played our own version of basketball, just as we played our own version of soccer: kick, chase, tackle. Freaks (like my brother-in-law Steve) played basketball; foreigners (like my friend Tom who'd come to Canada from Ireland) played footie. What was more complicated about playing hockey than playing basketball? In basketball the ball needed to bounce; in basketball you needed to mount baskets on a wall or a post somewhere. It was no easier to get a b-ball game going than a street hockey game. So, what's the deal? All I can figure is it's a race thing; it's a weather thing; it's a technology thing. Hockey is still mainly as white as snow, seen by the rest of the world only during the Winter Olympics, and played with all sorts of gear in a highly controlled space. Who could identify with that? One time I was channel surfing in a hotel in Dar es Salaam and happened upon an NHL game: Detroit versus Chicago. I was so excited. But also completely confused: who was watching this? Granted, it was a satellite feed carried by a South African provider, but still, who anywhere in Africa other than a Canadian ex-pat was watching this game? I got up from my chair in the hotel room and hustled outside, looking up and down the walkway for an unsuspecting victim. There was a guy sweeping jacaranda flower petals off of the flagstones and into a big purple pile on the grass. I called him over. He spoke no English, but was happy to play along with the crazy Canuck. I got him to come into the room where I pointed at the TV. The game was in full swing. 'Do you know this?' I said, making shrugging motions with my shoulders. He stood motionless and watched for perhaps twenty seconds. He looked at me. I shrugged again. He looked back at the TV, then back at me, and shrugged his shoulders too. We couldn't communicate properly, but the message was clear: he didn't have a clue as to what was going on. And why should he? There was nothing about this sport that resonated with anything about his life, his experiences, his surroundings. Nothing. That's how it is with the rest of the world. A marginal curiousity at best. But not to me or my two friends sitting with me in the hospital room. Hockey was life. And we'd love it to our dying breath. Which, I hoped, wasn't anytime too soon.

'How many Canadians are even on the Canadiens?' I asked no one in particular, and knowing the answer well in advance. I just wanted to spark a bit of controversy, get my blood moving around. There was a bit of hemming and hawing before the devices came out and we checked 'the google', as my mother-in-law would say. Without doubt, Toronto was Canada's team. Only Chan, the big Swede and Horton, who was an American, came from away. This edition of the Leafs marked a high point in a trend toward stocking up with home grown talent across the league: blonde-headed surfer dudes in L.A. and San Jose; bible thumping cowboys in Texas; hillbilly guitar twangers in Nashville and Carolina. For the rest of the U.S.-based teams, longitude largely determined whether you drew from the WCHA, the Big Ten, Hockey East or the ECAC. The Bruins, for example, were led by a mighty-mite named

Sam Anas Jr. who, like his dad, had played college hockey at Quinnipiac before moving on to the NHL. Who could have foreseen thirty years ago that one of the premier players in today's NHL would hail from Potomac, Maryland. The big exception was Montreal which, aside from the Westmount-born Subban twins, and a just-turned-40 year old journeyman defenseman named Nick Welsh who hailed from Halifax, Nova Scotia but played junior with the Cataractes in Shawinigan, looked to be the spitting image of the Red Army 1970s style. They were chock full of what the Don Cherry types called heartless 'East bloc robots'. More than 60 years after Borje Salming came into the league with the Leafs, and many thousands of often brilliant European players later - remember Petr Klima? Ziggy Palffy? Hakan Loob? - and the 'buy Canadian' crowd remained as myopic and xenophobic as ever. On the other hand, one couldn't deny how weird it felt to watch Montreal play with nary a 'habitant' in the bunch.

'What with all the Euros and Russkies on the Habs, and all the home-growns on our team, this looks more like the '72 Summit Series than the Stanley Cup Finals. Never mind Tronna, we gotta win for the sake of national pride.' This was Peach, seemingly having a revelation. I began to wonder what was in that tea.

'Come on, man, who cares where they're from? Can they play the game - that's the question that matters,' I said.

'O! Ca-na-dah!' Hutchie sang, hand over his heart, but I could see he was just trying to wind me up.

'Besides,' I continued, not one of the three of us can claim Canadian heritage back more than one generation. All of our families came from away.

'Remember when you were first at school and you'd meet new people, they'd always ask "where're you from?" We did too. And we didn't mean Pickering or Bolton or Sioux Lookout. We meant what country did your forebears hail from.'

'Forebears hail from'? I mimicked Hutchie. 'You sound like a CBC Heritage Moment. Better watch out, you'll pop your dentures with future phrases like that.' I could feel my own about to pop; an eff-based alliteration often led to an embarrassing moment for many a hockey player.

'I've got a lot in common with the big Swede,' said Peach.

'Ya,' I said. 'You can both pass a puck into a teammate's skates no problem!' We all laughed.

We all made so much out of this Montreal-Toronto thing. Rue St. Denis versus Bay Street. Joie de vivre versus all work and no play makes little Johnny a Toronto banker. But really it held no more substance than did the my sweater versus your sweater argument. In a way, what we were rooting for, inside the sweater, was not just the current team of our dreams, but for our memories as children growing up, of crowded public rinks where you innocently chased after Lee Ulrich, not sure what you'd do with her if you ever caught her; of flood lights shining across a sleek patch of backyard ice, your dad standing stock still with the hose in his hand, dishing out an even spray, trying to make sure the ice was a smooth as glass by morning; of red cheeks and snow-frozen woolen mittens, toes as cold as the ice they skated on; of our dads lacing up our skates, steam rising from their brylcreamed heads; of puck after puck lost in the snow; and of Heinz tomato soup and buttered white bread or ritz crackers waiting for us when we came in, mom's smile as warm as the air that embraced us as soon as we entered the house. Toronto versus Montreal: this was a battle to keep memory alive, to pack more experience around it, to build up your bank of remember whens, and, ultimately, when you're a geezer like we three, to keep the old ticker beating, the blood flowing, so as to keep the grim reaper - in her hospital shoes - at bay for at least another day. Of course, we'd never admit to such a lame-assed nostalgia, because we're guys, we never admit to anything even when it's staring us straight in the face. If someone was to ask me right now, while I'm lying here in this hospital bed, whether I was a candidate for a heart attack, I'd say 'What? Me? Never!'. And I'm not the only schmo out there either. But if hockey isn't as much about nostalgia, of lives lived where and when, as it is about two teams playing a game today, then why do we keep making more kids of our own, building the backyard rinks, buying the kit, and pulling the little gaffers out there?

The HNIC theme music drew our attention to the screen. There was Ron and Cassie rinkside, roof-mounted searchlights dancing across the red and blue lit ice, the crowd filtering in to their seats in the background, almost everyone decked out in their bleu, blanc et rouge. It was all so very familiar. And, to me, dead boring. People say that your life flashes before your eyes just before you die. I wonder if perhaps, instead, you end up with a kaleidoscopic triptych of every pre-game ceremony you were saddled with through time. Maybe if you've got a date with el Diablo. It would be a suitable warm up. On the other hand, the opening and closing ceremonies of the Olympic games clock in every year as two of the top 10 shows viewed on Canadian TV. I'm not sure what this says about us, or me, who always preferred to just cut to the chase. Drop the puck. Get on with the show.

'What would be worse,' I said, 'a never ending loop of opening ceremonies or a never ending loop of CBC TV "news", you know, all the shit moving around in the background while Suhanna Marchand tells us about the Queen's gout?' Nobody answered. We'd been together for too many decades for them to bother reacting to yet another one of what they believed to be "Killer's pointless queries".

'Hey, when did Ron McLean become Don Cherry?' I asked.

'And when did Cassie Campbell become Ron McLean!?' Asked Peach.

18.

GAME 2

The game began with a bang. Literally. The Leafs coach started the checking line - Hutchinson, Pappin, the Big Swede - against the Cosmonauts - Titov, Popovich and Bykovsky - of the Habs. Right from the draw, the puck was flipped into the Montreal zone, Subban (PK1) turning to give chase, Papps right on his tail, Subban's brother (PK2) skating backwards toward his own net, keeping an eye on the other two Leaf forwards. Everyone watching could see what was coming. You could almost feel the air sucked out of Central Canada, as we all took and held a deep breath. PK1 had only a half-stride on Pappin who had come down the wing as though fired from a gun. Head down, facing the end boards, fishing for the puck, a sitting duck, and wham! The tall glass rocked before cracking where PK1's head had made solid contact with it and then, like time lapse photography, a million fissures angled out from the crack and the glass collapsed in a clatter of tiny pieces. The defenceman was down and he was out, out cold.

Papps, adrenalin flooding his system, first went for the puck before realizing what had happened and, inevitably, what was coming. What was coming was PK2, gloves off, helmet pushed to the back of his head. He was loaded for bear, the bear being Pappin. Papps quickly dropped his gloves and managed to get his arms up just as PK2 laid into him. Usually in a hockey fight there is a bit of awkward grappling, especially if it's spontaneous and not a goon square-off. This time, however, PK2 came in fists flying and cold-cocked Papps square on the jaw. He dropped like a bag of cement.

'Two down, 10 to go!' Said Peach.

Little Hutchie then flew into PK2, Popovich tried to pry them apart, and the big Swede tried to peel Popovich away from the other two. A sort of square dance ensued. You know the kind, grab your partner, doe see doe, and all that stuff. Not very interesting to watch actually. Gloves and sticks everywhere. The goalies pairing off at centre like two wallflowers at a high school dance, tugging at each other's arms, looking terribly foolish. There's nothing graceful about goalies once they have left the crease. Team medics had raced out amid the chaos and were attending to PK1 and Pappin, both of whom they had managed to rouse, but both of whom lay still on the ice.

'Old time hockey,' joked Hutchie, though clearly concerned about his grandson.

Once the hubbub had died down and a semblance of order had been restored, the result was two players lost due to injury, one of whom received a 5 minute major for boarding and a game misconduct. PK2 was also ejected for his bad behavior - a 5 minute major penalty for intent to injure and a game misconduct - though this announcement was greeted with a deafening chorus of boos from the partisan crowd who firmly believed in 'an eye for an eye', though they often pretended they didn't. There were assorted other off-setting minors, meaning, in the end, that teams simply would play at full strength, as though nothing had happened. Though, in fact, everything had, and by everything I mean the Habs had lost their number one defense pairing, the Subban twins, less than ten seconds into the game. Without PKs 1 and 2, the Habs were just another very good team.

In the crowd, buried deep in and among the few hundred Leafs fans, clustered together in Sections 123 and 124, close to the visitors bench, Steve audibly groaned, holding his head in his hands. Christine would have none of it, and a sharp elbow to the ribs let him know which side she was on. The she bear was in the house! And she was surrounded by a small but tenacious group of like-minded moms and dads here to cheer on their boys. Logan stepped onto the ice.

'Well, there goes the game,' said Steve.

'Good!' Said Christine. 'How you can not cheer for your own sons is beyond me.' She was wearing a Leaf jersey with CASH across the back but no number; wouldn't want to seem to favour one boy over another now would she?

'I support my sons! What're you talking about? I want to see them do well. Excel. Succeed. Just, well, preferably not here.'

'Traitor,' said Chris. She leaned forward, squeezed Eve's shoulders, whispered in her ear, 'Your grandpa can be such an ass.' Eve was Andrew and Bianca's first born. She was born exactly 10 months into their marriage, in St. John's, during Andrew's first year with the AHL club. She'd made the trip by train to Montreal at the invitation of her father. 'It's only 5 hours, with one change at Union Station, she'll be fine. Fifteen is more than old enough to travel on your own,' he said when Bianca raised a fuss. 'Besides, she'll be chaperoned by the good people at Via Rail', he had said to his wife over the phone. 'Whew! Now that's a relief!' she was mocking him, but ultimately relented. Eve loved hockey, played for her high school team in Milton, and fantasized about making the Canadian Olympic team.

'Vive le Quebec libre!' Said Steve, who, when dressed in a white turtleneck sweater, bore a striking resemblance to Gilles Vigneault, minus the pork-chop sideburns of course. Today he was wearing a bright pink golf shirt with grey slacks: deliberately non-partisan colours. But, in his pocket was a laminated, original O Pee Chee Guy Lafleur rookie card, 1970-71, which he decided to carry for good luck. No one need know. What harm can it do? he had said to himself, slipping it into his pocket unnoticed by the Leaf police, aka his wife.

'Would you two please stop arguing and watch the game!' This was Lisa Walton, Joshua's mother. Next to her sat Bob and Lori Pappin, who had calmed down once their son, though clearly still woozy, was back on his feet. He'd been helped off the ice by the team medics and gone straight to the dressing room. A tweet had come through to them that he was alright though having suffered a mild concussion.

'He's out for the game,' said Bob quietly to Lori, both looking at his mobile device.

'Maybe longer,' she whispered back, not wanting to risk gaining the attention of hockey's capricious gods.

Up in the Leaf corporate box, Ged and Eric watched the hit and ensuing melee like two kids watching waves at a shoreline: build, unfurl, crash, subside. Ged didn't say a word, neither did his son. They didn't have to. They were thinking what every other hockey fan was thinking: this is now Toronto's game to lose.

The period passed without incident or major event. Evenly played, Toronto had not been able to turn lady luck to their advantage. At least not yet. The shots on goal were even at 9 apiece. Neither team had taken another penalty, though the game was played at a very high tempo. Meanwhile, the dressing rooms were both very quiet. In the Leaf room, Logan took centre stage to utter the obligatory platitudes of encouragement, of opportunity knocking, and all that. It was more to break the silence than anything else. It's not wise to let a dressing room stay quiet for long, otherwise the boys will begin to think something's up, something's wrong, get inside their own heads, perhaps let in a narrow sliver of doubt. Better to get the tunes going, talk about nothing, rah rah rah go fight win. Hockey players are creatures of habit and often very superstitious. Over a player's lifetime the noisy room meant confidence, meant wins, while the quiet dressing room generally means something is, in fact, wrong: we lost when we should have won; we were playing poorly and the coach just ripped us a new one; that sort of thing. So, like Pavlov's dogs, a quiet room makes for an anxious pack. Logan nipped it in the bud, said what he said, got the tunes going. Kardinal Offishal never got old in hockey dressing rooms: 'Reppin' every where I go!'. - Yo! Let's go homes! shouted Andrew. Everyone responded, the younger players also exchanging glances, rolling their eyes, as if to say: Geezers, what next, Miley Cyrus?

The quiet in the Montreal room told an important story. A team that had its top two D knocked out in one go, one for who knew how long, maybe the whole series, should be riled up, madder 'n hell, ready for vengeance. But the boys in bleu, blanc et rouge were passive; not pensive, just silent. A passerby would have wondered who died, or who had flipped the switch to 'off' on these East bloc robots. It was a team without passion. Make no mistake, it was a team, a very very good team. Won the President's Trophy as the best team in the league this year. Sometimes incredibly creative on the ice. The Cosmonauts could give the Harlem Globetrotters a run for their money in that department, no problem. They were also tough as nails, absorb hit after hit, and still keep coming. When asked to explain this ability, Montreal's coach simply said: Weebles wobble but they never fall down. You could warm to their talent, admire them, respect them, but love them? You could love the Subbans. They were cut from the same mold as every Subban who had played before them. Charismatic. Fun. Fun to watch and hell to play against. They were a coach's dream and every marketer's fantasy. They were the kinds of guys who could balance perfectly and effortlessly the complex demands of the media, community outreach, personal life and the game. Together they were the face of the Montreal Canadiens. But, in behind them, were a talented crew of awkward, hard-to-get-to-know foreigners who, despite their skills, could never measure up to the Habs of yore. When asked to name a player on the Montreal Canadiens, people were most likely to say Lafleur or Lemaire, perhaps the Subbans, even Patrick Roy, but rarely one of the current day Cosmonauts or any of the others who remained, somehow, out of focus.

Playing for the preeminent sports prize in Canada - sorry Grey Cup! - is no walk in the park. The long season, the ramped up tempo of the playoffs that seemed to never end, the scratchy beards, the endless hours between games and in transit, reporters and paparazzi at every turn, everybody with a device suddenly fancying him or herself a Hot Stove guest specialist, everyone playing hurt or sick, your family wondering who is this ghost that walks the wee hours of the morning in our house. The grind has sunk many a lesser man, and many a family. To succeed, then, requires something special, both within the self and within the team. Within the self: steel and determination, the ability to block out the noise, separate the essential from the inessential, health, youth - physical, but especially mental, and if not experience then ignorance in its unreflective form; think too deeply and you may not like what is revealed to you, may give rise to an 'OMG!' moment and scare the shit out of you, better to just focus on the game and let those with experience guide and lead. As a team then, you need this balance of youth and age, strength of body and strength of experience, you also need trust in each other and faith that the job will get done, you need talent and balance, straight men and comedians, guys to simmer you down and guys to get you pumped up, followers and leaders. Phil Esposito could barely skate but he could lead. Anyone who watched it, will never forget Espo's post-game, off-the-cuff, wake-up call to Canadians to get behind the boys in that now long gone series. And Phil could fill the net. The greatest teams are not those that are filled with danglers and snipers, but those that have, in addition to the pure scorers like Esposito, the muckers and grinders, the guys that will go into the corners and dig out the puck, the guys that will stand in front of the net and take crosscheck after crosscheck, the pain in the ass, the hound dog, the D man who will go down to block shots on an April afternoon with no hope of the playoffs for his team - anyone remember Jim Schoenfeld? You need guys that you hate to play against, with nicknames like the Rat and Knuckles. You need guys with flair - clear the track here comes Shack! - toughness, even meanness, and speed. The funny thing is that everyone knows what makes a team great, but no one really knows how to make a great team. I've just laid out the key components. It's not rocket science. But even if you think you've got the pieces put together just right, you can never force the final ingredient which is a combination of heart, passion, cohesion, togetherness. In this silent Montreal dressing room, with or without the Subbans, you could see that they didn't have it. Could they still win this Cup? Well, did the Russians ever win a Canada Cup? A Summit Series? There's your answer.

19.

The second period unfolded pretty much like the first until a questionable penalty call - against Toronto - seemed to turn the tide in the Leafs' favour.

'What the fuck is that, ref!'

'It was a dive! A dive!'

While the Leaf players complained, the crowd jeered. A chant of 'Go Habs Go' started up and the fake organ music joined in.

'OK, Ellis. Keon. Let's go.' That was the Leafs coach, setting up the penalty kill. Pronovost and Horton were on defence. The face-off was to the right of the Leafs net and was won by Titov who drew it straight back to the point. Ellis angled in to attack the D man who had already wound up for a slapper. As he came down and through the shot, the puck took off like a rocket straight into the right shin pad of Ellis where it rebounded out toward centre ice. Without even breaking stride, Ellis side stepped the defender, deftly collected and settled the rolling puck, and took off on a breakaway, two Habs in hot pursuit. He crossed the blueline near the right side boards, to the left of Habs' keeper, Blahoslav Brambory, who got himself into his set position, skating out a few strides and gliding slowly back to the top of his crease. At the top of the circle Ellis dropped his head and wound up for a slapshot. Instantly, sensing his opportunity, Brambory came out to cut off the angle. But, at the last second, Ellis faked the shot, leaving Brambory high and dry, took two strides into the slot and slid the puck home into an empty net. 1-0 Toronto. A smattering of applause and cheers could be heard around the rink. For the most part, though, the Bell Centre was silent.

'Woo! Hoo!' Shouted Peach, almost spilling his tea.

'Remember the '76 Canada Cup?!' Shouted Hutchie. 'Just like Sittler: fake it and go around!'

The boys were in a good mood. There was a lot of ruckus to be heard down the hallway, as every room had the game on.

'That's exactly what Duke used to say to me.'

'Only ever met him the once,' said Peach. 'During the 2016 world rec hockey championships down in your old hometown. Remember that?'

'Oh ya,' I said with some enthusiasm, though I didn't really. 21 years is a long time. Why we remember some things and not others is anyone's guess. How Peach, self-proclaimed king of CARHA, could keep all the adult rec tournaments straight in his head, like they were on a rolodex, was quite amazing.

'Who's Duke?' Asked Hutchie.

'He was my old coach,' Hutch. 'He's been gone a long time. He was a lot more than that, though, when I think about it. Mentor, friend, teammate. A lot of things. But somehow I always think of him as a coach, first.'

Duke's real name was Terry Snyder. Like Steve born tall and given a basketball, it seems every guy with the last name Snyder gets nicknamed 'Duke'. Who the hell was Duke Snyder anyway? A baseball player I think. My Duke was a teacher at Riverside High School. I never took a class from him but his antics were legendary. He'd established a reputation as being quick with the yard stick. This is back in the day when corporal punishment was the norm for kids of all ages both at home and away. 'Spare the rod, spoil the child', the saying goes. In middle school, we had a gym teacher whose name I have long forgotten, who had a plastic whiffle bat that he named 'Clem'. Step out of line and you'd risk the wrath of Clem. Being a natural born troublemaker, I'd been made to bend forward at the hips, keep the legs straight and, yep, wait for it, wait for it, wham! There was Clem across the hamstrings of your bare legs. It would hurt for days. Duke was cut from that cloth. Having been a teacher all my life, I waffle between 'WTF?' and 'Get me a yard stick!' I'll never forget the first time I went to Botswana in the 1980s. I was staying at a flop house for volunteers across from a primary school. In the morning, drinking instant coffee out back on the veranda, I'd watch the teacher in charge of the playground chase the kids around with a sjambok, which is a flexi leather whip used to herd livestock. At the ages of 6,7,8 I guess there's not much difference between kids and goats in the minds of most teachers. Those in Botswana were just more open about it. Duke used to get the teenage miscreant in his classroom to come to the chalkboard and bend forward so the kid's head was below the little metal shelf where you put the chalk. Then he'd give the kid one across the back of the legs with the yard stick. The kid would involuntarily pop up, whanging his head on the metal shelf. Vicious stuff. But somewhere along the way, Duke found God and became born again. With God comes understanding and a predilection toward pacifism: swords into ploughshares and all that.

'How do you think that got there!' he'd say, placing his watch on the table. We were in the bar, having a post-game cold one. We'd just sit and wait for the punch line. 'Someone put it there. That's how. Someone put it there,' he'd say in a very self-satisfied, teachery type of way. Like: case closed. We were arguing about the existence of God, which often happened at the bar with Duke on a Monday night during hockey season. We all played together in the Civic League, which was the premier industrial league in Windsor back in the day. All the washed up pros, semi-pros, recently graduated with nowhere else to gos landed on the shores of the Civic League. Maybe it still is a great league; I don't know. Is there still industry in Windsor? Gambling doesn't count. Anyway, we'd argue back and forth, a never ending battle between belief on one side and proof on the other side. If nothing else, it was highly entertaining. Our Civic League team was really 'Team Snyder'. We'd all been coached by Duke over the years, played together in the Duker Hockey League or DHL, which ran Wednesdays in the winter and Tuesday/Thursday in the summer. In the early days, when the ice came out for a few weeks in the few arenas in town, we'd engage in 'dryland training', i.e. soccer and basketball at Riverside High. After the games, Duke would open the pool and we'd go for a dip. We always got a kick out of the fact that he had the keys to the school pool.

Duker hockey was a highly sought after hour of ice time. Since Duke had been around for ages, he'd taught a few generations of students, so the list of potential players was very long. Around a solid core of Duke's fellow teachers, friends and a few parents, there was a sliding scale of participants aged anywhere from 15 to 50. Duke would make teams, which would play a best of 7 series, after which he'd rejig the teams for another series. Player preference was given to his current high school team. If you played for Riverside you were automatically included among the 20 skaters and 2 goaltenders. Duke needed to keep an eye on you. I, however, was on the 'call-up' list. And I'd wait patiently by the phone hoping for the call on every one of those nights, until eventually, having ticked several boxes in the 'makes the cut' list known only to Duke, I'd become 'a regular'. I'd been coached by Duke, but it was football not hockey. For some reason, I was always the last one cut from the hockey team. Even when I'd played well, once scoring a hat-trick against Windsor's top high school goalie, Mike Freeman, in the tryout game, it was always 'thanks for coming out, maybe next year'. At 80, it still bugs me, but, then again, I'm like that. Over our many years together Duke never explained why, in his view, I just wasn't good enough. But he was happy to have me play after high school was over, and even help him coach the team for several years while I was a student at the University of Windsor.

Summer hockey drew crowds. All the young guns were home from their stints in Europe, the OHL, US College hockey, the NHL. The pace of the game went up several notches and we played for keeps. And Duke kept playing well into his 70s; though he was always slow as molasses he got the job done on D through a combination of positioning, clutch-and-grab, and the fact that the young guys respected him, so they'd slow up around him, give him a fighting chance. Duke taught us all about respect, about team play, about comradeship. If you didn't fit Duke's 'code', you'd be out the door, 'thanks for coming'. But not being one to hold a grudge, if you cleaned up your act, he'd give you another chance. I guess, somewhere along the line, Duke thought I'd cleaned up my act.

'Looks like the kids have cleaned up their act, eh, Peach,' said Hutchie, feeling optimistic.

'There's a lot of jump in those young legs. That Ellis kid reminds me so much of his great granddad. Remember those guys, Hutchie? Ellis, Keon, Pappin. Funny to see the same names here. I hope that young Pappin is OK. He was out cold. The Subban kid too.'

'Weren't we all a bit too young to remember the 67 final with any real clarity?'

'YouTube can make you feel like you were present for pretty much everything but the birth of Christ.'

'I remember Sawchuk's face mask. Rogie Vachon in the other net. No mask. Crazy. Goalies, eh?'

'I dusted off my copies of Shea and Cox,' said Hutchie. 'The Cox book is an interesting read. Gives you real insight into the collapse. Left a sour taste in my mouth the first time I read it. Left the same taste 50 years later.' Hutchie was smacking his lips and making an odd face, eyebrows creeping around like a pair of albino caterpillars.

'Imlach. What an a-hole.'

'Better to leave those sorts of books on the shelf,' I said. 'Keep the childhood myths alive. For me, a guy like Mahovlich was larger than life. When he got traded to the Wings, I just couldn't believe it. I felt bad for my dad, 'cuz his buddy Henderson was moving up the road, but, man, Frank Mahovlich in a Wing uniform! Paired up with Gordie. Delvecchio in the middle.' We all looked off into a mythical middle distance, where youth was recaptured, but the wisdom of years retained.

20.

'Atta way, Elly!' 'Great move, buddy!' 'Woo hoo!' The glove slap skate through routine, gap-toothed smiles up and down the line. And from there it was off to the races. The big guys played big. The pests were as bad as the deer flies on the lake in June. The danglers dangled. The speed merchants wheeled and dealed. The keeper came up big when he had to. And the veteran captain led the way, scoring a pair of third period goals, the last one an empty-netter to salt the game away. 3-0 to the Leafs. Their first victory in a Stanley Cup Final game since May the second, 1967, that game salted away too with an empty netter by their captain, the 36 year old George Armstrong.

'Who's too old?! Who's too slow!?' This was Naz, as the kid line had Logan down in the corner of the dressing room in a sort of group headlock, Keon getting ready to dump a big plastic container of ice-filled Gatorade over his head. It was a boisterous few minutes, as the boys let loose while the Leaf coach held the media at bay out in the hallway.

'Well, what can I say?' said the Leaf coach. 'The boys played their hearts out. Gave 110% percent. I think the

Cash boys showed that they've still got what it takes. 38 is the new 28, or what?' He was trying to be loose, jocular, a good 'ole boy, but all he could think was, 'don't say fuck on TV'. The questions came in thick and fast, just like the Leafs around the Habs' net. This was hectic, a bit stressful, but, man, he felt good.

Up in the corporate box, Ged and Eric had played it cool. One win does not a series make. But it's a start. They were standing, white shirted, black suited, corporate tied, shoes shined to the nines, arms now folded, watching the Leaf coach on the post-game show. What a rube, thought Ged. Eric looked at his dad, nodded, said 'you can say that again'.

Down at the Ryerson arena, Lori and Martha were happily soused.

In the crowd, Christine said to Steve, 'How about we head down to the dressing room to see the boys?'

'Nah,' said Steve. 'It'll be a mad house down there. Everybody will be wanting a piece of them. Let's just head over to the Marriott, leave a message, they'll drop in when they're good and ready.'

'But what if they head straight home?'

'Send Andrew a message, Eve. Tell him not to dare to leave without seeing his old mom and dad.'

'Just because he doesn't listen to you, doesn't mean he listens to me either,' she said, smiling. Just think, she said to herself, my dad got a shutout in the Stanley Cup Finals. And her smile got bigger.

21.

'All tied up,' said Hutchie happily, his grandson having displayed some of the grit and fire that makes a hockey playing grandpa feel young again.

'You know what's funny about this game? The way the role of the enforcer comes and goes. Especially as league policy on fighting goes up and down. Clamp down on fighting and guys like Colton Orr or Frazer McLaren would have to learn to skate or back to the minors witcha.'

'Why do you bring that up?'

'There's not a goon or enforcer on either team here. Just tough hockey players. Guys who will stand up for themselves and watch each other's back. None of that staged fighting. Remember that league? The one that guaranteed a fight per period or something like that? No different than lingerie football in my view.'

'Hey, don't knock lingerie football! It's a helluva lot more entertaining than that other stuff the Yanks play.'

'But guys like John Ferguson could play the game.'

'Ya,' I said, 'my alltime favorite tough guy was Bob Probert. I mean, he got caught up in all that "we're going to Toronto tonight so I will have to fight Domi" nonsense, but Proby scored 29 goals one year, made the All-Star team. What year was that?' Everybody looking off dimly into nowhere land again, it occurring to no one that the google was ever ready to put an end to speculative sorts of conversations. Proby was a Riverside boy, used to drink at our bar. Was always out of control. Hung with a tough crowd.

'Who was the toughest guy on the 67 Leafs? The Habs had Fergie, I remember that.'

'Tiger Williams?'

'No, he came later. With Sittler and McDonald.'

'Allan Stanley?' This brought a hearty roar of laughter from us all. But really, there was nobody on that Leafs team you could label an enforcer or goon. Somehow the game just wasn't played that way, with everybody segmented into strict categories: grinder, goon, sniper. Of course, teams were composed of these sorts of players, but there was no 'goon market' for example. Everybody had to play tough, even the Ellis, Keon, Pocket Rocket types. People forget that Bobby Orr could fight just as well as anybody. And why wouldn't they forget? There were very few people left alive anywhere who had seen Orr in his prime. I remember going to the old Olympia Stadium in Detroit with Mike Klimkowski, an older boy who was the son of one of my dad's best friends. This was 1966. I think it was a Saturday afternoon, though I could be wrong. It was

Orr's first game in Detroit. I had never heard of him. Why should I? I was 9. And at that time my whole hockey world revolved around 9 - Detroit's no. 9. We were at the bar where I was saying goodbye to my dad. And my dad was telling Michael to drive safe. There were a bunch of regulars standing around the bar at the time. My dad, rocking on his feet behind the bar, arms crossed across his chest, white dress shirt with the sleeves rolled back to the elbow, said, 'keep your eye on number 9'. Which, of course, I would. But the guys at the bar all protested, 'No. You keep your eyes on number 4 for Boston.' Which meant nothing to me at the time.

'If Bobby Orr were alive today he'd be, what? 90?' I said this apropos of nothing except the whir and spin of my own memories. But this never stopped the boys from jumping straight in to the conversation.

'Born in '48, I believe.' This was Peach, the walking encyclopaedia of hockey.

'Remember the hit Pat Quinn put on him?' Said Hutchie. Heads nodded all around. But our heads were starting to nod for different reasons. We were all ancient history. It had been a big day for the Leafs and their faithful, and for those, like me, who were guilty by association. Dawn, Peach's wife, poked her head into the room. 'Hey boys, time to go home now,' she said. Like me, Peach had also married a younger woman. Who knew it would pay off years later in the form of rides home particularly since the State had, in its wisdom, deemed us to be road hazards and refused to renew our driver's licenses. I bet every citizen who opposed mass transit in their 40s, are thanking their lucky stars that the State, again in its wisdom, built the LRT so we could ride it - to Shoppers, Tim Horton's, Sobey's, the proctologist, the ear nose and throat guy, cousin Betty's - in our 80s.

22.

Why does sleep come so furtively to the aged? Creeping up on us, caressing us, teasing us with promises of quiet bliss, only to get up and walk out leaving us here in the deep dark middle of the night wide awake and alone? Back when I was trying to finish my PhD and teach full time at the University of Windsor, I used to get up at 330 and, moderately groomed, some 30 minutes later, head in to my office at the U. It was a 15 minute peaceful drive along the waterfront road. I used to play a game with the lights, trying to figure out their exact time count so I could gauge my speed in such a way as to try and catch every green. Some mornings I'd stop in for coffee at the 7-11 at the corner of Lauzon and Riverside Drive. The shop was kitty corner to our hotel, and the big öld building would look like it belonged to the Addam's Family in its street-lit spookiness. One morning I ran into Jim Peck who had pulled in to the 7-11 on his bike. Mr. Peck was a popular figure in Riverside hockey circles and was known, behind his back, as 'The Grizzly', for he was bear tough and bear mean. As a player you didn't want to get on the wrong side of him, provoke the bear so to speak. To see him on a bicycle at 4 am was a bit incongruous. He must've been 60 at the time but still cut a rugged figure in his sweats and ball cap. 'Mr Peck!' I exclaimed, 'What are you doing up at this time of day?!' 'Well', he said, 'I don't want to miss nuthin'. Maybe that's what it is, then. Sleep is more difficult for the elderly because while we appreciate it, we know the clock is ticking on us, and we don't want to miss nuthin' - even if, like my mother, this meant mostly a date with her daytime TV family, Montel, Ellen, and so on.

So, let's take stock. The witching hour makes for a ruminative octogenarian. A hospital room is never really dark, even at the darkest hour of the day. Hallway lights, a little wall socket night light, too thin curtains revealing the incessant, persistent, intrusive light of the city. The only good thing about this is it makes my little foray to the toilet less hazardous, even without my glasses which are, where? Somewhere, anyway, what does it matter? I don't need to see with my eyes to take stock. I need to feel my way around the old self. Covers pushed back, legs flung, a firm grip on both the edge of the bed and the IV holder contraption, and off we go. It's only 5 steps and a turnaround to the toilet - I like to sit when I pee. The old prostate is holding up quite well, thank fully. Not like some of my age mates, whose urinary woes are the stuff of legend in dressing rooms across the GTA.

Once back in bed, I lay very still and listen to my body. Test everything out. The joints ache but not abnormal- ly. When things have ached for 40 or more years, what does that really mean anyway? Wiggle this, rotate that, snap, crackle, pop. Everything ship shape. The lower back though is a bitch, and my ass is so friggin sore. Like I'd been at a bloody opera, or an orthodox catholic midnight mass. Too much down time. Use it or lose it and I haven't used it at all now for what a week or so. Even a stretch would help. I need to speak to the nurse about this. Get rid of this bloody IV tomorrow too. It all looks pro forma to me anyway, a simulation of health care rather than actual actions constituting health care. If truth be told, I feel good. OK, I'm 80, so I'm nothing to look at. Too many years in the African sun and I look like I've got a bit of bushman blood in me. Wrinkled like a prune. Muscle atrophy. Space where there used to be mass. Thighs firm but thin. Where did the meat go? And when? You don't even notice the change in yourself until you catch sight of that guy looking back at you in a dressing room shower mirror. It always gives a bit of a shock. Who's that old fucker? Me! Well, at least I'm not alone in that department. You look around the dressing room and you see sags and bulges where once all was firm and taut. What once was flat is now round. Muscle replaced by what? Nothing at all. Not everybody of course. I've managed to stay lean, but the result is that I look preserved, like I'm a half step from an ancient Egyptian display case. The more rotund of us, those who just can't say no, who live in a land of plenty and partake of it every day, they don't look preserved so much as pickled, like eggs in a jar behind the neighborhood bar. 'I'm full as an egg', a friend used to say after they'd eaten too much. A quick gander around the dressing room reveals about 60%

plumped out egg and 40% stringy chicken neck. A bit of both on several guys. Young at heart, though. And not only do clothes make the man; they make a train wreck of a body look like the Japanese Shinkansen.

So, I feel creaky but good and look my age. But what does this mean? I've had a heart attack that no one, least of all me, saw coming. Is that it, then? Am I about to check out, or do I have a few or several or even many good years left to me? To be 'on the right side of the ground'? The whole 'he's had a good life' is fine for those not the object of discussion. If I was a religious man, like the Duke, I'd be heading off to the next world singing hallelujah, Lord here I come! Belief is a powerful narcotic and the Duke was high as a kite. Good for him. Lord knows we've buried so many of our teammates - and all through our lives. Car accidents, suicides, cancer, childhood leukemia, aneurysms, drug overdoses, an endless array of tragedy among the hockey playing community. Just like the rest of the world. Too many gone before their time. Only the good die young, goes the saying. But I always had a theory about that: the truly good seemed to succumb to all sorts of things, whereas the mad bastards hang on and on and on. Pick your world's worst ruler, let's say, Robert Mugabe. The bastard is still alive! He's 110 for God's sakes. And still rules poor Zimbabwe with an iron fist. Many people believe the Chinese have some special medicine keeping him alive. Every time he goes to China for medical treatment he comes back looking younger. Want to live long? Pull a kid's ear. Kick a dog. It will add years to your life, is what I used to say. But now that all of us are hanging on into our 80s, I need to revisit this theory. I mean, it holds for me. You don't get a nickname like Killer by being a nice person. There's many an old adversary out there who, if not suffering from Alzheimer's, would flinch at my name and say 'is that asshole still alive!?' But Peach and Hutchie are still going strong, and two nicer guys you'll be hard pressed to find.

Anyway, i'm kind of off topic. I was taking stock. Ruminating. Wondering the big WTF? Men - so much goes unsaid. Maybe that's a good thing. I don't know. Maybe most of what's going on in the heads of men is not worth knowing in the first place. Just look at the state of the world. That should give you some idea about the way the rabbit wheel spins in the noggin of average Joe. But we never talk seriously about aging or death. We lament the passing of friends. We mock each other mercilessly about our failing physiques. But we don't ever sit down and hash out the what next. The closest I've ever gotten to speaking about this with another man was all those years ago with Duke, sitting around the bar, arguing religion. One time I had the temerity to lament the passing of one our friends and Duke said matter-of-factly, 'Why be sad. He's with the Lord now. We should rejoice.' Ya, well, that's not a good enough answer for me. I don't even know if I want an answer, or expect an answer, or even want a discussion. It's just that well, I'm 80. My friends are in their late 70s and even early 90s. We're falling apart at the seams. Some of us are barely even what you'd call sentient beings any more. It's the late fall of our generation and we are withered flowers, browned and crispy leaves, spindling in the wind, ready to detach from the tree and flutter to earth. End of story. Eish. Such thoughts. This is what happens at 3 in the morning when you're stuck in a hospital, listening intently to the tick, tick, tick of your fading heart. It is a muscle. It must go like all the rest.

23.

The latest incarnation of 'Maple Leaf Gardens' - ie the Samsung-Blackberry Centre - is a 25,000 seat state-of-the-art arena complex located just off the 401 on the property of what used to be the Milton Heights Campground. The campground had been around for donkey years, but had been encroached upon by development to such an extent that, one, there really was no point in camping there if you wanted to 'get away' from the urban world because it just kept whizzing by your tent flap, and two, the land was too valuable not to sell. The Leafs all lived north of the rink, from Eramosa in the west to Erin in the east. While most of the guys were either in condos or in relatively well established monster-home developments with names like 'Meadows in the Glen' - you know the kind, with the twin garages out front, each one so filled to the brim with stuff that no car could possibly be parked there - Andrew had bought an old farm on the Tremaine Rd just a few minutes drive to the rink. He and Bianca had the whole place redone so that it was entirely environmentally friendly. 'It's off the grid, you know', said his 9 year old son, Charles, his twin sister, Marie, nodding her head, cradling a basket of eggs.

Over the last fifty years, Highway 7 had entirely filled in, swallowing up small town centres such as Acton, making it resemble Dundas St. as it runs through the core of Toronto, rather than a highway of any kind. Logan, and a few of the other single guys, were in a condo in Georgetown on MacFarlane Drive. Georgetown had evolved to feel a little like Bloor West Village meets the Danforth (without Rob Ford and the crack houses).

The team had taken a red-eye charter, getting into Pearson around 2 am, onto a team bus for the half-hour ride to the arena and then into a variety of vehicles for dispatch to their respective homes. Andrew had parked his Brammo Empulse in the Zamboni room. He poked around a bit to make sure the battery was charged, before hopping on, motoring silently out of the building, through the parking lot, out onto the road and up to his house precisely 5 minutes later. Home sweet home, he thought to himself.

In the morning, the sun shone down on a happy Toronto. No one under the age of 70 had been alive the last time the Maple Leafs won a Stanley Cup Finals game. Imagine the number of generations of hockey fans that had come and gone since 1967. My father was born in Toronto, the middle child in a household of 14 kids. All of them Leaf fans and all dead and gone. Many of their children, also Leaf fans, are also dead and gone. And many of their friends and friends of friends, all Leaf fans, all six feet under. How sad to think of the millions of Leaf fans who each fall returned to the NHL with hope, year after year, like lemmings over a cliff. Streaky Leaf teams were the worst: win 10 and it's Lord Stanley here we come; only to find that this was swiftly followed by lose 10. There's nothing more difficult either than supporting a team that wins as many games as it loses. Because in such a team there is hope. If only this, or if only that, we will be top dog once again. It is easy to love a loser just as it is easy to love a winner. You know what you are getting. There's either no reason for high expectations (the chronic loser), or there's no reason to feel that we will not be 'right up there' again this year (the chronic winner). But the fifty/fifty team is another story. And for about 70 years the Leafs have been a fifty/fifty team. Such teams give rise to frustration, and to the expression of this frustration: remember 'the sweater toss' of 2014-15; the annual paper-bag-on-head 'I'm ashamed to be a Leaf fan' gag? And it usually is annual. But today is another day. The Maple Leafs are fifty/fifty with Montreal and, as usual, this gives Leaf fans hope that maybe, just maybe, this time will be different.

Andrew awoke to the smell of coffee brewing and eggs frying. He also awoke to the dog, Ginger Bell III, licking his face. It was early. Too early, but hey, they had two days off. He rubbed the dog's head and rolled out of bed, stretched, scratched what itched, made his way to the can, wondered where everybody was. Somebody for sure was in the kitchen; that much he knew. Dog and man both padded off in that direction.

'Hi honey, I'm home,' he said in a Ward Cleaver sort of way. Bianca was no June. She was much better. Running a household with 6 kids in her view was a piece of cake. She came from her own large Cape Breton family and had learned from her parents that the trick to managing the kids was to have enough of them so that they managed themselves. So, in her view there could never be too many. The trick was determining a minimum threshold. According to Bianca's mother, Blanche, four was probably the self-managing minimum, as long as you spaced them out properly. Have the first two in rapid succession. As they grow up they become playmates, friends, allies in the schoolyard struggle. If there's a gap, then the older one will not bond with the younger one, will not want to be seen with the 'kid' around school. Once you've got the two in train, wait a bit before you have the third and fourth, which you should then again have in rapid succession. Not only will they bond with each other, they can be looked after by the older two. Evidence shows that whoever comes last will either be left to raise themselves or doted on completely by the rest. Easy peasy, thought Bianca. The proof is in the pudding, and I've proved my theory with this lot, she'd often think to herself.

It helped that Bianca was both easy going and cool under pressure. Nothing fazed her. Her personality was the perfect balance to Andrew's 'drama queen' approach to life. It also helped that her in-laws, Steve and Christine, had bought a big chunk of farmland just over the road, built a relatively modest three bedroom bungalow with finished basement on the property, and moved in. Well, howdy neighbor.

Bianca poured Andrew a cup of coffee and asked him if he wanted eggs. They ate a lot of eggs. Mainly because they had their own chickens. If your land is zoned as farmland, well, you may as well do a bit of farming. They also kept a few goats, mainly to keep the grass in check. The majority of the farmland was under hay. Nobody else on the team had livestock, and given Andrew's advanced age - in hockey years, though goalies seem to play on forever (remember Johnny Bower? Dominic Hasek?) - the boys had taken to calling him 'Billy' which was a play on 'here comes the old billy goat'. Andrew liked it, liked its creative aspect, better than the usual hockey nicknamification via 'er' or 'ie'. And since Logan was himself 'Casher', Andrew could once again be his own person.

The nickname is another element of the game, of team sports in general, that lends to it a timeless nature. That men in their 80s could be called Ace, Dog, Gator, Killer and Peach imparts to them a boyish air, to forever be one of the boys. How does a man named George Nickerson get a nickname 'peach'? Or a man named Gérard Séguin get a nickname 'dog'? Or a man named Joel Quenneville get a nickname 'Tinhead'? Someone nicknamed 'Ace' is obviously your best player, he's your 'ace in the hole', so to speak. But if he actually believes himself to be the ace, and carries himself in that manner, then the nickname can take on ironic undertones where, 'Ace' actually means 'Ace... the arrogant prick'. 'Killer' is not obvious when it comes to sports related nicknames. Often times the active, descriptive nickname is meant to connote the opposite. So 'Tiny' is actually a muscle bound hulk of a guy. And 'Bull' is the most gentlemanly of hockey players. I once coached a young guy in AA Major Bantam who was very small for his age, about 2/3 the size of everyone else. But he was our best player, indestructible, a marvel on skates, and, well, just so damn cute. He just turned 70 and he's still the best player wherever he plays. We nicknamed him 'Chilly' based on the cartoon penguin, Chilly Willy, which Wikipedia describes as 'a diminutive anthropomorphic penguin living in Alaska' - who writes this stuff? But over the years, Chilly grew into a strapping young man, which turned the nickname on its head. So, Killer, ya, you get the idea. Like a yappy Jack Russell ready to take on the world. Or a baby kitten, baring its claws. All you can do is smile and call it Killer. Peach, by the way, derives from 'Georgia Peach', George being Peach's real first name. And 'dog' is the back half of an anglicized pronunciation of the French Gérard - 'Geddog' - a nickname only an older brother could dish out to his younger sibling. 'Tinhead' derives from the fact that Joel's hair never moved when he skated. This is back in the no helmet days. It was like he had a tin head.

As you move through life, sometimes you'll end up accumulating two or three nicknames. As you move from team to team, context to context, people want to name you, because nicknaming is a way of marking you as one of us. Hockey is terribly tribal. If you have played hockey all of your life and no one has ever given you a nickname, you should reflect on that. Somehow these guys see you as an outsider, as inside the room but not of the team. Nicknames, at base, then, denote trust.

Nicknames also stay with you for life, sometimes popping up at embarrassing moments, where, for example, the last thing you need to be called, when at a soirée with the world's top bankers, is 'dog'. Or when running a workshop on conflict resolution and peacemaking, someone calls you 'Killer'. We once nicknamed a guy 'Head' because he had wild Buckwheat hair. Over the years he went bald, so 'Head' was not so appropriate anymore, bringing attention where it was unwanted, like 'Hey, look at that guy's bald head!' (which, of course, as kids is precisely what you intend with some nicknames). We shifted to the usual 'ie' at the end of his monosyllabic last name, which, to me, is just boring. A little less boring, but no less unoriginal, is the cleaving of a polysyllabic last name, replacing the last bit with 'ie' or 'er', so Hutchinson becomes Hutchie, Labute becomes Buter, Boutette becomes Boutter, and so on. Gordon Arthur Berenson never became Berrie because he had flaming red hair. He could only become 'Red', and as a natural sniper, 'Red' became 'the Red Barron'. When 'Head' coached Tie Domi in junior, we tried to hang the moniker 'Head' on Domi as well because we'd never seen a guy with such a big head. No helmet would fit him. But it failed to stick. There's no explaining the stick/no-stick of nicknames. If the nickname fits, then it sticks. And once it sticks, it means you're 'in'.

Wives never called their husbands by their nicknames, though they'd happily call other men by theirs. To Bianca, Andrew was Andrew, never Billy though with his current playoff beard he looked a bit more goat than man.

'Where's everybody?' Asked Andrew.

'The twins are tending to the chickens. Eve is coming back with your mom and dad on the train. Westin and AJ stayed over at a friend's where they watched the game. And Maggie is in her room doing I don't know what. Oh, and the dog is right there,' she said, pointing at Andrew's feet. Ginger Bell III stuck to him like glue. Bianca's theory was that it was because they both smelled funny.

'Excellent. We have to go in to the rink around 4 to review the films, but otherwise I've got nothing planned. Probably go back to bed after breakfast. What do you want to do?'

'Want to try for number 7?' Bianca said.

'What!?'

'Just kidding. Sort of.'

24.

Over at Logan's everything was pretty much as it always was the morning after travelling back home. Thick curtains pulled tight. Air con set to 180C. And Logan fast asleep, which would probably be the case until well past noon. 'The body's got to rest, repair, regenerate,' he'd say when his dad would complain that given the chance he'd sleep his life away.

Logan's alarm went off around 2 and he popped straight up like a jack-in-the-box. He wasn't the sort of guy to negotiate the snooze button. An hour and a half was plenty of time to get his bearings, reenter the world of the living, before going down to the rink. He pulled the curtains back, revealing a brilliant June day. Remembered how last year at this time he'd already had 15 rounds of golf under his belt. Smiled a half-smile, chuckled to himself. At the refrigerator he discovered not much of anything. No matter how long he held the door open and peered inside, the scenery never changed. There was milk. He took out the jug, unscrewed the blue plastic cap, ventured a sniff. It would do. Some butter too. And, of course, eggs. There were always eggs, fresh off the Cash farm. The road trip had been short, so these eggs were good to go. He'd do up some scrambled eggs, have a coffee, scroll through some headlines, see what was shaking in the world of sport - as if he didn't know - then head down to the market. A good thing about playing for a fair-to-middling NHL team is that you can navigate public space without being hassled by the press or the public. You might get a few teenagers excited if you happened to be in a place where teenagers hang out - movie theatres, video game emporium, skate park - but, well, the chances of Logan pitching up in such a location were slim to none. But even if you were Gretzky in L.A. or Messier in New York, you were pretty much anonymous. That is, until someone recognized you, after which a crowd would form to put a cramp in your attempt to get from A to B. Here, in the GTA, if someone recognized you they were more likely to poke whoever they were with in the ribs and discreetly head-point you out to them and then move on. Canada is just like that.

Logan wandered the market. Even though he was a head taller than almost everyone, and even though he was front-page news in the sports section of every Canadian news service, the absence of paper newspapers helped ensure an unhindered passage from fruit to vegetables to dairy to meat. The entrepreneurs knew him as the big, good looking shy guy. He was a regular, but they didn't know his name; neither did Logan know theirs. He addressed everyone as either 'sir' or 'ma'am'. Most of the shop keepers were either landed immigrants or first generation Canadians, the sons and daughters of landed immigrants. As he entered the butcher shop, a little bell rang. He looked around, the place seemed abandoned. Where's the old fella anyway, Logan said to himself. He made his way around the rectangular-shaped shop in his usual clockwise direction. To his immediate left, there was a freezer wall offering a mix of frozen pre-cuts. In front of him was a long traditional butcher's counter with all sorts of fresh meat - chicken, beef, lamb - behind glass. The pay counter was at the far end, and under the front window of the shop ran a squat long rack containing snacks of various dried meats and condiments for barbecues. Logan began to salivate. He carried a cloth shopping bag that already contained a bag of potatoes and a head of broccoli.

'Can I help you?' Logan heard a voice say. He looked up from the beef jerky and saw someone's reflection in the window. He turned around, remained silent.

'Hello, can I help you?'

'Yes, sure, hi. Say, where's the old fella today?'

'Mr Dowhaniuk is not feeling well.'

'I hope it wasn't something he ate,' said Logan, thinking this to be an hilarious piece of repartée, but only delivering a half-smile to the young woman behind the counter. She didn't seem to get it.

'So, what would you like?' She asked.

Logan thought for a minute, said, 'Some T-bones.'

'Some T-bones? How about you be a bit more specific. Come over here and let's have a look at what we've already got cut.'

Man, she's all business, thought Logan, as they ambled along the counter over to where the beef was on display. He eyed her intently, liking the idea of a young woman in a white butcher's smock. A non-traditional sort of job usually means a non-traditional sort of person. She had her left hand in the pocket of her smock, was jangling keys or something, while she pointed out the different cuts.

'There's only a couple of T-bones, but maybe you'd like a nice sirloin or flank?' She looked up, caught him staring at her.

'Sorry, what?'

'Flank? Sirloin'? She waved her hand, palm toward him, back and forth in a line with Logan's sight, as if to say 'Hey Buddy, wake up. Are you with me?'

'Say, what's your name?' asked Logan.

'My name? Why?'

'I don't know. Maybe you'd like to have coffee with me some time. Or dinner. I could cook you a steak.'

'Why, have you got some at home? Because, so far you haven't bought anything from me.'

Logan smiled. 'Sorry. I'm a little bit out of it. I got home late last night. It was a very long day.'

'Party?'

'No, no, nothing like that. I've been in Montreal for the last few days.'

It was her turn to look him over, consider his request. 'Sort of an odd place to ask for a date, don't you think?' She said.

'Hey, this place is a meat market isn't it?!' Again, Logan thought this to be the apex of humour. Like his aunt, Mary Adams, he considered himself to be very funny, though almost no one else seemed to get his humour, except for his aunt. 'Anyway, it was just a thought. Listen, why don't you give me everything you've got in this corner of the window.'

'Now you're trying to impress me,' she said.

'Nope. I just like my steak,' said Logan.

At the cash register, he handed her his credit card. 'Logan Cash,' she said, holding the card with both hands, angling it so that the light could catch the print more clearly.

'Yep, that'd be me.'

'You live around here Logan, or are you just passing through?' She asked.

'I live here. I've got a place just down the road, on MacFarlane.'

There was a quiet pause as she rang his purchase through, handed him back his card.

'Thanks,' said Logan, catching her eyes with his and holding them for a second before looking away. There was another pause. Logan exhaled, looked around, like a nervous mutt.

'I'm Bella,' she said, extending her hand.

'Pleased to meet you, Bella,' he said, taking her small soft hand firmly in his big paw and giving it a bit of a shake.

'I get off at 5 she said, how about we meet here then?'

'I've got to go in to the office for a couple hours from 4. How about dinner? Maybe 7. Or I could meet you for coffee in the morning.'

She thought about the offer for a few seconds, wiped her hands on her smock, thought about it a bit more. 'I work in the morning. But I think maybe lunch tomorrow would be a good compromise.'

'Great,' said Logan, thrilled to pieces but unwilling to give his excitement away. 'Where shall we meet?'

'Let's just meet out front of here at, oh, one fifteen. I open up in the morning, but Mr. Dowhaniuk has agreed to let me go at 1.'

Logan nodded, smiled, saddled the handles of his cloth bag over his shoulder, felt the weight of his purchase - ethically raised by the good farmers in Ayr - turned on his heels and off he went. 'Bella', he said to himself. What a great name.

Bella caught his smile in his reflection as he opened the door, the little bell going off again.

25.

Getting in to the building was like running the gauntlet at some fraternity hazing. Journalists of every stripe: cable and satellite TV, 590 The Fan, bloggers, e-zines, guys who report the world of sports in 140 characters or less, virtual newspapers, and even members of the last two large circulation print-media outlets in Canada - The Globe and Mail and the Toronto Sun. There were, of course, still many little small town and limited circulation papers hanging around, such as the Dryden Observer and the Wiarton Echo. But when it came to sports reporting, if they reported it at all, it was usually a local softball tournament, or charity run. Andrew, in his crazy colored helmet and tinted goggles, just whizzed through on his bike, beard blowing in the wind, beeping his little horn as he went, forcing the journos to dive out of the way. However, Logan, Wiener, Shakey and the Kid Line, who all travelled down from Georgetown together, were forced to park in the lot and walk through the media scrum. Never having experienced this sort of attention before, they all walked with their heads down, sun glasses on, giant headphones covering their ears. It looked like they were either on their way to a court sentencing, or were part of a rap group, microphones thrust into their faces, under their noses, everyone braying like a pack of mules in heat.

'Whoa, man, that's some crazy shit going down out there!' This was Peyton Tench Jr, AKA PJ, who had just walked into the main lounge across from the video theatre. 'Yo, FC, what did you think of that, man?' He meant Frank Chan, AKA Channer, but also FC, just to complete the 'all acronym line', along with Chris Ireland, AKA Buddy I, which was a play on 'Buddy Guy', since Chris played the harp in the line's off season blues band. Since PJ's are what you wear to bed, Peyton was sometimes called Jammer, especially on those nights where he had a particularly good game, otherwise known as Jam City, as in 'Yo, PJ you were the may-yor of jam city to-night my brother'. This would come from Elliott Horton, who was no relation to Tim but a distant relative of the Detroit Tiger's Willie. Horton had grown up in Port Huron, Michigan, just across the border from Sarnia, Ontario. He played Triple A, mostly on the Compuware circuit, but one year as a 13 year old with Petr Klima's gang, before moving on to star for Saginaw in the OHL. Known as a big hitting defenceman with a powerful shot, his style of play actually reminded many of the Leaf faithful - at least those still around to remember - of Tim Horton in his prime. Paired up with Rene Pronovost, who reminded everyone of a young Aaron Ekblad, they were a formidable twosome along the blueline. Pronovost had grown up in Shawinigan - not too far from the birthplace of his great great uncle

Marcel, Lac-à-la-Tortue - and played his junior hockey for the Cataractes.

Most of the boys were just sitting around, waiting on the Coach. It was almost 4 o'clock. Some were dicking around with their sticks, retaping, and so on. Others were in the weight room, but no one was lifting any weights. They were just sitting on the various benches, leaning against the different machines and chatting about last night's game. Logan was in the kitchen, looking in the fridge, for what, he didn't know. It just seemed to be something he always did. A habit he wasn't quite aware that he'd developed over the many years of, well, looking in fridges.

Andrew was hanging with Shakey and Wiener, both of whom were reviewing the 'talent' in Montreal. 'Boys', thought Andrew, 'some things never change'.

Promptly at 4 the coach walked in, looked around, smiled, and said 'OK, fellas, let's get at it. We've got the video loaded and ready to go.'

The meeting adjourned around 6. Several of the players made plans to meet for dinner. Wiener and Shakey gave each other a sly nod, after Shakey flashed an open right hand twice.

'Log, you gonna stop by?' asked Andrew.

'Now?'

'Ya? Mom and dad will be back. They'll want a briefing.'

'But I gave the kids a ride in. Wiener and Shakey too.'

'Let them take your truck back. You can stay with us or mom and dad. One of them would probably be happy to give you a lift up the road anyway if you don't want to stay.'

'Ya, ok,' Logan said and turned to look for Wiener or Shakey. 'Shakes! Hey, man. Catch!' Logan threw him his car keys. 'I'm gonna see my mom and dad with old Billy here,' Logan shoved a thumb over his shoulder in Andrew's direction. 'You guys take the truck home, K?'

'OK Cashman, no prob. We'll see ya later.'

'Ya, later skater,' said Wiener, taking them all back down memory lane.

'Grab your lid, Log,' said Andrew.

'Why?'

'I've only got the one helmet.' So Logan grabbed his CSA and NHL approved, Bauer manufactured (made in China), official Toronto Maple Leaf helmet, popped it on his head, and off they went toward the Zamboni room. There was barely enough room for the two big galoots on the bike, and they looked quite the sight as they silently wended their way out of the building, past the still waiting gaggle of media geese, and on up the road. 'Hey, aren't those the Cash boys?' one of them could be heard to say. 'Well it wasn't Evil Knievel and his ugly twin', said another.

As they scootered up the driveway, Steve's big, double-cab, Ford F-150 could be seen parked in front of the house. 'Can they make them any bigger?' Said Andrew, slowly shaking his head, but Logan couldn't hear a thing as the wind whistled through the ear holes in his helmet. Once they got around its girth - 'Who buys a truck cuz the guy on the ad has a deep voice?' Andrew would say - they could see everyone arrayed around the wrap-around veranda. It was a muggy but cloudless evening, the sun still high in the sky.

The boys loped up the steps, both still wearing their helmets.

'Geez, would you look at Logan. Whut ayre ya, b'y, a whahkin' advertisement?' Steve said with aspirated aiches peppering his most affected Cape Breton Gaelic. This elicited a giggle from Eve.

'Shush, Eve, don't encourage your grandfather,' said Chris. 'Hi boys, you look no worse for wear.'

'Hey,' said Logan.

'Hey,' said Andrew.

It was something about the sight of the parents that turned grown men back into teenage boys, like an autonomic response from the central nervous system.

Removing his helmet and goggles, Andrew surveyed the scene, said 'Where is everyone?'

'What? Are we not enough for you any more, then?' said his dad.

Bianca had been coming through the front door, wiping her hands on her apron. Obviously, something was cooking. 'Hi guys', she said, smiling.

'Where are the rest of the kids?' Andrew asked. It seemed to be the central element in any conversation with his wife on most days: taking stock of the brood.

'AJ and Westin are staying over again. I said it was no problem. The twins are taking care of the goats, and Maggie is in her room doing I don't know what. And there's the dog', she said, pointing at Ginger Bell III as she made a bee line for Andrew. 'So, all present and accounted for, Captain.'

'He's the captain', Andrew said, twitching his head in Logan's direction. 'I'm just a lowly grunt, cannon fodder on the best of days.'

'Makes for good practice', said Steve. 'Keep the cosmonauts in check, hold your team in there.'

'Like game 1?' Said Andrew, suddenly irritated.

'Well, no. Not like that. The boys seemed to have a bit of the stage fright. It seemed like that to me, anyway. Took a while to get the lead out. But you all looked great last night,' said Steve half-forcing a smile. For 37 years he'd been pussy footing around Andrew's 'moods'. Bloody artists, he said to himself.

'Home ice advantage now,' said Christine, genuinely smiling, ebullient even. But the boys were reticent, didn't really want to talk about the games. Didn't want to jinx things. 'Bloody superstitious hockey players,' she muttered under her breath. Anyway, they'd come round. Just needed to get some food into them. A beer or two. Loosen them up a bit. 'You guys must be hungry,' she said. 'Bianca's on veg and salad detail.

Charlie and Marie have agreed to help her out once the goats are dealt with. Your dad's gonna barbecue.'

'Steaks?' Said Logan, suddenly perking up.

'You want a beer, dad?' asked Eve. Andrew looked up, looked at his daughter, and saw that all was right with the world. Fuck game one, he said to himself. Let the critics and the analysts have game one. It's game three that matters now.

At the dinner table they all held hands and were led by the twins who said grace, thanking the animals for their lives so that they might live, thanking the goats for their tasty milk and for keeping the lawn so tidy, thanking the chickens for their eggs, and for providing the central feature in the occasional chicken salad sandwich, thanking nanny and papa for being there for them, thanking mom and dad for being such wonderful parents, thanking...

'OK, OK, Amen,' interjected Andrew. 'That was very well said kids, but the food is getting cold. Wouldn't want to insult the good cows of Ayr now would we? Having given their lives only to be dished up like a cold chip?'

They nodded their heads in agreement, said 'no, sir' in unison. They were such good kids, thought Andrew, looking at them with a fair dollop of puzzlement, saying to himself 'How did they turn out to be such friends of the earth, anyway? Must be Bianca's doing.' Bianca had a steak on the end of a big fork, said 'Andrew, give me your plate.' Logan was sitting up like a golden retriever on its best behavior, ears back, licking his chops.

'Are you going to see your uncle tomorrow?' This was Christine. She was speaking to Andrew and Logan.

'Why?'

'Cuz he's in the hospital. He had a heart attack. Didn't you know?'

They didn't know. Looked at each other over the beans and corn, looked back at their mom.

'Where is he? What hospital?' Asked Andrew.

'He's at Cambridge Memorial. It was the closest hospital to where he was playing hockey. He collapsed on the ice.'

'On the ice! How... How is he?' Logan looked worried.

'The doctor says he's fine. Lori was in to see him too. She tweeted me the "all clear". But he's stuck in there for a few more days and I'm sure he's going stir crazy. A short visit would help.'

'I don't know,' said Andrew. 'Coach told us to lay low. You should have seen the media at the rink today. It was completely crazy.'

'We'll give him a call at least,' said Logan. 'Get him on skype. If we can't go, I mean.' He shrugged his shoulders in an awkward fashion, pushed his plate away, put his elbows on the table, rested his chin on closed fists. 'Let's do it now. I mean, after supper.' There were nods all around.

26.

The day had come and gone without a single visitor. I was laying on my back, propped up by a few extra pillows, feeling sorry for myself. Well, not exactly. You know that feeling where you're alone and you're quite content doing whatever you're doing - watching the non-news on some specialty news channel, listening to CBC radio while doing the dishes, or screwing a screw into some wall or device - but there's this lingering sense in the back of your mind that everyone's forgotten you. Many have. Once you pass 80 you begin to feel that you're basically just the space capsule, a wee sputnik, left out there in its singular orbit, family and friends jettisoned at various stages of life's long, sometimes too damn long, journey. Why do you think so many old folks sit looking out of windows? Maintain a land line when nobody calls except to sell you some thing or idea whose time has come? Why do you think we chatter like mad people when someone does visit, does enter our orbit? We treat you like a visitor from another planet, or, if an old buddy, like Peach or Dog or Ace, as if we are survivors in some Sci-Fi movie, like Peter Ustinov in Logan's Run. Stunned. Stunned by time, by events. Mobility is one of the main problems. Just like a space capsule stuck in an orbit, most oldies lack mobility, have, at best, worn the hall carpet threadbare, to the kettle and back to the La-Z-Boy by the window, holding the channel changer at arm's length, it's giant buttons a problem because several of the numbers have been rubbed off. I've been so lucky. I had my driver's license up until this year. However, the State, in its infinite wisdom, says my eyesight is just too poor to risk having me on the road anymore. OK, fair enough. I'd like to get a driverless car, but they are still too bloody expensive. Besides, as long as I've got someone to take me to the rink I'm fine. Otherwise, the LRT is my link to the world beyond my front window.

The boys called me just now. It was good to hear from them, see them - sort of - on the skype. My handheld device is a bit too small for these old eyes. Funny that. Because I can usually see what I want to see, like the puck whipped toward me cross-ice. I can see that no problem. But point out something that reveals my shortcomings and I will claim advanced cataracts. But I'd like to see the boys a bit better, on a bigger screen. They are so big themselves anyway. They fill up a screen pretty damn quick. They're in great spirits. Having the time of their lives. The toast of the town, of Canada really. It's a funny thing, this Stanley Cup Final. Even hardcore Leaf haters seem to be pulling, if not for them, then at least not openly against them. There's been a lot written about this being 'Canada's team', with Montreal really being a mostly Euro squad. This, of course, has got the Subbans - all nine thousand of them - in an uproar. PK1 has been trying his best to paint this as 'old time hockey', as the best the 'original six' can offer, and may the best team win, which, in his view, certainement, is Montreal. Either way, it's great for Canada and for the game. Bla bla bla, lah de dah. Je ne sais quoi, dude.

I told them not to worry about me. That I'd be out of here in no time at all, and they'd see me rinkside for Game 5 in Montreal, or, if necessary, Game 6 back here in greater hogtown. 'Bite your tongue!' Andrew had said. 'There ain't gonna be a game 6.' Logan said he was just taking it one game at a time, one shift at a time, to be truthful. Focus on the task at hand. They told me about all of the media and so on, and I said to not let it stress you out. Just go with the flow. Enjoy it. Just don't say 'fuck' on TV.

Nurse Ratchett had been in earlier too. OK, I exaggerate, she's probably not pure evil, but it's somehow unsettling to think that the Grim Reaper will be heard as a squee-kee-gee squee-kee-gee of little white shoes coming down a hallway toward you. She said the IV had to stay in, and that they still had to monitor my heart for I don't know what. Which, as the little machine by the wall showed quite clearly, got my heart rate up a bit. She took my temperature, looked at me like I was out of focus, told me to ring for a nurse if I wanted to go for a walk, said I looked a bit sallow - oh really? Do ya think? - glanced at my chart and squeaked her way out of my room, her back arrow straight, her uniform a flawless white. Nice legs too. And speaking of nice legs, I hadn't heard anything further from my wife, though I'd been hashtagging 'peacetalks', 'MiddleEast' and 'ArabIsraeli' on twitter to see if there was any news. But, nothing. When she said it was hush, hush she wasn't kidding. Then again, my wife is no kidder, there's not a funny bone in her body, though for some unknown reason she fancies herself to be a comedic raconteur non pareil. Logan seems to agree with her, but that kid's all business too. Birds of a feather I guess. Now Andrew - just like his father: that kid can tell a joke.

The boys said that Steve and Chris would probably drive down tomorrow for a wee visit. I gotta be sure not to talk their ears off. Hello, ground control? This is Major Tom.

27.

Steve had driven his son home after dinner. Though it was only a little before 9, Logan began to feel the cumulative weight of the day, said as much, said his goodnights and goodbyes. It was mostly a silent ride, denoting comfort as opposed to tension. Steve had ferried the boys around for so many years in so many towns that this just felt so, so, normal. Logan went straight to bed. He was still bagged from yesterday's very long day, the win in Montreal seeming more and more like a dream than a reality, Logan's sore lower back, tender groin, the only reminders that the hockey season was still in full swing.

He awoke around 4 am, the room as dark as pitch. He fished around for the little switch on his bedside lamp, gave it a flick, produced a dim light that was kind to the eyes. He felt wide awake. 'I wonder what time is it in Seoul? Or Ouagadougou?' he said out loud, counting time zones on his fingers. He booted up the Xbox. An hour or two of Tom Clancy's latest wouldn't hurt. He loaded *Splinter Cell: Pandora Chaos Forever,* before making a quick trip to the loo. He opened the curtains a bit, made a promise to himself that he'd quit as soon as it started to get light out.

Logan was wired, or, rather, as he would say 'stoked'. Lunch with Bella was just around the corner. He pulled out his device, checked the time, scrolled through his messages. Checked the twitter, hashtag 'Leafs'. A directive had come down from on high many years before regarding social media. The Director of Public Relations and Communications for the Leafs indicated that it was official team policy for each player to have a Facebook and a Twitter account. If a player resisted, the team would set up and manage the accounts for them. That was fine with Logan. He searched for himself on Twitter to see what he had to say. It was the usual stuff: go, fight, win! The media people made sure he was cookie cutter clean. He got a kick out of this, set up a fake account, started following himself. It was like he was watching his own life from a distance, from a ledge twenty stories up along the side of a big glass dome. Often he really felt like that. He'd get these weird moments during a game, sitting on the bench, standing apart from everything, marveling at the way his life had turned out. His linemates would catch him zoned out like that every now and then, give him a discreet elbow in the side, say, 'Earth to Log, come back to us, man. We need ya down here.'

'Down here' was currently the corner of Harding St and Dominion Gardens Dr. He was heading into the Dominion Gardens Parks for a short walk to kill time until his 115 appointment with Bella. The market was located next to the park, on the grounds of a former

Catholic high school. The school had closed about a decade ago. Not only were there too few children around to keep the school going, there were hardly any Catholics, or even Christians, as far as Logan could tell. The school had been transformed into the market's centre piece, full of stalls selling knick knacks, coffee, deli foods, bear claws and other pastries. The butcher shop was part of an annex that included a bakery as well. Both the park and the market fronted onto Guelph St., the old Highway 7. Logan was wearing a ball cap that had 'Mighty Hurricanes' stenciled on it - a gift from his uncle - wraparound sunglasses, golf shorts, flip flops, and a maroon colored St Mary's Huskies t-shirt. Not the best way to be dressed for a date, he supposed, but he didn't want to give Bella the wrong idea. Better to keep everybody's expectations right where they belonged: as low to the ground as possible. Slow and steady wins the race, as his grandpa would say.

At precisely 115 the little bell ding-dinged and Bella looked up from behind the counter. Logan gave her a shy wave. Bella smiled.

'Ready to go?' Logan asked.

'Hi, Logan. I'm fine. Thanks for asking,' she teased.

'Oh, sorry. Hi. How are you?'

'Not so good. No.'

'Why?'

'Mr Dowhaniuk is still sick so I'm stuck here for the whole day. I mean, until 3. That's when we close on Sundays.' As a regular, and a connoisseur of fine meats,

Logan knew their hours by heart. Where had this young woman come from, anyway, and why had he never seen her before?

'Oh.' Logan visibly deflated, his shoulders slumping forward. 'So, I guess lunch is off, then, eh?'

'Maybe. Maybe not,' she said.

'What do you mean?' asked Logan.

'Well, you could pop into the main building and bring us back something to eat. We could have our lunch here. I just can't leave the shop since I'm here on my own. If you want, you could even stick around til 3, help me out, take some of the pressure off. As you can see, we are very busy today.' Bella waved her arms around as if to say, look at everyone, but the shop was totally empty. Oh, thought Logan, she's making a joke. She does have a sense of humour.

'Sure, I'm cool with that,' said Logan. 'You can make a butcher out of me,' and he smiled at the thought of himself in a big white smock. 'What would you like to eat? You a vegetarian?' asked Logan, thinking this to be yet another example of his capacity for witty banter.

'Why, yes, I am a vegetarian. What makes you say that?'

Logan was momentarily lost for words. 'It's just that you look so, so healthy,' he said and smiled. Bella went flush from the neck up, looked back in at the meat display, then up at Logan.

'How about some domalthes, rice only for me. And some salads, you know, 3 bean, 5 bean, 7 bean, how ya been. Maybe a nice baguette.' They were both quite hungry.

'OK, I'll be back in a flash,' said Logan and out the door he went.

Upon his return, Bella was just finishing up at the cash with a customer. -Thank you Mrs. Farooq. You have a nice day.

'Please extend my best wishes for a speedy recovery to Mr. Dowhan,' said Mrs. Farooq. 'You are a very lovely young woman, my dear, so helpful and polite.' When she heard the door open and the bell ring, she turned to see the doorway darkened with the strapping figure that is Logan Cash. 'Oh,my,' she said. 'You are a big one.'

Logan just smiled and waited for Mrs. Farooq to shuffle her birdlike frame past him and out into the daylight. Bella laughed. 'Oh my, you are a big one!' She mimicked. Logan, who had been called 'a big one' his whole life found no humour in this remark, but neither did it bother him. Like water off a duck's back, as his grandpa would say.

'Look what I've got,' he said, holding up a large paper bag.

'Set it down over here by the cash. The counter will have to do.'

'It's really only finger food,' said Logan. 'I've got plastic forks for the salad.' As he extracted the small plastic containers he recited, '3 bean, 5 bean, 7 bean,... just joking, there's some couscous in here too.'

'Yum!' said Bella.

They were at ease with each other. Logan was an easy guy to be with, not too complicated, not high maintenance like his brother, though Andrew had calmed down considerably over the years. Six kids and a very successful hockey career will do that to you. The little store began to smell less like a butcher shop and more like a Mediterranean delicatessen. Bella had fetched an old school auditorium style chair from the back room for Logan to sit on, while she stood behind the cash counter. He's almost as tall sitting as I am standing, she thought, looking down at the top of his blond head. Logan had removed his cap and glasses, placed them on the windowsill in behind the halal beef jerky and chicken curry-flavored potato chips.

'So, I come in here all the time. Why haven't I met you before?' Logan asked Bella.

'Because I just started this week. I run a Healthy Foods catering company with my mother, Camilla. We live over in Caledon. We've been all greens all the time. Or just about. You get the picture. It's gotten so boring. And our clientele are boring. Lunches for the 'new age' types which, in my opinion, is really 'old age' and really 'old news'. They're all so self centred. Anyway, I've talked my mom into branching out. She suggested that I learn about meat. The good, the bad and the ugly.'

Logan raised his eyebrows. 'Ugly meat?' he thought and imperceptibly shook his head.

'So, aside from endless hours on the internet, I thought it would be a good idea to work in a butcher shop, learn the ropes from a master. You get the picture. But I didn't want any old shop. I wanted a shop that specialized in the sourcing and selling of ethically raised and slaughtered animals. So here I am, and three days into the job, my 'master' has taken ill and I'm stuck here on my own. Ho hum,' she sing-songed.

'Whoa. That's totally cool. That's why I come here. "Green beef",' he said raising his index fingers in quotation marks. 'You know, just healthy meat from animals not subject to all the crap and stress that goes into industrial farming. My uncle used to say that countries like Botswana are missing the boat when it comes to selling beef to the world. Rather than fall in line with EU and other regulations, passports for cows and all that stuff, better to buck the trend. Market all natural, range fed beef. Why they haven't done it, I don't know,' he said, shaking his head.

'Maybe because of corporate pressure to fall in line.'

Logan could relate to that. One day he'd tell her about his Twitter account. After they'd finished eating and cleaned up their various messes, Bella asked if Logan would man the counter for a few minutes because she needed to go into the back and deal with a flank.

'Whattaya mean, "deal with a flank",' asked Logan.

'I need to cut some flank steaks, make some rolls. Mr. Dowhaniuk left me strict instructions. Besides I'd like to get in some practice while the store is quiet. If you have any problems just call me back out. OK?' She didn't wait for Logan to answer. 'Now, let's see if there's a smock big enough to fit you.'

While Bella was in back, Logan strolled up and down looking at everything on display in the counter: fresh brisket, tip kebabs, short ribs, stewing beef. Judging by quantity, these seemed to be the cuts most in demand for the sort of clientele that came into the shop. Logan, on the other hand preferred the quick and easy: a big hunk of steak on a barbecue, a few boiled potatoes, a bit of broccoli for colour and regularity and Bob's your uncle. There was also plenty of lamb and chicken on display. His stomach rumbled; he was starting to feel hungry again. Just then the door opened and the little bell dingled. Logan looked up. It was a man in his early 50s. Judging from his face, which was beet red, and his attire, which was golfer chic, the guy had just finished his round, possibly over at nearby Granite Ridge. By all appearances, he'd also had a very successful 19th hole and was probably in the market for something to drop onto the barbecue for a leisurely Sunday afternoon lunch. His golf buddies were probably on the way to his house now. I hope he called the wife to let her know what she's in for, thought Logan.

'Whoa!' said the guy when he looked up, and up, at the big guy in the big white smock behind the counter. Logan smiled, said 'Can I help you sir.'

'Sure, sure. A few steaks would be good. Say, you know, you look at lot like Logan Cash. Anybody ever tell you that?'

'On occasion,' said Logan. 'Why, who's he?' Logan thought he'd have a little fun with this. 'By the way, what kind of steaks would you prefer. There's some lovely top loin over here,' said Logan nodding his head toward the far end of the counter, which, by the way, was Logan's area of expertise.

'Sure, sure. I'm gonna need 6 nice big juicy ones. T-bones maybe. You sure do look like Logan Cash.'

'Who?'

'Cash, Logan Cash, the captain of the Toronto Maple Leafs.' The guy looked again at Logan, let his gaze linger for a bit, wondered if he was losing his mind. After all, what would the captain of the Leafs be doing in a butcher shop on a Sunday afternoon anyway. Na, it can't be him, thought the guy, while visibly shaking his head.

Once they'd sorted out the order, Logan wrapped the steaks expertly in butcher's paper and plopped them on the scale. It was a simple process to key in the cut with a press of a button, the gizmo did the rest of the work. Logan pressed the sale button and a sticker was produced. He used it to seal the package as he'd seen many butchers do just in this way for Logan over many years. Easy as pie, he thought. 'That'll be $98.75,' said Logan. The guy produced his credit card and Logan repeated a process he'd witnessed a thousand, tens of thousands of times before. 'Oh, one more thing,' said Logan.

'Yes,' said the guy.

'Have you got any kids?' asked Logan.

'Ya, two. But they're almost your age I'm sure. Why?'

'What's their names?'

'The oldest is Gabe. They're both boys. The younger one is Aidan.'

'Is their last name... Ravenscain?' asked Logan, looking at the guy's credit card as he handed it back to him along with his receipt.

'Ya, ya. Say, what's this all about.'

'Do they like hockey, Mr. Ravenscain?'

'Leaf fans born and bred, just like their old man, I'm sorry to say. Brainwashed from the start.' The guy smiled an ironic smile known only too well by Leaf fans around the world. The whir of a circular saw could be heard coming from the back room, followed by a slight whiff of cooked meat.

'Listen,' said Logan, taking a magic marker down from the counter, uncapping it, and then writing across the steak-packed butcher's paper: "To the Ravenscains. Go, Fight, Win. Logan Cash" followed by his number. 'Listen, I'll leave you 4 tickets at the will-call booth at the Samsung-Blackberry Centre for tomorrow night's game. In your name, what's your first name?' he asked.

'Phillip,' the guy gulped, his eyes and mouth hanging wide open.

'It'll be my pleasure to have you as my guest tomorrow, Mr. Ravenscain, er, Phillip.' Logan extended his hand.

The guy took it and shook it, said 'Say, what is going on here. Am I on TV?' He looked around. 'What sort of gag is this? What is Logan Cash doing working in a butcher shop the day before Game 3 of the Stanley Cup Finals?'

'Coach said to lay low. Take it easy. That's what I'm doing.' And the transaction was completed with smiles and chuckles all around. 'Enjoy the rest of your day, Mr. Ravenscain, especially your steaks. Come again soon.'

Phillip Ravenscain, bag under arm, left under his own steam, but he was clearly bewildered. Logan wondered what the price of spontaneity would be. It suddenly dawned on him that the little shop would be inundated by reporters as soon as Phillip recounted the story just once. He might be on his mobile as we speak, thought Logan. He took out his device, checked the time. It was 245. Fifteen minutes to closing. He would have to gut it out. Hope for the best.

Bella emerged from the back with a platter of meat. 'What do you think?' She asked.

'I don't know what to think,' said Logan. He stood stock still for a moment, really unsure of his next move. 'Listen, Bella, I don't mean to be rude, but do you mind if I cut out of here for a while?'

'Aren't you going to help me close up?' She looked terribly disappointed.

'I can't explain right now, OK. Please, you'll just have to trust me on this, just this once. Can I have your number so I can call you later, maybe around 5? I really enjoyed our time together today, and I don't want it to end. Not yet, OK? But I really need to go. Just for a few hours.'

'OK, I guess.' She was visibly hurt. What have I done here? she asked herself. Forcing a smile, she gave

Logan her number and said 'Typical man, I guess. Afraid to clean up!'

Logan, a bit rattled, handed her his smock, muttered a sort of 'hey, hey', bent down and kissed her on the cheek, and took off out the door, the bell dinging more insistently given the speed of his departure.

At 3, Bella locked the door, flipped the sign over so that it read 'closed' to the public. As she was closing up the display case she noticed a small crowd beginning to gather outside of the shop. First there were only two or three people, but within a few minutes there were at least 50 people crowded around outside, pressing in upon the shop window. There were microphones and TV cameras. She could see CTV and CBC trucks parked across the street. It was a scene she simply could no longer ignore. Bella went to the door and opened it a crack, making sure the safety chain was secure.

'Can I help you?' she said to no one in particular. In response came an unintelligible cacophony of sound. 'Please, one at a time. Someone, can you tell me what you want? What seems to be the matter?'

'We heard that the captain of the Toronto Maple Leafs is here. Is he here?' asked a reporter.

'Who?' Bella asked back. 'Toronto Maple Leafs?' She looked puzzled. The reporters looked at each other, some began to scatter. Others thought perhaps this was a ruse, that he was in fact on the premises.

'Who is that? The Captain of the Toronto Maple Leafs? '

'Lady, don't tell us you don't know who that is.'

'But, who is it?' She said again.

'It's Logan Cash. Logan Cash is the Captain of the Toronto Maple Leafs.'

Suddenly things began to make sense.

28.

5 o'clock came and went. As did 6, 7, 8 and 9. It's not that Bella was hanging by the phone waiting for Logan's call. That sort of behavior had gone out with the invention of the mobile hand held device. But Logan's promise to call and to get together did cramp her plans, not that Sunday nights were anything to brag about. One measly lunch and she was reduced to the stereotypical 'girl waiting by the phone'; this infuriated her. Bella was determined, and had been determined her whole life, neither to 'wait for' nor to 'hunt down' a man, however perfect, or more likely, imperfect, he would be. She was mad that she had given Logan her number but not asked for his in return. If she had his number right now she'd call him and give him a piece of her mind.

But while she had a right to be angry at his behavior, she was wrong about cause and effect. True, Logan had gotten spooked by the prospect of having to face 'the media', which, in his mind, was this ever hungry monster that loved to devour the innocent, the honest and the unsuspecting and spit up rather than digest whatever facts they could -most likely accidentally - get their grimy little paws on. He'd seen too many friends abused by the media during his years as both an amateur and a pro. Quite rightly, he was skittish. The coach had asked them all to lay low, and here was the captain dishing out freebies to some guy in a butcher shop. What were you thinking, b'y, he said to himself. Logan felt sick. It would be all over social media by now. He was afraid to give it a google. He was also worried about what he'd done to Bella and the little butcher shop. Of course, a simple phone call would sort it out PDQ, but Logan had built it up in his head to be such a big deal, he thought that surely Bella would never speak to him again. He also hated the fact that now she knew who he was. He liked the idea of being with someone who liked him for himself, not some puck bunny who liked him because of, because of what? That he could play hockey. How stupid was that anyway? People are freaks. He'd agonized over the whole afternoon to such an extent that he'd knocked himself out with worry. So, 'I think I'll have a little lay down, chillax about this for a bit' turned into a 4 hour snooze fest. When he woke up at 915pm, he didn't know where he was, what time it was, and, glancing at himself in the bathroom mirror, he was sporting a pillowcase crease across one side of his head that made him look like the star attraction in a Bela Lugosi filmfest (Logan loved old black and white horror movies). You Jabroni he said out loud. He decided to call his brother.

'Yo, Andrew. Whutup?'

'Log, where you been all day man?'

'Why? You been looking for me?'

'No. Not particularly, I've got my own thing going on down here. The twins are teaching me how to make cheese.'

'Cool. Say, listen, have you watched the news or seen anything on social media about me today?'

'About you? Why, what happened?'

'Nothin' really. I was in a butcher shop in Georgetown and promised a guy 4 tickets for tomorrow's game.'

'So? What's the big deal with that?' Andrew was ruffling the furry head of Ginger Bell III as he talked. Half of his kids were now in bed. Two were still missing. And one was, well, somewhere. Bianca could be heard clattering around in the pantry. Andrew hoped that meant a snack was on the way.

'Well. At the time I was sorta, kinda, working the counter.'

Andrew began laughing so hard he thought he'd wet his pants. Bianca raced into the room. 'What's the ruckus?'

'Logan was working the counter at a butcher shop today,' he managed to squeeze out before collapsing into fits of laughter. Ginger Bell III began barking at him.

'Good for him,' said Bianca. 'A man should diversify his interests, build up new talents.' It was her theory that a one-note wonder may make a big impact on the world -

say, Einstein - but he'd make a crap husband and an even worse father.

'Why were you doing that, Logan?' asked Andrew, suddenly sitting upright on the couch, leaning forward, waving one hand around in the air.

'Well, I sort of met this girl. Woman, I mean.'

'So,' said Andrew, 'the plot thickens!'

Andrew's advice was straightforward: give the girl a call. She was either fine or not fine, but the only way to find out was to dial the number and ask. 'OK,' said Logan, ready to face the music like the good captain he was.

Bella's device buzzed on the coffee table. She was eating hand made yogurt with fresh mint and berries and watching Netflix. She was home alone, though she shared the big old farm house off of Airport Road with her mother. It doubled as their place of employment, with an industrial kitchen out back and a big sign out front saying Healthy Foods. She put her bowl down and looked at the device. She didn't recognize the number. She'd let it ring. If it was him, he could leave a message. She'd deal with it later. The phone stopped ringing, went over to voice mail.

Logan didn't leave a message. Hung up and straightaway tried again. The shortest distance between two points is a straight line, his grandpa would say. He wasn't sure how this quite related to what he was doing now, but it felt right to say it to himself, out loud, with determination.

'Hello,' Bella said. Who was she to hold a grudge. She wasn't even sure why she was mad at him.

'Hi, Bella, this is Logan. Logan Cash.'

'Ya, the captain of the Toronto Maple Leafs,' she replied.

'Oh my Gawd, I'm so sorry. I didn't mean for that to happen.' Logan paused. 'What did happen anyway?'

'Nothing much. A bunch of people showed up shortly after you left. I told them I didn't know who they were talking about, so they left.'

'Did they at least buy a few steaks?' asked Logan, and suddenly they were back to where they'd left off earlier in the day. Logan apologized, told her about the guy he'd promised tickets to; said he'd fallen asleep. Bella said that's OK, at least you sold a few steaks. Logan said he wanted to see her again but it would be a bit complicated over the next little while. Bella said, well at least I've got your number now too, so I can stalk you if I want.

'Are you on twitter?' he asked.

'No, but our company is,' she said.

'If you do a search for me on twitter or facebook, just know that that's not really me. It's somebody at the front office writing stuff in my name. Maintaining my public profile "as best they see fit".'

'I wonder what they'll say you did today.'

'Shit. I better do some creeping on myself.'

'Logan, I don't know what that means, but I hope you enjoy the rest of your evening.'

'See ya, Bella. See ya real soon, K?' said Logan.

'K,' said Bella. 'Have a good game tomorrow,' she said.

'Thanks.' And they rang off.

29.

'Geez, b'ys, would you look at him!' This was my brother-in-law who could fill up a hospital room pretty damn fast.

'Hi Jack,' said Chris, leaning in to press her smooth warm cheek against my cold and, according to the Grim Reaper, sallow one. 'How are you?'

'I've been better.' Going right out of me mind, if truth be told. Funny how quickly I'd adopt the lilt of a Maritime accent whenever in the presence of a couple of Maritimers. 'Have a seat, take a load off. Tell me something I don't know,' I said.

'What did the doctor say?' asked Christine.

'Not much to me. Just that I'd live - for now - and that I was to stay away from the arena until further notice. Forced retirement, it seems, at least for now. At least I've done a bit better than Eric Lindros in that category.'

'Lindros... remember him!? Said Steve.

'Of course. Logan always reminded me of him. Same sort of upright skating style. Different sorts of skulls on the two boys though.'

'We build 'em tough out there on the island,' said Steve.

'Down with the causeway!' said I.

We then commenced to chat about this and that. A bit later I said, 'You'll be going to the game tomorrow night of course.'

'Can't wait for it. It is sure to be a humdinger.'

30.

GAME 3

The super-metro conurbation that is Toronto was buzzing with excitement. The Leafs were home, having achieved a split in Montreal, shifting so-called home-ice advantage their way. Travelling to the rink was a piece of cake, as though the State in its wisdom had foreseen the importance of the LRT to Maple Leaf hockey. None of that stupid, endless bus ride or pointless drive out to the nowhere land that is Nepean as is still the case for Senators fans. Just a twenty minute whoosh in air conditioned comfort whether you are coming in from Hamilton, London, or old Toronto. There's a bar car too, since if you're riding there's no need to worry about drinking and driving.

The boys had been instructed to lay low over the short break. Try to minimize the distractions. To the rink and home. Stay out of the clubs. This was meant in particular for Wiener and Shakey, both of whom were notorious skirt chasers, and not the most elegant of drunks. They'd each - separately and together - had more than one run-in with the law, mostly in relation to parking lot fisticuffs with mouthy non-fans. Channer, that is Frank Chan, was their coach-designated handler for the duration of the playoffs and to this point in time he'd done an excellent job. They'd reviewed the films, talked strategy, sat in the cool dark cedar-panelled positive visualization room, engaged with their sports psychologists, had their massages, sat in their saunas and steam baths, pumped some iron, pedaled bikes, had bandaged that which needed bandaging, iced what needed icing, shot puck after puck, stopped and started, done crossovers along the blue line, talked it up, played with their kids - if they had any - supped with wives, girlfriends, and family members, and, most of all, laid low. And now it was game on.

The joint was jumpin'. The boys could hardly hear themselves think. The anthem had been played - Canadian, though Russian also would have been appropriate - and the puck dropped. They were still without PK1, as were the Leafs without Pappin. Montreal decided to go with 5 D, doubling up the ice time for PK2. The Leafs, however decided to fill the gap, calling up Keney Dramiuc, a smart, tough kid, from their Marlies farm team. Montreal came out with fire, as was expected. The Habs laid siege to the Leaf goal, but Andrew stood tall, shouted instructions, led from the rear. Horton and Pronovost banged and crashed. Prince and Shaw cleared the front of the net, fired the puck around the boards, relieved pressure. Forwards held their positions, let the centre men do the running around. Going the other way, Shakey and Wiener chipped and charged. Ellis and Naz dumped and chased. Tench and Buddy I cycled down low. The big Swede played big. The centremen - Casher, Channer, Wee Ian, Hutchie - danced across the ice like water bugs on a frog pond. It seemed as though the Leafs had successfully weathered the storm. The score remained zeroes through period one.

'That's it boys, keep 'er goin'! '

'Lookin' good boys!'

The locker room chatter. The Leafs were upbeat, feeling confident. As were the Habs.

In the second period, Montreal struck first. A momentary lapse. An errant pass through the middle of the ice. A turnover. And suddenly it was 1-0. One of the Habs' nameless, faceless Russian robots. In as quick as a cat, slipped one through the five hole. Andrew remained calm, just fished the puck out of the net and flipped it back toward centre ice. This calmed the crowd, let a little shadow of Leaf doubt slip into the building.

Steve was on his best behavior. After all, this was enemy territory. But when the goal light went on he could almost hear the Bud light horn go off in his man-land basement at home. He looked down at the back of his number one son, who remained monk still on the bench. He looked up at his number two son, who seemed unusually calm given the circumstances immediately preceding the goal. He glanced ever so slightly to his left at his wife, clad in her Leaf jersey, shouting encouragement, a hockey mom to the end, and to her left he saw Eve sitting quietly, keeping her opinions to herself.

A collective groan went up at Ryerson arena where Lori and Martha had accidentally bumped into their old high school friend Rita. They were sitting together on the main floor, sipping at vodka coolers or beers, alternatively chatting about decades gone by, or quietly watching the action on the big screen. 'Doesn't Ireland remind you of Darcy Tucker?' she said to no one in particular. 'Who's Darcy Tucker?' asked Rita. 'Really?' said Lori. 'You must be joking.'

Play see-sawed through the period. Back and forth, chance after chance. Very uncharacteristic for a Stanley Cup Final which, over the last few decades increasingly became a series of games played along the boards, behind the nets, and where goals were increasingly scarce and those that did come were always ugly. A scrum in front of the net, a deflection off a knee, a wild swing at a loose puck. Winning had become so important in hockey that the beauty of the game was too readily sacrificed for effectiveness. This was because winning equaled money. And hockey was a business. Just like it was a business, an ugly deceitful business, the last time the Leafs won the Cup.

Montreal struck again. Titov to Popovich to Bykovsky and goal. It was like time stood still: Makarov to Krutov to Shepelev and goal and goal and goal. The 1981 Canada Cup final. Remember that? 8-1 for the Soviet Union. When you look at Team Canada's lineup for that game you may be forgiven for thinking that the score would be 8-1 for Canada: Gretzky, Lafleur, Perrault, Dionne, Bossy, Trottier and on and on. But we Canadians always underestimate the opposition. For some reason we've claimed the right to hockey supremacy as God-given. We dismiss others as charlatans, wimps and wussies, as faceless robots incapable of playing with passion. But then we forget that in a competition you must defeat the other team, and to do so means you must try your best because that is what they are doing. They don't care that you claim winning as your right; in fact, they probably find it a bit insulting. That's a beautiful thing about hockey. If you watch a well played game, most of it consists of failed attempts because each team is getting in the other's way: a deft poke-check, a knocked-down pass, an open ice hit, and that damn goaltender. It is a game of failure populated with moments of brilliant success, born of hard work and dumb luck. I had a coach who once told me 'Stop being so hard on yourself'. It was the best advice in sport I ever received. His argument was that there will never be a shortage of people in the world who are more than happy to say you aren't good enough, a bum, a failure, no matter how good you are. So why add to the pressure. Be your own best friend, stick up for yourself, and recognize that most of hockey consists not of mistakes but of failed attempts. Why do attempts fail? Because there are two teams out there on the ice, with one objective: to win. So, if you go out on the ice assuming you will win, you will most certainly lose. Just look at that Team Canada lineup. And they got smoked.

That night in Toronto, there were at least 20 people who were not there to anoint the Maple Leafs as 2036-37 Stanley Cup Champions. Euro robots and faceless Russians they may be, but they were professional hockey players who wanted to have a Stanley Cup notched on their belts more than anything else. Just because they didn't beat their chests about it, didn't mean they didn't care.

The second period ended with Montreal up 2-0. There was a palpable tension in the Leaf dressing room. It's not that they weren't trying. It's not that they were being outclassed. It's not that Montreal was the better team. In fact, they had done pretty much everything right. Played smart. Played the percentages. It's just that Montreal had taken advantage of two of their chances, and the Leafs hadn't. At least not yet. It's a complicated feeling in a dressing room when you're down but feel you've played well enough to be up. At least if you are all hungover and sucking wind, you can point the finger at yourself and say, see, you stupid piss tank, I told you this would happen. But when you are in the prime of your life, playing to the best of your ability, and you are still down by two, there's little to be changed, nothing really to be tinkered with. The challenge is therefore to 'Keep pluggin' boys. Things will turn around.' This was what Logan was saying in the dressing room. 'Our chances will come.' 'Let's get one early, turn this thing around.' You want to believe it, but because you're down 2-0 and playing your hearts out, you can't quite believe it. Like I said, it's complicated.

Early in the third, Montreal was once again buzzing in the Leaf zone. Andrew turned away puck after puck. The crowd 'baa-aad' like goats at every miraculous save. Off of a scrum in front of the net, the puck squirted into the corner. Horton was first to it and faked a slapshot around the boards before circling the opposite way. When he got to the dot, he ripped a high looping shot down the ice to relieve the pressure. The puck bounced to the right of the Habs' goalie about 10 feet inside of the blueline, then took a crazy hop to his left where it landed on edge and skipped back to his right nipping between his body and his arm. He sort of waved at it with his blocker but missed and it landed up in his net. The crowd went wild.

'What the hey...' I said, removing my glasses and rubbing my eyes.

'Did you see that!?' said Peach.

'Sure did,' said Hutchie. 'Turn about is fair play boys. Remember the Coyotes' goal against Bernier? Who scored that, anyway?'

'Oliver Ekman-Larsson,' said Peach, ever ready with the trivia. 'And don't forget the one on Toskala. When was that?' He paused rubbing his chin. '2008 I believe,' he said, answering his own question, 'against the New York Islanders. Somebody Davidson, wasn't it?'

'What are you eating anyway, Peach, you can remember all this stuff? Carrots? Helps you see into the past?'

Peach just smiled as he watched the replay for about the fourth time in 30 seconds.

As sometimes happens in an evenly played game, a mishap such as this can tip the balance ever so slightly. In this case, the Horton goal tipped the balance into the Leafs favour, gave them renewed belief. The chatter up and down the bench was full of energetic platitudes regarding effort and teamwork, of direction and purpose, of will and way. The chatter on the Habs' bench, by the way, was much the same. Of still being ahead, of not losing focus, and so on. No matter what level of hockey, the chatter is the same. It's another way we can all relate to the pros. And how we can imagine ourselves to be Dionne or Lafleur, Robinson or Sittler, Crosby or Ovechkin, Cash or Chan. To be tribal, to retain a sense of shared purpose, requires a sense of relationship, of empathy. As Frank Chan led his line over the boards, following that flukey goal, everyone who had ever played hockey knew that a window of opportunity had creaked open and it was up to the Leaf players to squeeze through it, to bust it wide open.

On the ensuing face-off, Chan nipped the puck past Titov, stepped around him and lofted it into the corner to the left of the Habs' goalie. PK2 turned and gave chase. Tench was in on his heels, and PK2 tried to just hold the puck up until help arrived. Instead of help, Buddy I arrived first, digging the puck out from the corner boards. He looked up and saw Frank in front battling for position with the other Hab defender. Buddy I wired a low hard shot toward the front of the net thinking that maybe Channer would get his stick on it. Instead it hit the Hab defenseman in the back of the boot and ricocheted into the far side top corner. Game tied 2-2. Two goals in twelve seconds and both were crap. As I said earlier, just dumb luck.

'Woo hoo!'

'This is our game, boys!'

'Atta way Eyezee!'

The high five skate through never gets old.

The Habs' heads drooped, just for a second, but they most certainly drooped after that goal. Steve saw it. And, again, he knew they were done. Little tell tale signs that indicate persistence has broken down dogged resistance. The Leafs couldn't see it, except for Andrew, who was always looking for such signs. A student of the game. It's no accident that most hockey colour commentators are former goalies, at least the good ones are. Nevertheless, the Habs did not give in, turn turtle, pack their bags and go home. They gave it their best shot, but when Frank Chan tipped in a Prince point shot to give the Leafs the lead, there was a sense of inevitability about it. Like, OK, we'll give you this one. But only this one. Wouldn't want to ruin your party after a 70 year wait.

Ebullient would be the best way to describe the feeling in the Leafs' dressing room, though no more than two or three of the players would have ever heard the word, and maybe only one know its meaning. Again the coach ran interference outside the room, fielding questions, feeling 'exhuberant, buoyant, cheerful, joyful, cheery, etc' himself, all the while trying to maintain a poker face. 'The boys gave 110%' 'Played like a team' 'Gotta give credit to the opposition' bla bla bla. The post game interview never changes, but it doesn't stop reporters, or fans happy with the outcome, from hanging on every word. But there is a subtle difference here. While the words never change, while the context is always the same and if you wait long enough another Cup final will come your way to start the cycle all over again, while this is true, the subtle difference is that this is a coach of the Toronto Maple Leafs uttering these phrases. They are simultaneously empty and full of meaning. Empty in the sense that they reveal nothing about the nature of the game, but full of meaning because they are meant to convey a sense of how a Toronto Maple Leafs team performed in a Stanley Cup Final game. So listen carefully folks, such words have not been uttered for 70 years, and who knows how many years it will be before they are uttered again.

31.

Another off day tomorrow, Andrew thought happily, his body heavy with exhaustion, but his system still shot-through with excitement. He hopped onto his bike, tooled down the hallway and out of the building. He loved the short ride home: to your own bed, the unique and sometimes puzzling smells of your own home, your kids, your pets, your goats. Despite the brevity of the ride, it was midnight when he trotted up the front steps, tossed his helmet and goggles on a cushioned wicker porch chair, eased his way into the darkened house. Once inside, he moved to the moonlit kitchen where he stood quietly, listened to the old farmhouse settle and sigh. He closed his eyes. If he concentrated he could almost see the rise and fall of the chests of his children, hear their own quiet sighs. Opening his eyes, he looked down to see Ginger Bell III looking up at him, as if she knew exactly what he was thinking. The reverie broken, Andrew nosed around in the fridge, cracked open a beer, and went back outside to sit in the two-person swing, sip his beer, listen to the crickets sing. In the morning, about half the team was going golfing. The coach had dished out the same instructions: 'Lay low,' he said, 'Try not to raise a ruckus by working a meat counter or a fun fair', he turned his head and looked over the top of his glasses at Logan. Everyone in the dressing room laughed. Despite Logan's misgivings about his behavior, the front office had loved it and adjusted his social media profile accordingly. 'Take a selfie next time, wouldja?' some Joe Blow had said to Logan.

The coach had arranged a block of tee-times at a local private course, received assurances that there would be 20 minute gaps before and following their tee off times, to give the guys some privacy. They also agreed to keep the media out of the loop, but had warned him that 'the walls have eyes'. 'And ears,' said the coach, 'so if you see a reporter try not to say 'fuck'.' Everyone chuckled, thought 'the coach, gotta love the guy, but he's such a dweeb'. Andrew and Logan said 'pass' when asked if they were going to golf.

'Too good for the rest of us, are you?' said Wiener, who was a self-acknowledged hack.

'No, no,' said Andrew, who played off of scratch, just like his brother. 'You guys go ahead, have some fun. I'm gonna spend some time with my kids, if I can find any of them,' said Andrew.

'And I've gotta work the meat counter,' said Logan.

32.

In the morning, Andrew was awakened by the lilting sounds of a Cape Breton fiddle. Maggie. She was in her room practicing. She was a natural. After an initial few days of scratching and screeching about, she quickly got the hang of it. -At least one of the Cash clan will follow an island tradition, he said out loud, though his only companion in the bedroom was Ginger Bell III. 'Isn't that right, Ginger Bell the third?' he said, patting the dog roughly on her head. Both dog and man went back to sleep.

At noon, the twins came in and woke him up. 'Dad! Dad! Get up!' they said. 'Get out of bed you sleepyhead!' Sometimes, he thought, it was really creepy the way they said things together. They were on the bed with him, trying to tickle him. It looked like the Lilliputians trying to manage Gulliver.

'OK, OK,' he said and rolled sideways away from all the action. They jumped up on the bed and grabbed him, one hanging off his shoulder, the other with her arms clasped around his neck, both giggling uncontrollably. Andrew made an 'AAAARRRR!' sound like some monster pirate, and walked out of the room being sure to put an arm around each one lest they lose their grip and fall. As his mother used to say, 'It's all fun and games, 'til someone loses an eye'.

Once in the kitchen, the game quickly got old. 'OK, kids, your dad needs a coffee, plee-eese, leave me alone.'

'There's fresh goat milk, they said.

-In the big jug, said Charlie.

-In the fridge, said Marie.

He found Bianca out on the veranda, scrolling through the news on her tablet, drinking iced tea.

'The twins made some iced tea,' she said when she saw Andrew come through the door.

'Coffee first,' he said, and smiled, sat in the wicker chair next to hers. Between them was a small wicker table with an inlaid glass top. He took a sip of his coffee and set it down on the table, looked out over the front yard, could see the arena not too far off in the distance.

'No golf today?' she asked.

'Nah. Wanna hang out with you. We could play nine later. With the boys. Whattaya say?' By "the boys", he meant Westin and AJ. 'Where are they anyway? Not still at their friends' house? Who are these friends anyway?' He picked up his cup and took another sip, set it down again, said 'Delicious!'

'The boys are at the course,' she said. 'I will fetch them before dark.' Andrew nodded his head. Bianca had a theory about trouble and boys. Left to their own devices it would be a short trip to blowing up frogs, shooting birds and, eventually, one of them drowning in a pond. Better to get them addicted to a sport early, one winter, one summer, and then drop them off in a semi-supervised recreational space, like a golf course or tennis club (summer) or a ski hill (winter). (A hockey arena was a different story: plenty of room for trouble there, including girl trouble.) No doubt they'd still get up to testosterone driven nonsense, but at least it would be circumscribed by the rules and procedures of the place where there were penalties attached to poor behavior. And work too. 'Idle hands are the devil's playground', she often said when one or other of the kids complained about household chores. Develop a good work ethic as early as possible. Don't turn them into child slaves, of course, but make sure they understand that running a household is teamwork, so requiring everyone to pitch in. Eve was now 15 years old and would soon be old enough to legally drive. She'd learned to drive the tractor when she was 12, helped bring the hay in, which, as you can imagine, required all hands on deck. Eve worked part time during school and full time in the summer at a burger joint in town. That's where she was now. Even though she was morally opposed to the entire fast food industry, she believed it was her duty to understand the whole production-consumption thing if she was ever going to be able to change it. 'Do you know the average meat pattie is made from the meat of 78 different cows in as many as 15 different countries?! This is outrageous! Unacceptable!' she'd exclaim.

Her dad liked to egg her on, so he'd say things like 'Still?' or 'Only?' or 'Stop, you're making me hungry', which, of course, she did not find funny at all. 'And sugar! In everything!' She'd shout. 'Don't even get me started on that!' To which her father would often respond with 'Yum', or 'That reminds me, I gotta pick up some ketchup', or 'Anybody want a timbit?'

She knew he was joking, but it drove her crazy anyway, especially when she'd come home from work still in her work clothes and her dad would approach her, sniff the air around her like a dog, and say, 'Wow! Do you ever smell good! What is that perfume you are wearing? Come here Ginger Bell the third and get a whiff of your big sister!'

'Just ignore your father, he's only teasing,' Bianca would say. Which of course he was. Andrew was proud of his daughter, his first born, admired her for her strong, informed opinions, her willingness to speak up particularly for those not able to speak up for themselves. She's just like her mother, he'd often think. 'You're just like your mother,' he would say to her, 'only you smell delicious!'

'How's your brother?' Bianca asked.

'Why?'

'It looked like he took a pretty good two hander across the back of his skate. Second period? Didn't you catch it? That big defenseman, the Canadian, not the Subbans, the other one. What's his name?'

Andrew didn't respond. He hadn't noticed, but Logan didn't say anything or look to be hurt, like limp to the shower or anything like that. His brother was so rarely injured that Andrew never gave it a thought. 'I'm sure he's fine,' he said after thinking it over. 'What've we got to eat?... And please don't say eggs'.

33.

GAME 4

Andrew had a sense of unease. He felt it from the moment he got into the dressing room. The room was quiet and, as he looked around, he could see that Wiener and Shakey were both flushed and breathing hard, their flow seriously disheveled even though they were still in their street clothes which looked rumpled. He also noticed that PJ and FC were breathing heavily, looking equally disheveled. The room smelled funny. I mean, funnier than usual. There was something more than the roasted sweat sock, stale popcorn and cat piss smell of hockey gear in the air. He had passed Logan in physio on his way in. He was face down on a padded table, clad only in gym shorts. It looked like he was having his left Achilles iced. His face was turned away from the window, so he didn't see Andrew go by. Whatever had gone down in the dressing room, no one was saying anything more about it, least of all to Andrew - or Logan, the captain, who, the boys thought should be left out of it completely if possible.

And now, standing between the pipes, ceremonial pucks dropped, sweet chorus of children rolled back up with the red carpets they came in on, soldiers and their flags safely stowed backstage, Andrew still felt uneasy. Something was amiss, and that something became painfully clear from the opening shift. Logan's line started. From the way he bent forward to take the face-off, Andrew could see that something was physically wrong, that Bianca was right. Having lost the draw, the Leafs had to back check straight away as the Habs wheeled in over the blueline, PK1, back in the line up, leading the way by ripping a slapshot on Andrew, just to see if he was awake. Andrew caught the puck, dropped it off to one side for Horton to collect and regroup. A heavy forecheck was on, and Horton was forced into trying to backhand it around the end boards to where Shakey could pick it up. But Shakey wasn't there, for some reason he had come down low to the bottom of the circle so all he could do was watch the puck whizz around the boards past him where it was picked up at the blueline by PK2.

For the next thirty seconds the Leafs were hemmed in, finally icing the puck, which took the pressure off momentarily but also meant that Logan's line had to stay on the ice. As they lined up for the draw, Logan could hear Shakey and Wiener breathing like twin combines. He backed off, straightened up, looked at them both, reset. Wiener was leaning on his stick when Led Stroj, the Habs' winger, said in a thick Slovenian accent:

'Boy, you stink. Like booze, cigarettes.' He sniffed. 'And pussy. Smells like... your mother?'

Off came Wiener's gloves! Wiener was outweighed by at least 30 pounds, the guy had a neck like a bull. But that was no deterrent. Hungover and sleep deprived though he was, Wiener came at Stroj like a madman. Which, if truth be told, is the wrong attitude to bring to a hockey fight. Better to keep a level head. Anger will only lead to rash judgements and, like now, to Stroj simply stepping aside and reefing Wiener across the back of his head with a still gloved hand, which sent the Leaf forward skidding and twirling all the way to the blueline. Once back on his skates, he came at Stroj again, this time with Logan stepping in to hold him back. With his sore Achilles, however, Logan quickly lost both his balance and grip on his linemate which sent him toppling to the ice. Wiener, barely breaking stride, went head first into Stroj with an attempted head butt, which didn't work very well, but ensured a phone call from the head of the NHL's disciplinary committee.

With order restored, the Leafs found themselves shorthanded for 5 minutes. Stroj had received a roughing minor as had Wiener. But Wiener also received a major penalty and game misconduct for intent to injure, as well as a 10 minute misconduct for his use of abusive language toward the referee. The coach made Logan sit out the major, and Shakey sit out the misconduct. The Leafs were now without their number one line - which looked more like number two, if you know what I mean - and number one penalty killer in Logan Cash.

The coach sent out Channer and PJ up front, Morgan and Kell on D. Montreal countered with the cosmonauts up front and PKs 1 and 2 at the blueline. Andrew didn't like this line up one bit. He thought of how PJ and FC looked in the dressing room before the game. Well, hang on to your hat, he said to himself, banging the paddle of his goal stick on one goalpost, the top of the handle on the other. Then he set himself into his crouch, glove hand held high. Frank moved in to take the draw.

But there's a big difference between looking ready and really being ready. For the next five minutes the Habs pummelled the Leafs. It's Game 1 all over again, thought Andrew, but why? What's wrong with everybody? Popovich to Bykovsky to Titov: goal. Titov to Subban to Popovich via a clever little slap pass: goal. Loukat to Lopatou to Stroj: goal. The Habs wheeled around in the Leafs end like a well oiled machine.

'Attaway Hazet! Way to win that draw!'

'Howzat Zat! Nice pass!'

'Awesome shot, Ledder, c'mon boys!'

-Keep the hammer down!'

Another Habs high five skate through. 3 nothing already and barely five minutes into the game. There's nothing worse than having to watch that skate through in your own building. Andrew was unhappy, but he wasn't as upset as he was in Game 1. He knew something was up before the boys even got dressed, and here was the proof. All I can do is try to hold us in the game until we sort ourselves out. He said this to himself as he lifted his mask, put his gloves and stick on top of the net, drank some water, skated in a little circle, got himself sorted out.

The period ended 3-0. Logan had not played another shift. Once he had served the major penalty, he skated confidently across the ice - obviously not wanting to give anything away - had a brief word with his coach, and disappeared down the tunnel with one of the trainers. He did not return to the bench. Andrew found him right where he was about an hour earlier: in physio. This time, however, he was sitting up, watching the between periods telecast, his left foot in a big plastic bucket full of ice.

'What up, dog?' Asked Andrew.

'It's my Achilles tendon,' said Logan. 'Took a chop to it on Monday. One of the Russkies I think. Every time I try to push off I get this wicked pain radiating up my calf. The boot of the skate hurts like a mother too.'

'So, now what?' asked Andrew.

'So, I sit here chillin' with this bucket of ice until buddy gets back here with my x-ray assessment.'

'Sucks to be you,' said Andrew. Juvenile banter, just to keep things light. But an injured Logan was a major blow to the Leafs chances of finally winning a Cup. Andrew turned and trundled out in his sweat soaked gear, walked through the carpeted lounge and kitchen area and into the dressing room where hell was breaking loose.

The coach was tearing a strip off Wiener who sat sullenly at his cubicle, still dressed in his gear though he'd been tossed out of the game during its first shift. He smelled of cigarette smoke, so he'd obviously been having a puff somewhere within the confines of this non-smoking complex. But that wasn't what angered the coach. It would be added to the end if necessary, but it was already a long list: a) let your teammates down; b) selfish bastard; c) weak willed; d) a slave to the sins of the flesh; e) short-sighted; f) coulda got yourself killed; and g) not even a very good skater on the best of days. Shakey was stifling a chuckle, but he knew it was his turn next. The coach had come in shortly after all of the players. In the gap, where he'd been out in the hallway running interference with the media again, threats of violence had been meted out by several players to several others. It's better to leave the details out, for it was indeed an undignified scene. Certainly a scene not befitting a potential Stanley Cup Champion. When the coach entered the dressing room, having passed Andrew who was speaking with Logan, he came in upon a chaotic scene populated by a great deal of shouting, but no actual physical violence. He thought this to be a good thing. To restore order and some class to this bunch of classless spoiled brats, he thought he needed to play the bad cop, which he didn't often do. It wasn't his style. So, for the coach to lose his shit, and even say 'fuck' a very many times, came as quite a shock to the players. Without doubt Wiener and

Shakey were full of remorse. Most whoring drunks are the morning after, especially if they've lost their keys, cars and wallets along the way. But they start to feel like their old selves usually before the sun goes down. In this case, however, what had happened - and what the coach didn't know, didn't want to know, but could probably accurately guess at if you really wanted him to - was that after golf, the boys had had a few pops over at a teammate's house, then they barbecued some steaks, then most went home. Only Wiener and Shakey decided to take the party into the public arena, so off they headed to La Club Sexe or something like that - you get the idea - and, well, one thing led to another. When they regained consciousness, about 4am, they discovered that they were at the bottom of a dry roadside ravine, no car, no keys, no phones, no wallets. What had happened, neither one could recall. After managing, albeit with great difficulty, to crawl up the side of the ravine, they picked a direction and walked until they came to an intersection. It was the junction of two country roads east of Georgetown. -What the fuck? Said Wiener, looking at the signs and rubbing his head. -Ya, you can say that again, said Shakey.

Rather than try to flag down a passing vehicle which, admittedly, were few and far between at that time of the morning, they decided to walk, hoping that they could cover the several kilometres before daybreak. This they did, so avoiding the possibility of their photos showing up all over social media. What would head office do about that? Shakey didn't want to think about it. Once they got to their building, they had to buzz FC since they had no access to their condos. Frank, who had just awakened feeling refreshed and excited for the day, resisted dishing out a lecture. Better to get these two into bed and fast. So, he let them sleep in the two spare rooms, and tried not to let them spoil his day.

Of course, that wasn't possible. There goes our first line, he said to himself. How to make up for them, he wondered? Maybe the Russkies had their own set of pisstanks and we could pair the lines against each other. Fat chance, he said out loud. Nobody can hold their booze like the Russians, Boris Yeltsin being the lone exception. There was a team meeting at 2, so FC had to rouse the boys not long after they'd finally gotten to sleep. In the space between noon and 2, Wiener and Shakey had tried to piece together what had happened and make numerous phone calls cancelling credit cards and so on.

'You'll have to go to the police too. Report your vehicle as stolen.'

'Fuck that. It can wait,' said Wiener. 'The last thing we need is to draw attention to ourselves.'

'Like I'm sure you didn't do that last night already,' said Frank.

Wiener and Shakey shook their aching heads. 'Madre de dios!' said Shakey. 'I'm such an asshole.'

'That you are,' said Frank. 'That you both are.'

34.

The second period had gone much better. Sometimes a coach's motivational speech, which may or may not include some unexpected and even unusual behavior, will have the desired effect. Sometimes it won't. Go figure. The Leafs had played so badly in the first period that, really, there was only one way to go and that was up. Despite losing both Cash and Morris, the coach didn't have to spend too much time thinking about how to juggle the lines. This was because Walton was in no condition to compete. He would have to be content with watching the game from the most dreaded position of all - middle of the bench. D at one end, everyone else at the other end. And you, feeling totally useless, not to mention full of remorse, stuck right there in the middle, leaving the crowd and the media to speculate what it was that was wrong with you, whether it was health - the mysterious 'lower body injury' - or doghouse that got you there. With Walton right where he belonged, the coach would simply rotate the three remaining lines.

The Leafs had a lot of speed in their lineup. The entire kid line, PJ and Buddy I, Hutchie and the new kid, Pappin's replacement, Keney Dramiuc. Only Frank and the Big Swede had what might be called 'ordinary speed'. But the Big Swede had power and a magnificent wrist shot, and Frank was second only to Logan in the smarts department. Figuring he had nothing to lose, being already down 3-0, the coach let the boys loose, let them play a little run and gun. Give the Habs a taste of their own medicine. The only problem with this, of course, is that while they were rolling 3 lines, Montreal would roll 4. But, well, let's just see how it goes for the next little while, said the coach to his assistant standing next to him. For this to be effective, at minimum the Leafs would have to stay out of the box. Take a penalty and the whole machine grinds to a halt. Guys get cold on the bench. The rhythm gets broken. Momentum shifts to the team with the extra man. 'Gotta stay out of the box, boys, stay outta the box!' The Coach shouted up and down the line. 'Come on now, Hutchie, get your guys moving. Let's win this period!'

The new kid, the import, Dramiuc, had an outstanding period, scoring both Leaf goals. Hutchie and the Big Swede were in with helpers on each one. Montreal had failed to add to their total, so the team was only down by one. If things work well, if a coach's plan - against the odds - pays dividends in the short term, this can really give a team a boost. Shift momentum back to the team that is down, in this case the Leafs. It helps, too, if you've got young, talented kids up front. Not only do they not know they have limits - so making many things more possible - they are also like little weathervanes: if the team is feeling good, then I am feeling good; if the team is down, then I am down. Like puppies really. So effort plus reward equals confidence which then often leads to further reward, and so the team is set off in a virtuous circle of behaviour. Pappin watched from the corporate box, and what he saw gave him mixed feelings. The team was doing better, was on the comeback trail, partly thanks to my replacement, he said to himself. Would there be room for me in the lineup? What is up with this friggin concussion? It's been a few days now. I feel fine. And what's with Shakey in the middle of the bench? He must've gotten pissed last night. That boy will never learn.

Dramiuc had come to the U.S. at the invitation of Petr Klima's player development organization. Klima had established a vehicle for young Europeans, initially only Czechs but now open to the rest of the old East Bloc, to play minor hockey in North America. In this way, they could learn how to deal with the shocks of living in an alien culture before they were draft age. Though Klima had long retired, the organization had gone from strength to strength. It was Horton, on a visit home, who had spotted Dramiuc, flagged him for the Leafs. 'The boy can fly,' he said over the phone. 'And he can hit, and he dangle.' Which is exactly what he was doing from his position on Hutchie's left wing. From his position at the end of the bench, Horton looked on in wonder and chuckled to himself; sometimes you hit the jackpot.

35.

'That was quite a period,' said Peach. 'Only down by one.'

'That new kid, Dra-Dra-what?'

'Dra-moo-ich,' I said.

'What the hell kind of name is that!' said Hutchie.

'He'd be better off with a number,' said Peach.

'Helluva hockey player.'

'You can say that again, Hutch.'

Peach was occupying his usual seat in Jack's hospital room. Hutchie was in his. Hockey players are creatures of habit. If there's a guy on a team who likes to move around the room, sit in different places, well, let's put it this way, the guy's a bit weird. Pick a spot and stick with it. If you want to move around, talk to different guys, do it after the game, preferably with a beer in your hand. The new guy in any group, of course, will often get his knuckles verbally wrapped when trying to figure out where to sit: 'hey, sorry there buddy, but that's Bergie's spot.' 'Hey fella, you can sit there... at your own peril. That's Ricky's spot. Have you seen the size of Ricky?' I was in my normal spot, too, in the damn bed. I was feeling a bit chipper now that I had company for the game, but my mood was swinging wildly and often predictably throughout the day: go for a stroll, then I'm up; stuck in the bed, told not to move while they get this or that reading, then I'm down. I'm tempted to say, don't ever get old because it sucks. But, well, at least I'm still here and while I'm still on the right side of the grass there will continue to be ice cream to be eaten, the news of the day to be wondered at, and with any luck, friends and family to give you the odd hug every now and then. Don't underestimate the value of a hug, of physical contact. And just because I'm old doesn't mean I don't need affection and love just like everybody else. OK, maybe I'm just a sad, sentimental old geezer who should keep these thoughts to himself. But give it a try. Hug your grandma. I mean, really hug her, don't just sort of make contact and do the little shoulder pat thing, really give her a hug. Watch her light up, watch the years melt away, see the light of youth in her cataract clouded eyes. Give one to your grandpa too. I know he smells weird, but anything left untouched in the fridge for too long smells funny too. So touch him - come on don't be weird about it - and help get the stale off of your old grandpa.

'What did you say?' asked Peach.

'What? Oh nothing,' I said. 'An out of body experience. There's a young person inside me trying to get out while this old person who is me is trying to escape this friggin hospital.'

'Whoa. That's too complicated for me,' said Hutch.

'Like running the Leaf bench? Say, what's wrong with Walton? Why don't you think the coach is playing him? And where's my nephew anyway?'

'The word from my grandson is that Walton and Morris are party animals. They had two days off. Maybe that had something to do with it.'

'I think Logan's hurt,' said Peach. 'He took a two-hander the other night. I think it was one of the Latvians. On the ankle. Back of the leg somewhere.'

'I musta missed that,' I said.

'I hope it's not a Bobby Clarke sort of thing. You know, even up the sides by putting the other team's best player in the hospital.'

'I don't think so. He was skating around. It's probably a deep bruise. If it is broken, let's hope it's a Bob Baun thing instead. He can have the whole summer to heal.'

'Have they got the horses for the third,' I asked? The theme from Coach's Corner could be heard fading off in the background. The CBC was going to commercial.

'Cassie Campbell seems to think they do.'

'But Ron Maclean doesn't. And I'm with Ron.'

'Me too. Unfortunately.'

'Speaking of unfortunate, did you get a load of Ron's suit? What's with those collars?'

'And cuffs!'

'Go Leafs Go!' said Peach, unscrewing the cap on his thermos, asking 'More tea Hutch?'

36.

Up in the stands, Christine had finally unclenched her fists. 3-2 was much better than 3-0. There were deep fingernail marks in the palms of her hands. She vigorously rubbed her hands together, then rubbed them along her thighs. After that first period, it seemed like there was no hope. That it was going to be one of those days. She received a tweet from Logan about midway through the period telling her 'it's nothing to worry about.' Which, to her way of interpreting her son's cryptic communications, meant there was something to worry about. 'Logan says there's nothing to worry about', she had said to Steve. 'Then don't worry', he had told her, knowing full well that this was not going to happen. Let the worrying begin! he had said to himself. And though Logan had not returned to the game, the fact that Toronto had fought back, got themselves within one by the end of the second, did help ease her tension, allay her fears, give her hope. Leaf fans use the word 'hope' a lot. Almost as much as they use the word 'disaster'.

In the corporate box, Ged and Eric sat quietly, thinking their separate thoughts, each leaning forward with their arms resting on the railing. Ged straightened up, said to his son, 'So, want a hotdog?' 'What would mom say?' Eric said back to him. 'We just won't tell her, said Ged. 'Besides we're grown men. I'm 80 for god sakes!' And they both laughed.

At home in Caledon, Bella switched on the TV, hunted around for the hockey game, located it about halfway through the second period. Toronto was losing 3-2. She had never once watched any part of a hockey game, had only ever been in a big arena once to watch a rock concert, and that was 15 years ago. She thought the game looked slightly ridiculous. Without sound, it was actually quite funny. Like watching insects buzz around a porch light late at night. No rhyme, no reason. And always this wrestling with each other after play had stopped. Where is the red card? Send them out of the game. And where is Logan. At the end of the period she switched it off. Sent him a text message. Made some tea and went out back to read a book.

Down at the Ryerson Centre, Lori, Martha and Rita were having an off-day. This meant, in Lori's words, 'an old broad like me shouldn't drink alcohol every day', so this evening it was strictly soft drinks. 'Who wants a Tim's?' asked Lori. Having overheard her, about thirty people sitting in her vicinity raised their hands. 'Very funny,' she said. But upon return to her seat, 2 coffees and 1 steeped tea in hand, she also had a big box of timbits, said, 'Sorry about the coffee everyone, but who wants a timbit?' Which brought on a few cheers and claps. As she settled in, Lori thought how funny it was to be drinking a Tim's and eating timbits on the very surface where Tim Horton had once plied his trade. She'd trade the entire corporate behemoth behind a Tim's coffee for the return of the ghost of Tim Horton to the Maple Leaf lineup any day.

'This Horton, the Yank, does he remind you of Tim Horton?' she asked her girlfriends.

'Who's Tim Horton,' Rita asked back.

'Really, Rita? You gotta be kidding,' said Lori. She loved her old friend but. 'Them's fightin' words, Rita. You better watch yourself. Especially once this coffee kicks in.'

'Once the coffee kicks in,' said Rita, 'you better hope you can make it to the toilet in time. The old legs don't move as fast as they used to.' And the girls laughed. A white haired man sitting in front of them turned to look back at them and said, 'Boy, sister, you can say that again!'

37.

Ron or Cassie. Ron or Cassie. Ron or Cassie. Like pulling petals from a daisy. Who would you be left with? Who would be right? The third began much like the second, with the Leafs kid line buzzing around the Habs end. Brambory was up to the task, and as we all know, good goaltending beats good scoring nine times out of ten. I wouldn't quite say the Habs had played rope-a-dope. Letting the Leafs punch themselves out before turning the tables. For one thing, the Leafs were no George Foreman. Big tough and slow, with a right cross like a sledgehammer. The Leafs were fast, artful, in many ways they - not the Habs - were like Muhammed Ali who could float like a butterfly and sting like a bee. But for anyone watching the game, there was something to the metaphor. The Habs bent but did not break. The Leafs landed blow after blow but none of them had the desired result. As the Montreal coach often said, his team were like the Weebles: We wobble but we never fall down. Well, at least it appeared that way on this particular occasion.

For the first half of the third period the game was played mostly in Montreal's end. The Leafs had outshot the Habs 12-0, with Montreal's first shot of the period - a PK1 rifle blast from his own side of centre ice - coming just before the 10 minute mark. The Leaf faithful banged what could be banged, blew what could be blown, clapped what could be clapped, stamped what could be stamped, and hollered themselves hoarse with 'Go Leafs Go'. They sat on the edge of their seats. They rose as one as the Big Swede barreled in from the hash marks and snapped off a high hard one. And they uttered a collective groan when, totally against the run of play, Montreal scored first to build their lead to 4-2.

In the stands, Christine punched her husband hard on the arm. Steve looked at her, said -What did I do? In the corporate box, Ged and Eric simply stared straight ahead, showed no obvious feelings. On the floor of the Ryerson Centre, Lori said, 'That's it! That's it! My nerves can't stand any more of this. Who wants a beer?' About 30 hands went up around her, her fellow crestfallen Leaf fans uttering a collective 'I do'. And in the hospital, Hutchie let out a long sigh, said 'Well, boys, that'll be all she wrote.'

And it was. Run and gun had run out of gas. Not that the boys didn't give it the old college try. With 4 minutes left in the game and a face-off coming deep in the Habs zone, the Leaf coach called a timeout, gathered his troops around, squinted his eyes like Gregory Peck playing General Douglas MacArthur, gave a short Churchillian speech - which Shakey found truly inspirational - told Andrew to remain on the bench and ended with 'Now, let's go get 'em!'

'Six attackers,' said Peach.

'Won't help,' said Hutch, even though little Hutchie was out there with FC's line, Prince and Shaw on the blueline. 'They've shot their bolt.'

'Gave it their best,' said Peach.

'That's all you can ask for,' I said, knowing full well that that was a lie. As fans we always ask for more.

On the ensuing face-off, the Habs continued to bend but not break. Shots rained in from all angles. Bodies flew left right and centre, blocking puck after puck. Forty-five nail biting seconds passed before the Leafs were called for offside, Princey failing to control a bouncing puck at the near boards. The Leaf coach changed lines. Put out Ellis, Keon and Kadri, added the Big Swede. Horton and Pronovost on D. The young thoroughbred, Dramiuc, slid down the bench next to Shakey, champed at the bit, grew impatient. He ached for a chance to bring his team back from the brink.

The Habs won the draw and proceeded to bank a slow roller off the far boards. Like a shuffleboard shot. Horton reached the puck first, with Bykovsky right on his back. He held his left arm out to fend off the Montreal player, corralled the puck with the other, big Gordie style. But Horton was no Howe. Bykovsky leaned in and took a wild swipe at the puck. He made perfect contact. The puck shot out from underneath of Horton's blade straight into the centre of the vacated

Leafs goal. 5-2. One minute and thirty seconds left to play. The Leaf coach kept Andrew on the bench. 'Run and gun, boys, run and gun!'

But they were done. Dog tired and done like dinner. Montreal added a meaningless sixth, which pissed off the Leaf fans to no end. It wasn't Montreal they were mad at. It was the Leaf coach who they felt had made a poor decision. Pulled the goalie too early. Kept him on the bench. And now a close game, looked like a route, though it was anything but. Sure the Leafs sucked big time in the first period. But they'd shown the ability to come back. Not quite far enough, but there was a lesson in there somewhere for them. The coach would review the films and figure out what that lesson was, in time for tomorrow's mid-afternoon team meeting.

The dressing room was quiet, but not morose. Gone were all the hard feelings that had characterized their attitudes toward each other for most of the day, especially FC's feelings toward Shakey and Wiener. The coach was outside running interference. He was very calm. He'd have to give some careful thought to what should be done about Walton and Morris.

38.

Logan had no problem 'laying low'. He couldn't walk. He tried, of course, but the best he could manage was a one-legged hop to the toilet and back. He lay back in bed with a groan, bent his right leg and gingerly touched his achilles tendon. Just the faintest of touches. The point-source pain was incredible, but the radiation all the way up the back of his leg made it all the worse. He straightened himself out in bed, sighed, wondered what to do. Rest, ice, compression, elevation. These are the words hockey players live by, but don't often heed. We start off well, being good little boys, but usually lose patience quickly, just like little boys. He stacked some pillows at the foot of the bed, rested his foot there. Drugs. 'I need drugs', Logan said to himself. The pain of being awake was making him skittish. So he swung himself back out of bed, hopped over to the curtains which he pulled back to reveal blazing sunlight, then hopped back to the bathroom to rummage around in drawers and cabinets for some pain killers. Having found some Tylenol-3s whose expiration date had not yet been reached, Logan proceeded to the kitchen, put some coffee off, took two pills, and grabbed a bag of peas from out of the freezer. Back to the bathroom. 'There's gotta be a tensor bandage or three in here somewhere', he said aloud, slightly surprised by how completely his words broke the silence, let the reality of last night's fiasco seep in. 'Tomorrow is another day', he said, mimicking his grandpa, 'and now here it is'.

Having abandoned the bedroom for the living room, Logan settled in on the couch with his coffee, his device, and several pillows. He checked his messages, found one from Bella: 'You OK Mr Captain of the Toronto Maple Leafs?' Logan could almost hear her slight East European accent. He wondered where she was from. If she was born in Canada. No matter. She was here now. He smiled at the thought, texted her back: 'Yep am OK just a little sore.' Sipped at his coffee, looked out on another brilliant June day in southern Ontario. Briefly wondered whatever happened to global warming, all that. Anyway... he thought, sighed again. His device buzzed with another message. This time it was Andrew: 'Yo bro U up?' 'Yep', he texted back.

'How you feeling?'

'Hurts like a mofo.'

'RICE'

'Am on it.'

'Stay on it.'

'Will do.' Logan sighed. Andrew was like a friggin pitbull. Running herd over 6 kids wasn't enough, he had to keep me under constant surveillance too. Must be a 'dad thing', thought Logan. The phone rang.

'Hello? Bella?' said Logan.

'Hi. I'm wondering how you really are doing, she said. 'Players don't miss entire games because they are "a bit sore", do they?'

Logan chuckled. 'Well, ya, I guess you got me there.' He chuckled again, stopped himself, thought "man, I sound like a duffus". 'I took a whack on the back of the leg, my achilles, nothing serious, just… seriously painful.'

'Is there anything I can do to help? I mean, like, pick up groceries, or something like that? Can you walk?'

'Not so good right now,' he said. 'You could bring me a steak or two, if you like. I've got everything else I need.'

'OK, I'm at work now. At Mr. Dowhaniuk's I mean. I'm here for another few hours, until 3. I'll come by after that. What's your address? I know you said Mac something road.'

Logan gave Bella his address, said goodbye, hung up the phone. He didn't need any steaks either. But it was a good excuse to see her again.

39.

I've really had my fill of hospitals. Of injuries. Of ailments. Not just mine. Everyone else's too. If you play sports, you better get used to this quick. Parents make a mental note of this: your boy's or girl's first injury will be the first in a very long line of injuries. Also note, it will neither stop their determination to play nor hinder their love of the game. Emergency rooms. Broken this and thats. Cracked this and thats. Teeth, ribs, limbs, especially the bits that bend. Pulls. Tears. Hyper-extensions. Concussions. Stitches and splints and casts. Teeth knocked out. Blinded in one eye. Compound fracture. Injury prone. Never play again. In fantasy leagues and hockey pools the lists of the injured are studied and dissected daily and as closely as a Kentucky Derby racing form. People on the outside, at one remove, looking imperiously in. Like buyers at a cattle auction. Thumbs up. Thumbs down. But from the player's point of view, particularly the injured player's, it all looks quite different. So the wounded beast won't sell. Put it out to stud - hey, not a bad option. Put it down? Hey, not so fast buddy boy. When we're young we usually heal. That which does not kill you makes you stronger, something like that. But when you're old, the pulls stay pulled. The breaks take ages to repair. And the doctors look at you funny. Like you're some kind of freak. You're 75 and you broke your wrist doing what? When I was young the doctor often said, 'You're lucky. If you had done this at my age, you'd never play hockey again.' Liars. We still play. We just take longer to heal and play much worse. But playing worse is better than not playing at all. I often wonder about guys like Bjorn Borg or Boris Becker, guys who said 'no more' because they couldn't compete at the very top level any longer. What's wrong with a step down? With altered expectations? There's as many types of hockey as there are rinks in the world and hours in the day. Just because it ain't the NHL, doesn't mean it ain't worth playing.

And now this? Can a heart attack be counted as a sports injury if incurred during the playing of the sport? I wonder. I must say, I've been pretty fortunate in the health department. Almost all of my visits to hospital from the age of 13 onwards have been self-induced. I broke it, I cracked it, I pulled it, I strained it. I've only ever once had an operation in a hospital and that was decades ago. In Dakar, Senegal. I was visiting one of our university partners, and I'd been in the capital city for exactly 12 hours when overcome with acute appendicitis. Musta been something I ate, a wayward bone in the ceebu yap; or maybe a chunk of misguided gristle from my roadside dibi. So, I had my appendix removed. It was a Sunday and I took my Lebanese surgeon away from his usual game of pétanque. It was surgery 'old school'. In the operating room, which definitely could use a new coat of paint, I was laid out flat on a metal table, my right arm attached to a drip - the bloody drip, I still cringe at the very thought of swopping out the needle - and my left arm attached to the anaesthetist's kit, whatever that thing is. Like Monty Python's 'machine that goes ping'. The anaesthetist was a little guy who was as black as coal, wore giant late-80s style glasses with lenses as thick as coke-bottle-bottoms and wasn't much taller than me when I was laying flat out. He fiddled with the gizmos, affixed the ancient thick-plastic mask to my face and asked in French-accented English, "Ow eez it? OK?' I nodded. 'Can you count back from ten for me, please?' This I did. He nodded, said 'Sank you,' and fiddled a bit more with the knobs. I could hear gas 'And now, 'ow eez it now?' I started to fade, to babble a bit. He nodded happily, leaned in close to my face, raised a gloved hand, waved and said 'Bye bye, Jack.' Pegged out like Jesus on the cross, I only had a split second to wonder if indeed this was 'bye bye', before the anaesthetic kicked in.

Of course, I survived and returned to sport to face a few more decades of self-inflicted wounds. Like this one. What is more 'self-inflicted' than heart disease? Ya, ya, you hear about genetics and all that, but really we're just a slave society, bending to the master of sugar, salt and fat. Yum! I smacked my lips involuntarily, thought of a nice hot bowl of poutine. It was at that moment when Q walked in shattering my delicious daydream, bringing me back to the gag of hospital-room reality.

'Norm?' I said. I was momentarily confused at the spectre of Norm Quenneville before me.

'Russ?' said Q, obviously teasing me. But still I didn't clue in. Being bedridden will do that to you. Make a teething child out of you.

'Whu?' I muttered.

'Not Norm, Joel,' he said. There was a long awkward pause.

'Oh! Tinhead! Is that really you?' I said, smiling and laughing.

'Yep, Killer, it's me. How you doing?' He scanned the room. Q was very good at taking stock, making considered judgements.

'The all-time winningest coach in NHL history!' I announced, as though introducing him to a crowd of his faithful followers.

'And only had to coach 'til I was 70 to catch Scotty.'

We both laughed.

'Funny how time flies, eh buddy?' I said.

'Ya, funny as a crutch.'

'What brings you here, my old friend?'

'I'm a Leaf for a day,' he said.

'Oh ya,' I said. 'Remember that? I almost forgot you played for the Leafs before the Rockies.'

'Ya, most people do. But in this case, the Leaf brass wanted to bring me in and speak to the boys. Do a sort of 'rah rah rah' thing. Remind them of what it takes to be a Stanley Cup winner.'

'Well, if anybody knows, it's you.'

'Ya, but...,' he trailed off.

'No buts, man. You won almost as many yourself as the Maple Leafs have in their entire history. You gotta share the magic. Share the love, my brother.'

'I guess so, but I'm 79. Been off the bench and outta the dressing room for quite a while.'

'Just tell some stories. The kids will eat it up. Nobody tells a better story than you, Q.'

'That's sort of my strategy for the day. I'm only with them for an hour this afternoon anyway. Not much you can do in an hour. Maybe just try to light a fire under them. They'll have their tails between their legs after last night's performance. A few will have their heads down, too. I'll try to get them to lift their heads up, stay confident.'

'Ya, just tell them a tale or two from your "on the ropes" archives. That file's gotta be a foot thick. Almost as thick as the file detailing all of your league fines.'

We both had a chuckle over that, shook our heads.

'Anyway, Killer, I just wanted to drop by, say hi, get well soon and all that stuff. I'm glad to see you're your old self. You had me worried for a few seconds there at the start.'

'But geez, Joey, you look exactly like your dad.'

'You're one to talk. Hey, I'll try to check in later, but if not I'll see you soon eh?'

'Let's play some golf!' I said.

'I hate golf,' he said, pulling a face. I laughed. 'Oh, I see, you're just winding me up,' he said.

'You gotta admit, the knees can't handle the tennis anymore. So, what're we left with?'

'Poker,' he said, smiling, and hobbled out the door.

40.

Andrew woke up cranky and worried. Cranky about last night's game. Worried about his brother. He was still in bed and it was long after noon. He'd stayed there after texting his brother. Asked Bianca to please bring him a coffee. He wanted to brood in peace. But none of this played out quite as he imagined. Funny how kids take you out of yourself. Within half an hour of waking up he'd been visited by four of the six. The two older boys - AJ and Westin - were on a different time clock from their father. Straight to bed after watching the game, up at 530, at the golf course by 6. Once the bloody never-ending playoffs were over he'd have plenty of time to catch up with them. First to visit was Eve, who brought him his coffee, said she was sorry for how the game went, thought that he had played very well. -Thank you very much, said Andrew. Such a sweet kid, he thought, as she went out, telling him that she was on her way to work.

Next up were the twins. How a pair of 9 year olds could become ethical farmers was beyond him. They talked about the weather and how rain was much needed, what they had planted in the garden with the help of their mom, how the goats were doing, how the chickens were doing, what the prospects for the hay crop were this year, what with the no rains and all. Nothing about hockey. They neither cared nor knew anything about hockey. If they watched a game with the rest of the family, what they were really doing was joining a party, looking for an opportunity to shout and scream and jump up and down. If a game was going badly, they would simply take the temperature of the room, find it too cold for a party and head off to some other part of the house. What they did know is that their dad spent most of his waking hours in that big building down the road. It's where he worked. 'So I can bring home the ethically farmed bacon', he would tell them. This would not raise a laugh. To the twins, food was nothing to joke about.

Last up was Maggie who came in carrying a sheaf of papers. She hopped onto the bed, snuggled in under her dad's left arm and shoulder. He could feel the raging heat of her body. Like a miniature furnace. - Look, dad! she said, proceeding to haul out some of the paper. On each page was hand-written music. Andrew couldn't read music, but he knew what he was looking at.

'What've we got here, eh?' he asked.

'It's a violin concerto,' she said in her high and highly animated little girl's voice.

'Is it now?' said Andrew, truly amazed. He knew the kid was a bit of a musical prodigy, but all this stuff, like ants crawling across a page.

'Yes, my music teacher told me that I should try writing my own music. She said that I should try to "follow my inner voice".'

'Really? Is that what I'm paying her for? So that you can teach yourself? Follow yourself around?' Andrew laughed. Maggie laughed too, though she didn't know why. She was just laughing because her dad was. 'When am I going to hear some of it, then?'

'Oh, I don't know. Soon maybe. It's not quite finished.'

'Well, off you go, then. Get 'er done!' he said, mimicking his brother while giving his daughter's bird-like shoulder a light squeeze, then tousling her dark hair. Of all the kids, she looked most like her mother.

Who's next? thought Andrew. They came in one after the other making him feel like he was a patient in hospital. I was sick, but now I am healed, he said to himself. There was nothing left to do but get up and face the day.

41.

At the condo, Bella pressed the button adjacent to CASH, L. 'Come on up,' she heard a crackly voice say, the door buzzing shortly thereafter. Alighting from the elevator, she first looked left, then right, wondering which way she should go. As she looked to her left once again she saw Logan's head peaking out from near the top of an open door. She saw him smile, heard him say 'hey'.

By now the drugs and RICE had kicked into effect, so Logan was moderately mobile. While he felt pretty good about himself and his prospects for recovery, Bella, not having seen him earlier in the day, looked on with some alarm. Logan could see the concern on her face.

'How is your leg, really, Logan?' she asked.

'It's OK, really. It just looks worse than it is. I'll be right as rain in time for game 5.' "As right as rain", he reflected to himself, that's another of grampa's sayings.

'To me, you don't look so well,' she said. 'Anyway, you know best, I guess. But just in case you weren't feeling so well, I brought you a little care package. Look!'

She proceeded over to the kitchen counter where she placed the big paper bag she was carrying. She rooted around in the bag producing first two t-bone steaks. 'As you requested,' she said. Next up was a carton of homemade soup. 'Chicken soup is good for the soul,' she said, laughing at the sound of her "self-helpiness". Third was a loaf of homemade bread. 'Thick black Russian rye bread straight from the steppe, just like my great-grandmother used to make.'

'Really?' asked Logan.

'No. Not really. It's straight from my oven at home. But it is just like my great grandma used to make. And, lastly, courtesy of my mother, who learned the recipe from her mother, ta da!'

Logan looked at a non-descript silver thermos. 'What is it?' he asked.

'You'll see. Get yourself a glass.'

Logan took down a thick-glassed tumbler from out of the cupboard. Bella unscrewed the lid and proceeded to pour out a thick green liquid. 'It looks like liquid grass,' said Logan.

'And tastes just as good, too,' said Bella, pausing for effect.

Logan smirked. 'Oh, I get it,' he said. 'This is one of those devious plots to make me healthy.' He gulped down half of the drink in one go. Grimaced when he was done. 'I guess the worse it tastes, the better it is for you, eh?' He wiped any residue from his lips with the back of his hand.

'Don't worry. I'm not here to change your ways. And don't hold this drink against me. I don't like it either. I'm just delivering a present to you from my mother. She said it will make you better. I always listen to my mother. Don't you?'

'If I'd always listened to my mother, I probably would've never left the house. Scary world out there and all that sort of stuff.'

'I know what you mean. Mother protector: the she bear etcetera. Anyway, just drink it down. I want to see you better too. '

They shared soup and bread out on the balcony, their private thoughts shaded along with their eyes, cool and protected by the deep tint of their sunglasses, each wary of opening up too soon, too fast. At some appropriate point they each made space for the other's exit. Logan saying he had a team meeting at 5. Bella saying that her mother was expecting her about that time too. They had a party of 25 to cater and needed to prepare the menu. At the door to his condo, they exchanged an awkward kiss goodbye, Logan bending down aiming for Bella's cheek but hitting her sort of along the side of her head. Logan's towering height had been a persistent problem in the dating world. Bella tried to respond but kind of cuffed him along the bridge of his nose with her forehead as Logan leaned down to meet her just as she went up on her tiptoes to meet him.

'Oof! 'he said, straightening up and rubbing his nose with the thumb and forefinger of his right hand.

'Sorry!' she said, wrinkling her nose, knitting her eyebrows.

'It's OK. I'll see you later. Soon,eh.'

'Ya, soon.'

42.

It was about 730pm before things broke up at the Samsung-Blackberry Centre. Coach Q had been a big hit with the boys. He had entered the video screening room bearing a slick looking burgundy leather suitcase on wheels. There was a long table set up at an angle next to the easy chair he would sit in while addressing the team. The boys had fought for the front row, deferring of course to the senior members of the team - Logan and Andrew - who sat front row centre. Now they sat quietly spellbound as the living legend entered stage left. With some help Coach Q set the case up onto the table, opened it and began to set out its contents: not one or two or three, but ten champagne bottle-sized replica Stanley Cups he received during his career as a coach in the NHL. He could have walked out of the room there and then, and that would have been enough. But ever the gracious, engaging and funny raconteur, he took his seat, smoothed his moustache with the palm of his hand, and grinned his famous cat-got-the-mouse grin.

'Hello fellas,' he said. 'Welcome to the deep end.'

When it was all over, the Leaf coach had the final words. 'Thanks Coach Q. Boys, try to get a good sleep. We fly tomorrow morning at 11.'

43.

GAME 5

As Andrew looked out from his goal crease he thought how different was this game in comparison to the other four. The first four seemed to be played for the hockey purist, he or she who remembered the original six, the Canadiens of the 1970s, the Islanders and Oilers of the 80s, the Penguins and Red Wings of the 90s. End to end action. Plenty of hard hitting. Enough fisticuffs to show the people watching that the people playing cared about the outcome. A game played predominantly in open ice. Like a Junior A game, come to think of it. With just as many bone-headed mistakes too. But real beauty. Speed. Skill. Grace. The big three. This game on the other hand had perhaps one of the big three - skill - and it was ugly. Dump and chase. Chip and charge. Grind it out along the boards. Keep the opponent out wide. Avoid the centre of the ice especially through the neutral zone. Deploy the offside trap. A game like this was about as exciting to watch as watching paint dry. It was like watching the New Jersey Devils of any era.

Bor-or-ing, thought Andrew. To this point in time, about half way through the game, he'd had almost nothing to do. The boys had blocked almost every shot. What came through to him was served up on a platter. And it had been the same at the other end of the ice. 6-5 Habs shots on net in the first period; 4-3 Leafs to this point in the second. The score was zero zero.

What do fans do at a game like this? They ooh, they ahh, and implore their team on to victory. But mostly they chat to each other, drink a lot of $20 a pop beer and 50 cents a pop jumbo sodas (the industry had dropped into the tank; only Coke and Pepsi could survive and this mainly because they'd gone into the elite super health drink market in Europe and America while buying up competition, consolidating holdings and continuing to drop sugar bombs on the Third World). They also ate: popcorn, nachos, hotdogs, poutine, pizza, hot pretzels. No wonder everybody was fat. You are what you eat, and this crowd looked like 25,000 bratwursts on sour dough. And they had fun. The corporation shot t-shirts into the crowd out of cannons during every stoppage in play. Snippets of music boomed from giant roof top speakers, the giant scoreboard showed clips of the Habs' greatest hits: Robinson, Lafleur, Lemaire; Beliveau, Cournoyer, Gomez. Gomez! How did he get up there. Different sections played trivial pursuit against each other. The 'kiss cam' encouraged couples to kiss, fans sang along to all of the greatest francophone hits, and in between periods hordes of little kids play Timbit hockey, which never ever got old. So, the joint continued to jump while down below on the ice surface the boys continued their bump and grind. Uh-uh-gly. 'Hey, Titov, you play ugly hockey!' shouted Andrew as the Montreal player continued to hug the boards, corral the puck in his skates, hold Horton and Walton at bay, while the two Leaf players dug at the puck with their sticks, looking like two rink attendants scraping the ice from alongside the boards. Another whistle. Another stoppage in play. More t-shirts into the crowd. More ear drum shattering ancient rock. More poutine, Pepsi and 'original Coke' down the collective throat in between choruses of Mon pays and Je reviendrai à Montreal. No one is better at making a festival out of nothing than Montrealers.

So, the fans were happy. And Habs' management was definitely happier with this sort of game. Slow and steady wins the race. Grind them down. Easier on the old poutine-thickened ticker than the blood pressure raising fire wagon hockey which had gotten them into a spot of bother with the speedy Leafs over the course of the first four games. In management's view, Montreal was lucky to escape with a split in Toronto. Aside from a dismal first period in game 4, the Leafs were the better team throughout their homestand. And, if the rumour mill was correct, Habs management should send flowers and chocolates - or perhaps a case of scotch and VIP memberships to La Club Sexe - to Walton and Morris to say 'thanks for helping out'.

Walton and Morris, by the way, were having excellent games. Given their importance to the team, the Leaf coach's only choice was to act as if nothing had happened, play them, and let them do their thing. Casher was also in fairly good nick. Though tender, two days of intense treatment had managed to reduce the pain to a persistent dull ache, which for any pro hockey player at this time of the year meant he felt just fine thank you very much. As long as no one targeted him there again, that is. Then it would be back to the beginning, belly down on a physio table, let's start again. Given that they were playing the Habs, and the series was now down to a best two out of three, the Leafs' staff had plenty of ice buckets at the ready.

The party came to an abrupt halt with 5:38 to play in the period. That was when the goal light went on behind the Montreal net. This did not come as a surprise, however. Because about 15 seconds earlier, when Shakey intercepted a cross-ice pass 'No! Not through the middle!' you could hear the Montreal coach wail. Everyone stopped talking, chewing and swallowing. Pizzas, pretzels and poutine were held in slightly shaking hands halfway between cardboard plate and gaping mouth. There was a collective intake of breath as Shakey proceeded to split the defense, pumping his skinny bowed legs back and forth for all he was worth, head up all the way, puck flat on the ice, deked Brambury first right, then left and finally with absolute calm slid the puck through the five hole. Goal: 1 nothing Toronto. And just to align the metaphor with Shakey's bowed legs, you could say that the Leafs were off to the rodeo and out to rope some Habs.

From there, it all fell apart fairly quickly for Montreal. Toronto managed to put two more past Brambury before the period was out. Sometimes it's just one mistake. One little mistake. That's all it takes to send a game plan down the toilet. Instead of trying to stick to form, the Habs tried to get one back. It's unlikely that this was on coach's orders. But it's just as likely that the Eurobots would rebel on their own. There had to be a Canadian, a passionate embarrassed Canadian at the centre of the 'let's get even and quick' attack plan. Shakey had split the Habs D. Had intercepted a PK2 pass and then danced past both him and his brother, PK1. He'd made the Habs look bad. He'd made the faces of the Habs - the Subban twins - look bad. PK2 had brought dishonor upon the family that is les Habitants. It was up to him to restore that honour. Actually it wasn't, but this is how young men, in the heat of battle, sometimes let their emotions get in the way of the task at hand. I mean why else would you mount a medieval horse and engage in a joust if it wasn't for your crazy surfeit of testosterone. Who in their right mind agrees to a dual at 10 paces? Who willingly signs up to fight the Hun or the Jerries or the Commies, happily buying into the propaganda of your honour being at stake? Why men of course. Especially young men. What a bunch of fools.

So, in his attempt to regain the family honour, PK2 tried to go end to end, lost the puck, got caught deep, and left his brother out to hang when Shaw hit Naz with a beautiful bank pass off the near boards sending Kadri and Ellis in on a two on one. Naz to Ellis, back to Naz and before you know it the Leafs are up 2-0 and PK2 is dragging his ass back to the bench, head hung down in shame. However, as the saying goes, there is no rest for the wicked. As the Subbans were trying to regain their composure on the bench, Morgs, Buddy I and PJ pulled off a carbon copy from the wide side: bank pass, two on one, tic-tac-toe and in. 3-0 Leafs.

-Woo hoo! Shouted Christine, standing up and high-fiving anybody willing to do the same to her, accidentally spilling her beer in her husband's lap. 'Woo-hoo!' shouted Lori and Martha down at the Ryerson Centre, spilling coffee all over themselves in their rush to stand up and celebrate. 'Woo hoo!' shouted Killer, Peach and Hutchie in unison, Peach spilling his tea all over the front of his freshly laundered Maple Leafs white home jersey. Up in the corporate box, Ged and Eric were eating their hotdogs. Following Tench's goal, to give the Leafs their 3-0 lead, they looked at each other. Eric said, 'Dad, there's mustard on your tie.' Ged looked down at the nice yellow dollop looking very much like the ornament on a tie clip sitting square in the centre of the black silk. 'Oopsie,' he said, lifting the tie and licking the mustard off. 'It'll probably stain,' said Eric. 'Don't tell mom,' said Ged.

You would think that, what with the shoe on the other foot, the Ryerson Centre would have been in a party mood. That the pizza and popcorn would be flying from the concession stands just as fast it could be cooked and popped. That the overpriced beer and wine would flow like the mighty Ganges - but with significantly fewer pathogens. That the crowd would be swaying shoulder to shoulder singing the greatest hits of

Stompin' Tom, Blue Rodeo, the Tragically Hip or the Rheostatics. You know, some hummable hockey centred song that said something significant about the meaning of the game. But if you thought that, you would be wrong. Mostly people sat and talked in hushed tones, worried themselves sick and prepared themselves for the worst. A 3-0 lead heading into the third period was the perfect setting for yet another epic Leaf collapse.

'Will they collapse?' I asked Hutchie.

'Not a chance, not a chance,' said Hutchie in full hockey mode. 'The Habs are done like dinner. This is our year, Killer. I can go to my grave a happy man.'

'Yep, a life bookended by Leaf cup wins. You know what that means, Hutchie?'

'What?'

'It means you lived a bloody long time!'

'Who knows, boys, this could be the start of something big.'

'Dynasty!' said Peach.

'Let's not get greedy, fellas. You are starting to sound like typical fans: delusional to the end.'

In the third period, it was back to bump and grind, only this time it was the Leafs who promoted this excrutiatingly boring style of play. Gain the centre line, roll it in. Forecheck one man. Clog up the middle. Stand them up at the blueline, make them fire it in. Beat them to the puck. And, most importantly, slow things down.

'Slow things down, boys, slow things down!' shouted Logan to all within ear shot. 'Be patient. Be smart. This one's ours if we want it.'

I watched intently as the camera zoomed in on Logan, standing up, urging his team on. I could picture his words fluttering in the air like pages torn from the team captain's book of aphorisms. But words from the captain matter. Some guys are born to lead. And some guys are born to follow. Why there are fewer of the former and way more of the latter is anyone's guess. But Logan was that natural leader. He followed in a long line of beloved Leaf leaders, from Syl Apps and Ted (Teeder) Kennedy who most famously brained Gordie Howe, to the Chief, steady and strong George Armstrong, and from Keon to Sundin with Sittler, Vaive, Clarke and Gilmour in between - all prolific scorers.

With such a pedigree, one might wonder how the once mighty ship that was the Toronto Maple Leafs could have wandered rudderless for decades, foundered on the rocks and washed up on a shore of failure and ignominy. The answer, of course, is that a captain is not a team owner, and despite the best intentions of most able captains, the players are involved in a game of battleship: 'F5' says Harold; 'Miss' says Punch. So captains are no more than deck hands on a plastic ship that is glued in place, waiting, waiting for the next call: 'G9' says Gord; 'Miss' says Brendan. A captain can lead in any particular game, but ultimately there is someone behind the scenes shifting the pieces around, rolling the dice, calling the shots, in an on-going effort to sink each other's battleship.

I am saying this because, as with the 1967 Leafs, there is a tendency to glorify agency and forget about structure. That when we succeed, we believe that it was up to us, the guys on the ice with our tireless effort, and the fans in the stands offering up unfailing support; and when we fail, it was due to our shortcomings as players and as fans. That may be the case. But maybe just maybe there's more to it than that. And we should not forget that hockey is a business. That players will be sacrificed for the business as often as they will sacrifice themselves for each other. Should Logan be playing with an injured Achilles tendon? Yes, the hockey fan will say: it shows fortitude, a will to sacrifice for the sake of the team, like the true leader that he is. But maybe, just maybe, he's in the game against doctor's orders because a win will put bums in seats, sell season tickets, ring up the cash register and if it shortens or ends his career, well, there's another would-be captain out there waiting in the wings. I may sound like a cynical old bastard but as much as I want the Leafs to win, to see my nephew lift the Stanley Cup, skate around the ice with it, held aloft, I also want him to be well and to know that there's a life beyond hockey, believe it or not.

The teams traded goals in the third period and that was all she wrote, as Hutchie liked to say. The Leafs played the old 'kitty bar the door' game, successfully turning the tables on the Habs. Like I said, it wasn't pretty but it was effective. PK1 scored from the point, sliding a seeing-eye grounder through a maze of sticks and legs in front of the Leaf net. Andrew had no chance. That ended his bid for a second shutout in the Stanley Cup Finals. This goal gave the Habs some temporary jump, but the Leafs gave them no space at all. PJ got the goal back to restore the 3 goal lead about ten minutes later. A one-timer from the high slot off of a pin-point pass from FC. From a mad scramble in the corner, the puck had popped loose to Frank who, seemingly with eyes in the back of his head, turned and whipped a pass straight on to PJ's tape. The result was Jam City.

'Keep 'er goin' boys! Keep 'er goin'!'

'Jam City Jammer!'

'Attaway!'

The high five skate through was less boisterous than usual. The boys had been stung in game 4, and they were all business tonight. It wasn't quite 'Mission Critical', but if the Leafs were to win the Stanley Cup, they'd have to win another one in the Habs' building. Better game 5 than game 7 was Logan's view. Get 'er done, was his attitude. Let's get this geriatric monkey off our backs and bring home Lord Stanley to Toronto, and to Port Huron and to Halifax and Shawinigan and all the hometowns in between. If management could read Logan's mind, they'd have surely turned this thought into a timely tweet from the team captain. Inspirational but unstated. Action speaks louder than words - that had always been Logan's approach to the game. Lead by example. Show it don't say it. You get the picture.

As the horn sounded to end the game, there was a smattering of applause indicating that the Leaf faithful were happy but not hedging their bets. The best thing about a win in Montreal was that you silence the crowd. There's none of that 'nah nah nah nah, hey hey hey, goo-ood bye' bullshit that Habs' fans love to rub in your face. Dead silence was music to Leaf fans' ears.

'Well, it wasn't pretty, mostly, but it was effective,' said Peach.

'That last goal was a beauty, though,' said Hutchie. 'Reminded me of me and the Killer back in the day.'

'Yep, back in the day, eh Hutch. Funny how forty or fifty years can seem like yesterday. Do you remember when your dad would show you stuff from when he was a kid, a photo, or you'd sit and watch an old movie with him that felt to you like it came out of the stone age. And that was what, maybe 20 or 25 years in the past. It was like, why are you making me watch this ancient history?'

'And here we are, feeling the same way, only the gaps are even longer. Seventy years is a long time between Stanley Cups. There's not many of us left who can even remember those games, those players.'

'Half the time, things I remember, my sister doesn't remember at all,' I said. 'Or remembers in a completely different way. Crazy.'

'Remember Whitey? Glenn Whiteside. The potato farmer? Doesn't Frankie Chan remind you of him?'

'Whoa, Hutch, I said, you really are taking me back. But who could ever forget Whitey. Remember Ged saying he's got hands like potatoes... maa-aashed potatoes.'

'Ya, such a soft touch for such a big guy. Amazing hands.'

'I loved playing with him as my centreman. You're my number one of course, Hutch. But Whitey, boy he could elevate the play of everyone around him.'

'Don't you love playing with a guy like that? Somebody who makes you better. Who makes everybody better. Most guys seem to sink to a lowest common denominator. Especially with shinny. Even the really talented guys in shinny tend to play for themselves. It's a rare gift to be able to be better than everyone else, but to also be able to go down and lift everyone up. Whitey was like that. I wonder whatever happened to him.'

'Still over in Alliston as far as I know.'

'I still think about him every time I buy a bag of Lays potato chips. I remember how he'd promised 5 years of crop to Lays. I wonder if that still goes on.'

'It must. Monsanto owns the world of food, so everyone is giving up their newborns to them. Lays is probably a division of Monsanto by now. Creepy just to think about it.'

'Then let's not. Let's think about game 6. Coming up in two days.'

'Maybe I'll be out of here by then. Sit rink side for the victory skate.'

'Knock on wood,' said Peach, rapping himself up side the head.

44.

The boys returned home to an eerie sight. The entire Samsung-Blackberry centre was ringed with stuffed animals, mostly Paddington bears, three deep, five deep, ten deep in places. There were lots of other things too, rocks, marbles, Lord Ganesha medallions, four leaf clovers of all sizes shapes and colours, rabbits feet, various sorts of Chinese dolls, horse shoes, both plastic and real. It had started with an innocent comment coming from, of all people, Shakey. Walton, who had been in the nation's doghouse for a few days, but who also acquitted himself through stellar play in game 5, was asked how he managed to pick himself up after such a fall. 'Well,' said Shakey, 'when I'm in need of good luck or feeling a bit low and need to pick myself up, I just give old Paddington bear's head a good rub and say to myself "today will be a better day"'. When asked about the bear, Shakey told the media that he'd had it since he was a small child, carried it with him everywhere, it being the one constant in his life. Somehow this touched the hearts of Leaf fans everywhere, turning cold stone into warm mush, and just as quickly as he'd been blamed for the loss in Game

4, he was suddenly everyone's bad dog who just needed to be loved. And, hockey fans being as superstitious as the players themselves, took to the notion of luck. If one bear could help turn the trick for Shakey, then a thousand, ten thousand, fifty thousand bears, and all the other stuff, would surely supply the luck necessary to help bring home the Cup.

Traffic had been backed up for hours on the 401 with fans arriving to deliver their personal good luck talisman. Every line of the LRT was packed with people clutching some sort of cherished stuffed animal, an animal they had looked upon fondly for their entire lives both as children and as adults, an inanimate object alive with memory, with love and hope, chockfull of infinite possibility. Why, some of these bears had been around since the last time the Leafs won the Stanley Cup.

According to the Habs' coach, it would take much more than a sea of luck to defeat the formidable Montreal Canadiens. According to the Leafs' coach, the team appreciated such amazing fan support and would try to turn their good wishes into good actions and bring home Lord Stanley's finest to the GTA. The media were lapping it all up, trying to turn this into the feel good story of the year. While, at the same time, the Leaf communications people were working overtime trying to figure out how to deal with all of this stuff, which charities to get in touch with, the Tim Hortons Children's Foundation (can anybody explain to me why the second apostrophe is necessary but not the first?) and the Make a Wish Foundation being at the top of the list. 'Please don't let it rain for the next week or so', was the current mantra up in Head Office. 'Nothing's less lovable than rain-soaked fake fur', the head of Communications could be heard to say. 'And, since so much of it is made in China, who knows what sort of toxins might leach into the water table.' 'Oh my,' his assistant could be heard muttering in response, 'That would be a public relations disaster.'

In the meantime, the team had more important things to worry about. Like devising an appropriate game plan for Game 6. They'd won two by playing their own game; and they'd won one by adapting to Montreal's chosen style, beating them at their own game. In truth, neither team liked the 'paint drying' approach to playing hockey. But the slower the game, the less likely an uncontainable error might occur. Errors along the boards were not usually such a big deal, unless it was in a corner in your own end. Errors in open ice, especially those made in your own end, often were. Errors made at high tempo often led to turnovers and turnovers often led to goals. So, what would it be? Run and gun with four lines just might work, but there was no way the Habs, needing a win to stay alive, would be drawn into that sort of game. A team meeting had been called for 4pm the next day. In the meantime, they were all encouraged to go straight home - the Leafs had returned on another red eye - and get to bed. Arriving at 2am was not necessarily a deterrent to Wiener and Shakey heading for the clubs, especially in mid-season with an off-day ahead of them. But this was different. The ghost of Lord Stanley was on the plane, in the bus, in the room. So Coach had put FC and Logan on them as minders. Logan had spent the entire charter flight laying on his back in the aisle with his injured leg up, wrapped in a tensor bandage and resting on a big bag of ice. In that position it wasn't five minutes before he'd fallen asleep.

'Snores louder than the friggin plane engines,' said Horton.

'You can say dat again,' said Pronovost.

'Oldtimers, eh,' said Ellis, looking first at Logan but then over at Andrew who was also silently fast asleep in his chair.

'Whatever it takes,' said Keon, 'whatever it takes.'

45.

Logan texted Bella as soon as he woke up. It was almost noon: 'Hey, want to meet up?'

'OK. Where?' was her reply. Good question, thought Logan.

'How about Belfountain?' she texted again.

'The conservation area?' Logan texted back.

'Yes. I'm at home. It's only 15 minutes for me. Maybe 20 for you? Nice walk. Some tea. Lunch.'

Logan considered the option. If he took a painkiller now, he'd probably be good to go in about 40 minutes. The place was pretty flat, so a walk wouldn't hurt. What a funny sport, hockey is, he thought: a guy who can barely walk to the toilet or the fridge, can barely get up off of the couch, can fly around the ice like a perfectly healthy somebody. 'OK. Let's make it 1245, K?' 'K.' was her reply. He rolled out of bed, placed both feet on the cool polished wood of the bedroom floor, took stock. 'Not bad,' he said aloud. But when he stood up, the pain from his Achilles tendon shot up the back of his leg straight into his brain. Or at least that's how it felt. He sat back down. Reached for the oxycontine or oxycodone or whatever the hell they called the stuff.

In Belfountain, Logan and Bella crunched their way across the graveled parking lot, managed the pond loop, stood on the little wooden suspended bridge and watched the water gush over the weir. Bella had her hands atop the bridge railing. Logan reached over, placed a big paw atop one of hers. She looked up at Logan, and he down at her. The setting was so stereotypically romantic there was only one thing to do.

46.

I got my discharge papers from the hospital. According to Doc Holly I was good to go,

'But not too good, so don't get any funny ideas,' she said, wagging a schoolmarmish finger in my direction. People always think it's funny or somehow cute to treat an old guy like a child or a puppy. You baaaad dog! Sort of thing. It's friggin irritating really. I'm 80. I've been around. I'm an adult somebody. Show me some respect. North America. Drives me nuts half the time: the cult of youth. The cult of the me. It's enough to drive me back to Africa, back where you matter, but mostly in the context of the 'we', the collective, the social, the group, and where old people are venerated, treated like the knowledge banks that we are.

'Yes, Holly, I get your point, not to worry.'

'Oh, I won't worry, Jack; it's your life. I'm just laying out the appropriate range of choices for you should you wish to be here with us for a good while longer.'

She had a point. Peach and Dawn were there to collect me, take me back to my home, my stuff, my things, my own damn bed. Peach was particularly cheery this mid-morning, his beloved Maple Leafs within reach of hockey's Holy Grail.

'Top 'o the mornin' to ya, Killer, my good man.'

Eish... Leaf fans. If they win there'll be no peace for the rest of us for an entire year. God forbid they win and then repeat as champions. Hoo boy. Then you'd see how quickly the media and most of the rest of the sporting world would turn on the boys in blue and white. Nobody likes a gloater, someone who is on top of the world arrogant in victory, and a moody 'we wuz robbed' self-loathing bastard in defeat. Cautious optimism. This is what you want to cultivate in your kids. It's a necessary trait in the successful hockey player. None of this Christiano Ronaldo, shirt ripping, muscle flexing assholeness that seems to accompany so many athletes who sit astride the world of sport. You're a fucking football player, buddy. You kick a ball for a living. Have some class. Soccer's a team sport yet so many guys behave as though success grows out of their right boot. Somehow, hockey players have avoided that arrogance. Exhuberance, no, we have that in abundance: Ovechkin types who love the show, love the game. But no 'I, me, mine' types. Of course, they exist. In competitive hockey they can be found particularly at the lower levels - Pee Wee, Bantam, Midget - where the difference in maturation often gives one kid a major advantage over all the rest. I once coached a kid in Bantam Major who was like that. He shall remain nameless. Thought he was the cat's ass. Uncoachable. At fifteen. Imagine that. He had talent, that's for sure. But he was also a giant. He got big early, had none of the awkwardness that usually accompanies sudden growth spurts. As a pee wee major and bantam minor he could score almost at will. But he peaked at fifteen. Everyone else caught up to him size wise. But his long term problem was that he cultivated a style of play that was eminently selfish. He disrespected everyone else. His teammates. He never learned how to pass, play as part of a unit. So by the time he was in midget minor he was just an ordinary kid who had some skill. He faded fast. There's no room for those sorts of guys in hockey. Sure, such arrogant pricks can be found on any given rink on any given day, mostly playing pick up where no one back checks and no one gives a shit if Joe Hockey scores 5 or 10 goals in an hour. In fact, that sort of guy is usually the butt of locker room jokes: 'Still playing for the Stanley Cup eh buddy?' they'd tease him. Nope. Wanna reach the top rung in professional hockey? Learn to pass the puck. Be a team player. Respect your teammates and your opponents alike, until they turn out to be dicks of course. But that's a different matter.

Peach and Dawn were the consummate team players. And here they were, on a sunny June morning, ready to carry my bag, see me safely home. You'd go to the wall for people like that. Living proof that the selfish gene thrives in a cooperative environment; thank you Richard Dawkins - now there's a team player.

'Straight home, Squire?' inquired Peach.

'Can we stop at Tim Hortons along the way?'

'You betcha.'

47.

Over at Andrew's, Steve and Christine were sitting on the veranda, enjoying a mid-morning beverage of choice. Bianca was sitting with them, chatting about last night's game. Andrew was in the kitchen making brunch with the help of the twins. The delicious smell of fresh eggs frying in butter filled the house. Maggie could be heard working on the introduction to Mendelsshohn's Violin Concerto in E Minor Opus 64.

'Ya dee danh ya dah, ya danh danh danh duh dah,' hummed Eve, as she padded her way around the house getting ready for work.

'Do you have time for a quick bite, Eve?' asked her dad.

'Are you going to take me to work?' she asked back.

'No, gramma and grampa will. They've got some shopping to do.'

'OK, I guess I have time then.'

'How do you like your eggs? I've got fried and I've got fried,' Andrew said and smiled in her direction.

'Poached, if you don't mind,' said Eve.

'Gotta be different, eh Kid? Just like your mother.'

'Like my father, you mean to say,' and she smiled back in his direction.

Out on the veranda Steve asked after AJ and Westin.

'Golf course. They left before the rooster's first crow. They're prepping for a tore-nament, she said, her voice still retaining its Cape Breton lilt.

'How's your game?' Steve asked, knowing that Bianca hadn't had much time to play for a very long time. Nevertheless, when she and he did manage to get out for a round, he could see that she'd lost none of her talent, just a bit rusty with the short game. Andrew and Bianca had met many years before at Ben Eoin Golf Course where he was just a punk ass kid dressed up like Ricky Fowler and she the hottie working the cash register in the pro shop. Bianca was four years Andrew's senior, already a freshman in college at, yep, you guessed it, St. FX. What he didn't know at the time was that she also played on the women's golf team and, over the ensuing years, had won a number of local and regional events. The punk grew up, and ran into Bianca every golf season in Cape Breton where she eventually moved out from behind the cash register and over to the practice tee where she ran a golf school as the club's teaching professional. Eventually Andrew got up the nerve to ask her out and the rest is history.

Bianca managed to keep up her professional status and offered the occasional lessons, free of charge, at clubs around the area. She was particularly interested in supporting the mom and pop golf courses as well as the less privileged kids. She often dragged Logan and Andrew along as incentives for parents to bring their kids. Meet a real live Maple Leaf and get a golf lesson for free. For the moment this worked for her. She was happy raising the kids, but she also had a plan in mind: Once they are all in high school, then it's back to the golf course full time for me. She also had a plan to develop her own line of golf clothing. But there was no rush. 'Good things come to those who wait,' as her father-in-law used to say.

48.

The wait was over. It was game day. Across the hockey world people awoke with nervous anticipation. The Toronto Maple Leafs were on the verge of a Stanley Cup championship. They were stuck on lucky number thirteen for a very long time. Fourteen would be a very good number. Thirteen was good: Mats Sundin. No shame there. But 14, that's Dave Keon, and that's a very good number. And with one of Dave Keon's progeny in the Leaf lineup, the wee Ian Keon, and the Leafs playing at home, well, it felt as though the stars were in proper alignment.

'Lucky number 14!' said Peach.

'Davey Keon!' said Hutchie.

'Who wants a beer?' said Ged.

'A glass of red wine would be nice,' I said, 'Good for the old arteries.'

The place was a sea of blue and white. Sure there were lots of red and white sweaters being worn as well. After all, this is Canada and for about a century it had been Canadian tradition to hate Toronto. The country is a great big place, a land of many solitudes, a patchwork quilt of parochialisms held together by four things: a quirky red and white flag, the shared understanding that we 'are not Americans', Terry Fox and Tim Hortons. Beyond those four things, we are a people like any other, a consortium of 'not in my back yards', an amalgam of individuals standing on political correctness rather than standing up for hard truths, but happy to poke fun at each other from a distance, often through the medium of the stand-up comedian and the one or two still surviving CBC satires. So, why should we all get along? Be unified around one goal, one shared social project? All believe that it was Toronto's turn for a victory parade? Across the country the great debate had been long underway: Toronto or Montreal? And if Montreal, are you really a Habs fan or just a Leaf hater? I must admit, as I sat there in my rinkside seat, accompanied by Hutchie, Peach and Ged, all four of us wearing Leaf home jerseys, I was pulling hard for a Leaf win. We all were, but Hutchie and Peach were lifers, and Ged, well, Ged was rooting for his son Eric, up there in the corporate box, probably munching on a pre-game hotdog, trying not to get mustard on his tie or his shirt or his pant leg, or his shoe, or the guy sitting in the cheap seats down below. I was thinking about my brother-in-law, Steve, who I could almost make out sitting over near centre ice, several rows up behind the Leaf bench. He was relatively easy to spot in his lime green golf shirt. He'd told us he was wearing it so as to bring the luck of the Irish to the game, but he had failed to say to which team. Christine, of course, was in full Leaf regalia, including a pair of rattles that she planned to jangle in her husband's face every time something good happened to her Leafs. And make no mistake, in Christine's mind, in the mind of every hockey mom, whatever team her kids played on was 'her team'. She would defend them to the death. A pair of rattles, then, were perfectly chosen: don't cross the hockey mom, like a rattlesnake, she's all bite and no bark.

I had asked my sister if she wanted to come to the game, but she said she'd prefer to watch down at the Ryerson Centre, with her two lifelong buddies. She wanted to be on that storied ground, in that storied place, when the Leafs won. It was her version of bringing the team luck. Besides, there wasn't a single Habs fan in the entire place. This was hallowed ground. They would rise or fall as one.

If I am honest with myself, I was happier being out of the hospital than anything else. If this had been Stars on Ice, rather than Game 6 of the Stanley Cup Finals, I don't think it would have made a difference to my mood. And to sit here with these three old coots. We had been at it a long time together. I'd first met Ged when I was 10. It was in the fall of 1967, so we'd had no shared memory of the last Leaf Cup win. But we did have the shared memory of the expansion from six to twelve teams. Ged had been a Habs fan back then. He'd probably deny it if you asked him, but I'm pretty sure it was like father like son. And there is no one who ever lived - including Steve - who was as dyed in the wool Go Habs Go as was his dad, Roger. I was a few months older than Ged which, when you're ten, actually matters - in school systems, at point of entry into

284

hockey systems, and so on. It all seems sort of pointless today, now that we're both 80 and counting. But back then, it meant that I was a year ahead in all of these bureaucratic entanglements. So, we never played on the same team until Ged graduated from college and came home to sort himself out. We'd gone to the same high school, but while I'd played football and golf for the school, as I said before, Duke always cut me from the hockey team. Whereas Ged, a smoother skater you'd be hard pressed to find, was a high school star on D from the first day he stepped on the ice until he left for Colorado College - the CC Tigers - on a hockey scholarship.

It was through Ged's college experience that I got to know Peach, who also played at CC. Peach was a year ahead of Ged, so graduated a year earlier and upon graduation went off on his own guided and misguided adventures as we all tend to do. Peach and I climbed Mount Kilimanjaro for his 50th birthday. I was still living in Botswana at the time and happened to be in Toronto on a bit of a break. I was staying with Ged and Peach and his wife, Dawn, were in town to play in a volleyball tournament to help raise money for autism research. One thing led to another, and the following July, I found myself collecting Peach from the little airport in Maun. Among other things, he came equipped with inline skates. After all, Maun is the home of the Mukwa Leafs.

I still remember that first day when I took him over to Sandy and Ruth's for the Tuesday night skate. To get from my house to Sandy's you had to drive through dense African bush, over thick sandy ground, dodging donkeys at every turn, and even a very fat python on one occasion. As we came around a corner I could see something lying in path in front of us.

'What is that?' I said.

'A log?' said Peach.

After a very short pause, we both looked at each other and exclaimed 'Python!' a brief second after which we bumped our way straight over the great snake. Given the sandy ground, this caused the snake no harm and, as I watched it in the rearview mirror, it simply slithered off into the bush. Peach was a bit freaked out, but this was pretty much par for the course where we lived. I proceeded to tell him about the time when we were playing hockey and Ruth came out to say, 'Um, Sandy. I just saw a spitting cobra go in behind the fridge.' This was at a time when their son Charlie was only 2 or 3, so we needed to act fast.

'What do we do?' I asked Sandy.

'Bring your stick,' he said.

'And then?'

'I'll try to flush it out from behind the fridge. When it slithers out, just whack it as hard as you can. Whack it anywhere first. But then go for its head.'

So, dressed in our inline gear we skated from the rink, through the back room, and into the kitchen. And, just as planned, Sandy flushed the cobra from behind the fridge, whereupon Ruth and I proceeded to beat the snake to death.

'I don't know how it could have gotten in here,' said Ruth.

But, as I looked around at the numerous nooks and crannies, I said to myself, the same way the mosquitoes get in, through the holes in the mortar.

'The bloody Botswana Defense Force!' said Sandy.

'What?' I said.

'Ya, they get called into houses around the country, to "safely dispose of a deadly snake". What do they do? They catch it, drop it off at the wildlife sanctuary in Mokolodi, and then at some point gather them up and drop them by plane into the Delta.'

'Eventually they end up in our kitchen,' said Ruth.

'Where we beat them to death!' said Sandy, laughing.

'That's a funny sort of "conservation", I'd say.' I was still sweating profusely from the combination of inline hockey and nervous energy. It was my first snake kill, and I said as much.

'Better get used to it. There'll be more,' said Sandy.

Peach was also a Mukwa Leaf, having played in the annual Inline Swakopmund tournament in Namibia. I was away for work in Sweden, so missed the whole event which proved to be no Cinderella story. The team managed to score only 1 goal over the course of their 3 qualifying games. But the experience left a lasting impression with George, and over the years he and I often teamed up to collect and transport used hockey gear and inline skates to Maun.

I once ran into a married couple from Ottawa who were on their way into the Delta for their first 'African experience'. At the time, it was not possible to fly directly to Maun from anywhere else except Gaborone, Botswana's capital city. It was a wise choice I thought: you force tourists to spend some cash in more than one town. I had flown in from Canada the night before and was being dropped off at the airport by some friends. As the automatic doors opened, I gazed in upon the usual scene: 40 middle-to-old-aged white folks dressed in khaki colored clothes with zips and pockets everywhere. I was in a t-shirt, shorts and flip flops. While I stared at them, they stared at me, especially the two Canadians from Ottawa. What was so interesting about me was that I had some 25 wooden hockey sticks taped together and slung over my shoulder. The canucks gawked as I passed.

'What? Never seen a Canadian before?' I joked.

After I'd checked in, I went back to explain. 'Forget the Delta, my friends. You want the most unusual experience of your life? Go to Mukwa Leaf Gardens tonight. You will not believe your eyes.' I proceeded to tell them about the Mukwa Leafs and Sandy and the 'if you build it, they will come' arena of dreams out there in the African bush. And on that particular night, it was the annual Tequila Cup tournament. Teams were organized into three divisions: under 10, under 12, and everyone else. There were raffles and a potluck supper, annual awards, and plenty of tequila. All under a cloudless star-filled African sky. When I showed up with the sticks and a duffle bag full of gear, the cheers could be heard far and wide. My new friends from Ottawa did show up, were amazed, and no doubt to this day what they talk about, in addition to the hippos and elephants and lions and whatnot, is Mukwa Leaf Gardens.

Peach and I met Hutchie through Ged. When I was a post-doc at York University, I played in the Wednesday night league in Bolton, about 40 minutes' drive north of the university. That first year, Hutchie centred a line with me on the right wing and Mike Hall - Hallsie - on the left. The team wore Leaf colours, and that year we rolled through the league. 'Fear blue,' Mike would say every Wednesday as he entered the dressing room. 'Fear blue,' we'd respond.

Hallsie also played with a group of guys out of Brampton. They were in a Tuesday night league and they called themselves The Mighty Hurricanes. Not, The Hurricanes, no, that wasn't intimidating enough. They had to be 'Mighty' as well. These guys had been together as a team since the 1980s. Personnel had changed over the years, but the core remained, with Hallsie at the very centre. Ever the entrepreneur, Mike got the bright idea to run his own tournament, the first one going in 1994. From the beginning, Hallsie didn't want to run 'just any old tournament'. He wanted to run a tournament that everyone would want to participate in. He wanted to run a tournament that everyone who participated would remember and, whenever possible, return to again and again.

Tournaments as most guys, and many hockey playing women, know are a dime a dozen. Everybody runs a tournament as a way of generating some revenue to subsidize the costs associated with playing in a league. League hockey is bloody expensive. So teams run a tournament and if they run it well they will not only cover their league costs but may even generate a surplus to help fund a team trip somewhere, with Lake Placid, Florida and Las Vegas having been destinations of choice for the Mighty Hurricanes of the past. Now they all want to play in 'Super Geezer' tournaments. With the rapid aging of North America, there are now tournaments that cater specifically to those 70 and over. This was pioneered many years ago by Charles Schulz - of Peanuts cartoon fame - whose 'Snoopy Tourney' in California, with its 70A and 70B divisions, became immediately and immensely popular.

Mike Hall never did anything small scale. 'Go big, or go home', he'd often say. So there were live bands and celebrities, such as Wendel Clarke, to do signings and photo ops. And the Mighty Hurricane tournament grew and grew, eventually becoming so popular that Hallsie franchised it out, so that now there are Mighty Hurricane tournaments throughout Ontario throughout the year. Who would have thought that you could make a living running hockey tournaments? It took me a long time to understand the whole point of adult recreational hockey tournaments. In fact, it still seems to me that the term 'adult' is a bit of a misnomer. As a serious athlete, I understood 'tournament' to mean that you give it your all, you play your best, you have some fun but get enough rest, because competing is always more fun if you win. Sorry, I'm not of the 'we are all winners', everyone gets a ribbon, school of bullshit. But the funny thing with most men's tournaments - and this definitely goes for the mixed tournaments, with men's and women's divisions - is that while participants want to win, what they want more than anything is a weekend away from home where they can act like a bunch of adolescents. So, to me, the 'A' in CARHA should be reinterpreted as 'adolescent' rather than 'adult'.

My early experience with tournament hockey also misled me, because I was surrounded by a bunch of guys like me. Team first. Go, fight, win. Beers in moderation. Party at the prize ceremony. But over the years as I got invited to play with this group or that group, it all got very puzzling. If we wanted to win, then why did our best player go AWOL after the first game, only to show up at puck drop barely able to stand up? And guys who want to win, but are badly hung over, tend to be very cranky bastards. So as the days went by the chippier everything got. Anyway, now I understand it. That's why I steer clear of it.

OK, that's really a lie. I played oldtimer tournament hockey until well into my 60s. I just got more careful, picking my spots - a well-run tournament, a good bunch of guys. And I worked the Mighty Hurricane tournament for donkey's years too. It's all part of being one of the guys, more than being part of a team actually, it's being part of a hockey culture. Ged and I grew up together, Peach and Ged played College hockey together, Hutchie and Ged live in the same town so get to know each other in a league where they choose new teams every year so that all guys get to know each other so animosity doesn't build up. And Peach knows Hutchie and me through Ged. Different guys, different jobs, different interests, different classes, but all drawn together in a tight weave of hockey culture. One moves away becomes enmeshed with a different bunch of guys; comes back on occasion and is always welcomed (even if they make you wear pink booties over your skates as part of a hazing ceremony). Another guy arrives and gets introduced to the group, is made to wear the pink booties. Like I said earlier, if you can skate you will fit in somewhere somehow. And we all watched Hockey Night in Canada growing up; and the CBS Sunday afternoon games; and the NBC Saturday afternoon games; and read the magazines, especially The Hockey News. Then there was TSN and specialty channels and all hockey all the time. The drafts got televised, and the chat shows were everywhere via free to air, satellite and so on. No matter where you went there were many entry points to 'fitting in'. And part of fitting in was disagreeing: so Toronto or Montreal?

Peach, Hutchie, Ged and I are birds of a feather when it comes to competition. And, at 80, this means first and foremost, getting enough sleep. We'd had our afternoon powernaps in preparation for the long night ahead.

'Please, no overtime!' I said.

'Everybody wearing their depends?' asked Ged.

'Very funny,' I said.

'I'm serious. What are you doing getting seats so close to the ice? You know how far a walk it is to the toilet? Why do you think I like it up in the corporate box? Toilet's five steps away.'

'And the hotdogs are free. Just lay off the booze.'

'Bratwursts get awful dry without some suds to wash 'em down, you know.'

I ingored his comment, but did wonder if all of us, or only I, was wearing depends.

Kids with inflated plastic clackers in Maple Leaf colors banged them incessantly, still failing to dissipate their pre-game sugar buzz and wet-pants excitement. Back in the day, this used to drive me crazy. But now, well, it was all just a slightly annoying buzz, like living next to a major highway.

'It's a good thing we're all going deaf too. Don't need any earplugs in this madhouse.'

'What?' shouted Hutchie.

'Nothing,' I mouthed back to him.

'Game on!' shouted George.

49.

GAME 6

In the Habs' dressing room the coach spoke of pride, honour and glory. He spoke of the need to commit to the task at hand, to leave it all out on the ice, to support one another and to take it one shift at a time. He reminded his players that the eyes of the hockey world were upon them and that chances like this came along only rarely in a player's career. Revel in the moment. Carpe Diem! Lastly, he noted that God supported les glorieux. God Bless Montreal! He shouted. The last bit was surely over the top, but it was what the vast majority of Habs fans, the Catholic ones anyway, believed in their hearts. Had their fans down in the Jewish quarter been able to hear the coach, they would have cringed, for, in their humble opinion, God could be a real mean SOB. Be careful what you wish for, they would have said, reflexively ducking their heads.

The Habs players were inspired by this speech. Like the Subbans had said, it's not quite golf season yet, boys, we've got a job to do. They came out flying. This caught the Leafs by surprise, for they had convinced themselves that the offside trap was going to be the order of the day. There's no way management would have agreed to this mix of oldtime Montreal-style firewagon hockey combined with the oldtime Soviet whirling dervish game of gaining the blueline, refusing to dump and chase, back off if necessary and start again. From the opening face-off, the cosmonauts came at Logan's line with speed.

It was all very hectic, I thought. Hard for the old eyes to keep up. Gone was the calm of the hospital room, the sweet reminiscences of this game or that guy, the toilet five paces away, the giant flat screen TV, the endless replays in super slo-mo designed to show off technology while helping out the aged part of the audience. 'Did you see that?' 'Not yet, but I'll catch up to it from angle number five.' We were seated in the near-side corner in the Habs end where, down on the ice, very little happened over the first half a dozen shifts. Once in a while a Habs defenceman would show up to fetch an iced puck. Then back down the ice they would go. I watched Brambory in net, wondered what he was thinking. Wondered what language he was thinking in. He stood straight up but rested his right arm across the top of the net, the big goalie stick in his blockered right hand. The crowd around us were out of their minds with excitement. In whatever direction I looked someone was screaming something murderous toward the Montreal goalie, toward the whirling swirling twirling Russians, Czechs, Slovenians and the odd

Canadian or three that comprised the 2036-37 version of les Habitants.

'Hang on, boys, hang on!' shouted Hutchie. 'Weather the storm.'

But Hurricane Habs continued to blow. Andrew, aka Billy, was in the zone. You know how when from time to time you simply forget what you're doing, where you are, and inhabit the moment. Losing self-consciousness is an odd, kind of contradictory, thing for it can lead to your greatest performance about which, later on, you will have little specific memory. 'How did you do it?' the interviewer would ask. 'To be honest, Jim, I have no idea.' This was a sort of stock answer from sporting legends, from Tiger Woods to Peyton Manning, from Johnny Bower to Darryl Sittler. I could see that Andrew was in that sort of head space and I hoped he would stay there.

'Come on, boys, Shawsie, Princey, keep them out wide!' shouted Andrew.

The boys worked their hardest. Kept the Habs out wide. Cleared the front of the net. Cross-checked and slashed their opponents within a hair's breadth of the penalty box. Rammed them into the boards. Facewashed the cosmonauts at every stoppage in play. Tried every trick in the book to put them off their game, alter the flow, swing the momentum the other way. And the referees were letting the game flow, not sweating the small stuff, letting the players work it out for themselves. There were long stretches without a stoppage in play.

'Looks like the refs have put their whistles away,' said Peach.

'Good,' said Hutchie. 'Let 'em play. Let 'em work it out for themselves.'

Ged and I sat quietly, thinking our own thoughts, hoping shared hopes.

50.

Eve sat next to Christine. She'd switched shifts with another girl at the burger joint so she could come to the game. She'd only had time to run in the door, change her clothes, and join her grandparents who had been waiting patiently for her in the car. When she hopped in the back seat, grandpa Steve turned his head, wrinkled his nose and said, 'Eve, you smell delicious.' 'Don't start, grampa', she said settling in. At the game she quietly watched her dad at work. Watched him calmly steer each shot into a corner. Snatch puck after puck with a lightning quick glove. Send several pucks flying into the crowd with a blocker save. And once, using his patented kick save, he'd challenged a shooter standing straight up - no butterfly on this occasion - and when the shot came in low and hard, Andrew used his pad to boot it all the way out to centre ice.

'Did you see that!?' said Chris.

'Ya, my dad loves to do that. He's such a show-off.'

'Andrew always did love the crowds,' said Chris.

'And the crowds love him,' said Eve.

'At least this one seems to,' said Steve.

51.

The first period ended scoreless, but the Leafs were badly outshot - 18 to 7, which was clearly indicative of the play. There were indications late on not that Montreal was slowing down but that Toronto had finally got into the rhythm, into the flow of the game, and were able to give as good as they got from the Habs. In the dressing room they were chatty, loose. The period had been incredibly hectic, but in a fun sort of way. They had never felt out of control, or over-whelmed by events. Montreal simply came out with more jump and it had taken the boys by surprise. Sure they'd done some running around in their own end, but mostly they'd kept their shape, blocked what needed to be blocked, chipped what needed chipping and chased when the occasion presented itself. Most of the Habs' shots were from around the top of the circle back out to the blueline. The Leafs had given up only one or two odd man rushes and even so had managed to recover before Montreal was able to take full advantage of the opportunity. From the average fan's point of view, Toronto was badly outplayed. But from the Leaf player's point of view, however, it was more like we met the challenge, tough though it was, and now are well-placed to mount a challenge of our own.

Down at the Ryerson centre, a place full of average fans, there was a feeling of impending doom. Montreal had just kept coming. Wave after wave. Like water against a rocky breakwall, eventually the rocks would wear away, and the land would be inundated. But then again, this was the normal Maple Leaf fan response to almost every situation. If the Leafs were up by three it would be 'Oh no, this is the perfect opportunity to screw up. We'll be hockey headline news tomorrow.' If they were down by three, it would be 'ho hum, here we go again.' And even if the team came back from a three goal deficit to actually win, the Leaf fan response was normally, 'Well, don't get your hopes up.' Everything that went against Toronto was the fault of a Leaf player. Everything that went in favour of Toronto was because the other team had screwed up. But who could blame them? Seventy years of failure would make pessimists out of Howdy Doody and Buffalo Bob, neither of whom, to the best of my knowledge, was a Leaf fan. Though, in the opinion of many, a wooden head is a prerequisite for being a fan of the Toronto Maple Leafs.

'Things don't look too good,' said Martha.

'Nope,' said Rita.

'Now, let's not give up hope just yet, girls,' said Lori, ever the optimist. 'Old Billy looks unbeatable in the net. With a little luck we'll get things going next period.'

'Knock on wood,' said Martha, rapping Lori lightly on top of her white head.

52.

'Sure you don't want to go up to the corporate box?' Ged asked us three.

'Na, things are good here, man. Ice level action,' said Hutchie.

'Free food.'

'No thanks.'

'Toilet's only a short walk down the hall.'

'Nope. I'm fine,' I said.

Ged texted his son, Eric, who was up in the corporate box: 'Whattaya think?'

The reply came back: 'I got mustard on my shirt.'

'What did Eric say?' I asked.

'Same old, same old,' said Ged.

53.

Up the road a piece, Bianca had organized a Stanley Cup party for the kids. Westin and AJ had a few of their golf buddies over, as did the twins. Maggie was not interested in hockey, so mostly stayed in her room.

'What's she doing in there?' Charlie and Marie asked, looking at the closed door, at the little sign that said "Maggie is IN".

'Who knows?' Bianca said back.

'There's no music, so she's not practicing,' said Charlie.

'But she'll turn up when the pizza arrives,' said Marie.

54.

Over in Caledon, Bella had the game on the TV with the sound off. She was working with her mother in the kitchen out back. They had a party to cater. No meat. Every once in a while Bella would pass through the house and glance up at the screen: no score. On the rare occasion where she was able to pick out Logan - usually during a face-off - she'd pause and watch for a bit. But the game made no sense. In her view, it was like watching creatures from another planet. Or, like an anthropologist, she was gazing upon the other, some unknown tribe with indecipherable codes of conduct. Get too close to them, she mused, and you might end up in a cooking pot.

55.

Down on the ice, play was frenetic. A hockey fan's dream; coach and management's nightmare. Back and forth. Up and down. Crash bang boom. Bodies flying everywhere. Shots taken. Shots blocked. Sudden turnovers, sudden opportunities. Billy and Brambory equal to the task, leather flashing, each moment a Ken Danby painting in waiting. The Leafs struck first off of a broken play at the Habs' blueline, which began life as a normal breakout. But a bad bounce, a puck up on edge, a failed attempt to settle it down, and before you could blink twice, Ellis had stripped his winger of the puck, swooped down along the far boards, dropped a short pass to Keon trailing near the top of the circle who, without looking, feathered a backhand pass into the high slot where Kadri let rip a screamer, beating Brambory on the shortside, stickside, in the top corner.

The rink erupted in celebration. Across the hockey universe hands were clapped, feet stamped, bets won and lost, money exchanged, drinks were spilled and refilled, popcorn flew, hats were flung, dogs were petted, smiles smiled and kisses dished up happily by

Leaf fans ready to pucker up for any passerby. 1-0 Toronto.

'Nazzer! Wicked shot!'

'Woo hoo! Attaway boys!'

'Great pass, Keener!'

This was perhaps the most important high-five skate through of the boys' lives. Up one with Lord Stanley's Cup in the building. A confidence booster. A monkey killer. While Leaf fans around the hockey world immediately began to fret, as bits of fingernails began to litter the space between fans' feet at the Ryerson Centre and at the Samsung-Blackberry Centre, the players themselves savoured the moment, squared their shoulders, knew that the game was theirs to win, steeled themselves for the battle still to come.

'Casher, you're up,' said the Coach, tapping Logan on the shoulder.

'Let's go Shakes, Wiener, do what we do best,' said Logan, winking at the two of them, trying to keep things light, loose, stay in the groove.

From high in the crowd, Pappin looked on. He'd failed to return to the lineup. The import, Dramuic, was a keeper, no doubt. His one hope - that either Shakey or Walton would be made to sit due to bad behavior - had failed to materialize. In the business of sport, winning made every sort of bad behavior tolerable. The sports world was replete with guys who in any other walk of life would either be in jail or rehab or some other sort of facility: serial spousal abusers, rapists, child abusers, sadists, racists, homophobes, drug addicts and alcoholics. If you could score, or defend, put the puck in the net, or keep it out, help fill the seats and sell the merchandise you could find a place on a professional sports team. There were plenty of worse characters in the hockey world compared to Wiener and Shakey who were mostly just happy drunks. Can't find your car, your keys, your wallet, your phone? That's OK, we'll buy you another and another and another: just put the puck in the net.

Which is what Shakey did on the very next shift. From the face-off at centre ice, Logan knocked the puck over to Wiener who took a step over centre and rang the puck around the boards. Brambory went behind his net to stop it, but the puck caught a flaw in the dasher and ricocheted out in front of the net. Shakey had hit the blueline with speed, beating the Habs' D man to the puck and firing a bulls-eye into the net as Brambory tried to scramble back into position. 2-0 Toronto.

Outrageously ecstatic falls some way short of accurately describing the Leaf fan response. Two goals a scant 12 seconds apart, five minutes left in the period, this was simply too much to take in for the Leaf hopefuls. They screamed like teenage girls at a Beatles concert. The Beatles, by the way, played Maple Leaf Gardens in 1964, '65 and '66. My sister, Lori, was at that 1966 concert. And 70 years later she was once again screaming like a pre-pubescent girl, as likely to pee her pants today as she was back in the day. And she was not alone. The Ryerson Centre was awash in spilled drinks, tears, and, well, urine.

'Oh my God, this is so exciting!' Lori exclaimed to Martha.

Everyone was hugging and kissing and crossing their fingers. The two goals had already been replayed ten times each up on the giant screens.

The Montreal coach called timeout.

'What do you think he's saying to the boys?' I asked Hutchie.

'Five minutes left to play in the period. They're shell-shocked. Just look at 'em. I imagine he's just saying "let's get out of this period alive". Don't let it get any worse than it already is.'

'Live to fight on,' said Peach.

'Live to fight on,' I mused. 'Sounds like a plan.'

'Five minutes left,' said Ged. 'I'm gonna beat the rush to the loo. Live to fight on!'

The period ended as it had started. There was no slowing anybody down. But the old goat, Andrew, stood tall in the nets for the Leafs. With each save, the crowd happily baa-aad like the mad fans they surely were. Brambory was also flawless, and if truth be told, he couldn't be faulted on either one of the Leaf goals. When the siren sounded at the Samsung-Blackberry Centre, the Leafs held a 2-0 lead over the league's best team, the Montreal Canadiens, winners of the President's Trophy each of the last two years. Twenty minutes of play and a team desperate to stave off elimination, to avoid finishing second best, was all that stood between the Toronto Maple Leafs and the Stanley Cup.

In the dressing rooms, life went on. Routine matters. That's what practice is for. Do it again and again and again so that when the time comes, under pressure, you'll do it again. And in the dressing room, the routine helped keep the nerves at bay. Get the skates resharpened. Retape one or two sticks. Tell a few jokes. Talk about the cute girl sitting in row three. Utter platitude upon platitude. Stay present. In the moment. Don't let any thoughts like, 'Holy shit, we are gonna win the Cup!' or 'If we don't score, then we are done and I may never get another chance to win the Cup!' intrude into your consciousness. Keep it routine.

'How's the Achilles?' Andrew asked his brother, shoving in beside him, forcing Morgan to squeeze over.

'Not a problem,' said Logan, his hair matted flat with sweat.

'Serious?'

'Ya, serious. Just a little sore, feels weird when I push off, but the doctor says its just pain and nothing more. So, ya, not a problem.'

'Good,' said Andrew, patting his brother on the knee. 'Let's keep it that way.'

Logan didn't answer, just nodded his head, looked down, listened to the hubbub all around him, considered whether to make some sort of speech, but decided against it. He'd wait until they were ready to go back on the ice. Follow the coach.

56.

Bella saw that it was the end of the second period and that Toronto was up 2-0. She could see how excited everyone seemed to be in the stands, the talking heads saying something, it all so animated. She thought how good it was to have the sound off. Bella didn't much like crowds either.

57.

'Boy, your dad sure looks good tonight, eh Eve?' This
was Christine, and by "your dad" she meant "my son".
Both sons were having great games. Twenty minutes to
go. All those miles and miles of roads driven, of flights
flown, of walkways walked, of paths beaten to and from
one worry space to another, from one Tim Hortons to
another, from one arena to another, from one friend's
house to another. The small towns, the big cities, the
cold community rinks and the giant multi-plexes. All
the frozen ponds, and three on threes. All the miles of
tape, all the many skates, the boys outgrowing their
gear year after year. All of that and so much more. And
all for this. To reach this moment. This height. To be a
Stanley Cup Champion. She thought of her boys. Her
little boys. All the happiness and heartache, the drama,
the injuries, the physio, the hospitals, and the
questions, do we put them into hockey, do we force
them to play if they don't want to, can we afford all of
these costs, this travel, this stuff that goes along with
being a hockey mom? She thought of all the other
mothers and fathers of the players on both teams,

thinking these same thoughts about these big men who were their little boys.

'The other goalie is playing well, too,' she said, again to Eve but really to no one in particular. -But, there's got to be a winner and a loser. And, in this case, too bad for Montreal. You can have it next year, Steve. She poked her husband in the ribs with a game-sharpened elbow.

'Hey, what are you talking about?!' said Steve. 'I want the Leafs to win.'

'Oh. So suddenly you're on the bandwagon, is it?' she said in mock seriousness.

58.

Go fight win. That's the gist of what was said by both coaches and both captains in their respective dressing rooms prior to the teams skating back out onto the ice. Oh, there could be details but it's really always the same, isn't it. Funny how something so ordinary, that we so take for granted we hardly hear it, when uttered in a particular context by a particular group of people, takes on a certain poignancy. So, yes, go fight win you Leafs. It's been 70 years since those same words were uttered in a Leaf dressing room on a similar occasion. Seventy long years.

The folks at the CBC were having a party. The Leafs-Canadiens Cup Final was a license to print money. And the fact that the underdog Leafs, Cupless for 70 long years, were up 3 games to 2 against the mighty Montreal Canadiens verged on a global feel good story. Around the world people were paying attention to Canada. Imagine that. Once my wife spent a Northern-summer/ African winter asking everyone she met as we travelled through South Africa, Botswana, Tanzania: 'What do you think about Canada?' The answer, by a margin of 99 to 1, was 'Uh... we don't'. As a Canadian, I must admit, this hurt. Especially as someone like me who spent a great deal of his life working in Africa, for Africans, in support of social justice bla bla bla. Who as a graduate student attended rallies against apartheid, lobbied the government against 'constructive engagement', wrote super serious op-ed pieces about the tragedy of 'separate development' in South Africa as well as that government's aggressive posture toward neighboring countries. I fancied myself part of the 'helpful fixer' international Canadian community, part of the Lester Pearson approach to building a more peaceful world. But this was a position that pretty much went out the back door, with the trash, after 9/11. In through the front door came a Canada no different from the big bad neighbor to the south: big military, big prisons, and a big brother approach to keeping an eye on Canadians. Globally, we became Uncle Sam's little brother, following the yanks around the world as they bombed one country after another. The distinctiveness that was our Canadian identity seemed to just disappear in a puff of cordite-smelling smoke. 'What do you think of Canada?' Mary Adams would ask. 'We don't,' said pretty much everyone. Oh, how that hurt! And what did the one person who thought about Canada think about us? 'Tar sands', was the response. 'Global dinosaur.' Ouch! But now, here we are in the news again, the red Maple Leaf standing in behind the big blue one.

'The Toronto Maple Leafs stand on the verge of making history,' reported the BBC.

'The underdog Toronto Maple Leafs need one more win to break a 70 year drought for North America's top hockey prize,' reported Deutsche Welle.

'The world has long joked that peace in the Middle East would come before a Toronto Maple Leaf Stanley Cup championship, but here are the Leafs on the verge of just such a victory,' reported Russia Today.

Of course, the national broadcaster couldn't come right out in support of the Leafs. They had to sit on the fence. They played up the francophone angle in their global coverage of the contest, selling broadcast package after broadcast package to the French speaking world. People in Côte d'Ivoire, Burkina Faso and Senegal marveled at the puzzling images that flitted across their TV screens. What was this hockey sur glace anyway? And why were there only a handful of French speaking players on either team? Interestingly, Rene Pronovost of the Leafs quickly became an audience favorite with his charismatic smile and his Dieudonné wit. Of course, most of the non-white world took to the Subbans, Tench and Horton: who were these black people and what were they doing playing this violent game? For the Senegalese, the broad-shouldered, heavy-hitting, Horton looked to be a perfect candidate to compete in la Lutte - their traditional style of wrestling. Girls across south Asia swooned over Nazem Kadri Jr., as they watched the CBC feed of either the NHL in Punjabi or the NHL in Urdu. And the towering force that was Frank Chan ensured an audience draw in the hundreds of millions across China. Like I said, CBC executives looked on at the game, smiled, and listened to the cash registers ring. And into the media slipstream came the NHL, the Maple Leafs inc. and the Montreal Canadiens plc. Hockey sweaters flew off the shelves of shops around the world as fast as they could be produced in Bangladesh, Vietnam and La Belle Province (where the textile industry was still protected and heavily subsidized). Don't knock it. The inability to sell the game beyond the narrow perimeter of the circumpolar world had kept the NHL small-time. And limited exposure makes it hard to grow the game, as the continuing failure across the American southwest attests. Utter the words "Arizona Coyotes", and you can almost hear Jim Balsillie turn in his grave.

Why grow the game? To ensure its survival. And to build a bigger pool of talent from which to draw. Look at the success of the world's game: soccer. And of the European leagues in particular, where a global reach means significant revenue in order to fund soccer programs around the world, build the game, draw the best players into the spotlight and so fuel the dreams of young boys and girls across time and space. Who knows how many more Frank Chans are out there spread across the vast plain that is China.

Frank was out to take the opening draw of the third period, Tench and Ireland on his wings. They were matched against the cosmonauts who were sure to get as much ice time in this period as the other three Montreal lines combined. For the Habs, it was do or die, shit or get off the pot, go big or go home, win to bring the series back to Montreal or lose and unpack the golf clubs. Frank loved the idea of standing in their way, of thwarting the other team at every turn, of being the pitbull attached to Titov's ankle, never letting go, hounding him across every inch of the ice surface. Just before the puck was dropped, he looked up at Titov, bared his teeth, said 'Woof!' Then he won the draw.

And so it went. A 2-0 lead is more easily defended than 3-0 or even 4-0, if a team gets up by a big score early on. Two is not a big number. Two helps to concentrate the mind. Helps a player stay sharp, focused, determined, intent. Three is another story. It looks big, insurmountable. And 4 even bigger. The bigger the lead, the lazier the team becomes in defending it. The Leafs were anything but lazy. Two is too small to take for granted. They clutched, they grabbed, they clogged up the lanes and alleys, they used their sticks to full advantage, turning the timely hook or pokecheck into an art form. They backchecked and forechecked with zeal. Against form they forechecked two men in. Left only one man high. But were judicious in their choices and busted their humps to get back. They poked and prodded, they goaded and taunted, they were surly to a fault, scrums and facewashes at every stoppage in play. They did what had to be done to slow down the game, keep Titov, Bykovsky and Popovich in, at best, second gear. They went hard at the Subbans, chased down every loose puck, wingers stayed high covering the points in their own end, threw their bodies at every shot, looking at times almost clownish, like kids making snow angels. But it got the job done. It wasn't always pretty. OK, let's be serious: it wasn't pretty at all. But it was artful and stylish. In years to come the film of this particular period would provide the textbook case for how to defend a two-goal lead. It all went so well. Even after Montreal scored.

Yes, the Habs managed to pull one back. With about three minutes remaining in the game, at a point when even Toronto fans started to believe that they were going to win the Stanley Cup, that the drought was finally over, that out of the sands of the Kalahari came Lord Stanley with his Cup, and twenty cases of champagne. But then the bloody cosmonauts managed to nick one back. Granted, it was stylish. The usual Titov to Bykovsky to Popovich and goal! Around the horn, tic tac toe, and low and behold suddenly we have a new game. When the red light went on behind Andrew, you could almost feel the change in air pressure in the building, a collective groan followed by a collective sigh, carbon dioxide punched out, oxygen sucked in, like an old beater of an accordion. Make no mistake, there was panic across Leaf land. Down at the Ryerson Centre it sounded like pilgrims at the Wailing Wall as each and every Leaf fan beseeched his or her own chosen God to help deliver their team from every evil, which, in this case, meant another Montreal goal. Lori was ruffling through her purse looking for her rosary beads.

Eve and Christine put their heads in their hands. Uttered quiet "oh no's".

Eric up in the corporate box maintained a poker face.

The kids over at Bianca's stopped dancing and jumping up and down - having already started the celebration -

looked at each other, and, as kids who are too young to understand nuance, who see the world largely as black and white, immediately thought the end of the world was around the corner.

Bella and her mother were making California rolls along a shiny kitchen top. Mozart's Piano Concerto No. 27 in B Flat Major played softly in the background.

Steve sat calmly next to his wife. Whatever happened, as long as no one got hurt, it was all good as far as he was concerned.

'Woo hoo hoo!' I said. 'Don't look now, here come the Russkies!'

'It ain't over til the fat lady sings!' said Peach.

'You can say that again,' said Ged.

'Now's not the time to panic boys,' said Hutchie, who, aside from the players themselves and the Leaf coach, was probably the coolest cat in the building. 'Nothing to worry about, now, just be smart. Keep playing the way we've been playing all game long.'

As play resumed, a spontaneous chant of 'Go Leafs Go!' started up, first a bit spottily but very quickly everyone in the arena was into it. Even Steve. It was deafening. It was exhilarating. Hands were clapped. Feet were stamped. 'Go Leafs Go! Go Leafs Go!'

Gazing into shop windows or standing in corner stores and shebeens across the streets of Ouagadougou, Dakar and Yaoundé puzzled Africans looked at each other and asked, 'Qu'est ce que c'est 'Go Leafs Go'?' Whatever it meant, this crazy game was tros excitant, just too damned exciting.

With a minute to go, the Habs' coach pulled Brambory. The face-off was deep in the Leaf zone, to the right of Andrew, on his stick side. Logan was in on the draw. The Leaf coach had pulled Shakey off the line and replaced him with Channer, making sure that if Logan got waved out, he'd have his second best faceoff artist out there in the form of FC. But there was no need to worry, as Logan won the draw cleanly back to Horton who quickly turned with the puck and retreated behind his own net, two cosmonauts right on top of him. Horton shoveled the puck along the back boards to Pronovost who got as far as the hash marks on the far side before he was pasted to the boards by Popovich. But he was protecting the puck with his skates and the Habs, despite their efforts, failed to dislodge it. The whistle blew. Forty-five seconds left. The whole play had taken only fifteen seconds. For Leaf fans everywhere it was like time was standing still. Pure agony. The little clock up in the left corner of their TV screens teasing them mercilessly with its maddening tick... tick... tick.

'Mother of God please please please let the time run out,' said Christine, staring up at the jumbotron that hung hauntingly over the ice, like the giant spacecraft in ET, its illuminated time clock a menacing sight.

Once again, Logan stepped in to take the draw, this time to the left of Andrew along the far boards. In a pre-set play that they'd worked on day after day after day, Logan tied up Titov's stick, turned his big body into the Montreal player and kicked the puck back to Pronovost. Instead of retreating with the puck, Pronovost turned and fired a slap shot around back of his own net. PK2 hustled over to the near boards, blocking the puck from leaving the zone with his shinpads as he crashed sideways into the boards in front of the Leaf bench. The puck rebounded off his pads and as PK2 reached for it, Wiener beat him to it, chipping it off the glass and out. The crowd breathed a sigh of relief, but immediately became very animated. The puck landed on the Leaf side of centre and bounced once before being collected on his backhand by a hard driving Casher who, Mahovlich style, pushed off once with a powerful right leg, and swooped down toward the empty Montreal goal. PK1 and a passel of Russians gave mad chase. The crowd roared and stood as one.

Down at the Ryerson Centre the crowd also stood as one. Across the Leaf universe the people stood as one. In front of TV sets in family rooms and man caves, garages and back rooms, in bars and restaurants, in hospitals and old folks homes, in Tim Hortons everywhere they watched in seeming disbelief as their mighty captain, Logan Cash, calmly slid the puck home into an open net to cement the Maple Leafs victory. 3-1 Toronto.

'Game, set, match,' said Hutchie just as pandemonium struck. It was a happy raucous disorder, a cheerful bubbly sort of chaos, as the world as we had known it for seven long decades was suddenly turned upside down. After all, the Leafs, yes, the Leafs, were on top of the hockey world. 20-19-18, the clock ticked down. The

Habs had conceded defeat, 12-11-10. No one challenged Keon as he took the puck and turned back toward his own end, passed it to Ellis who passed it to Horton who stood behind his net, looked over at his defense partner, Pronovost, and listened to the crowd count off the seconds. 3-2-1 and wild cheers, tears, hugs, and kisses all around.

The Toronto Maples Leafs were, at long last, and once again, Stanley Cup Champions.

59.

The scenes were very familiar to hockey fans around the world. The NHL Commissioner, Gary Bettman Jr., booed by everyone as part of a long and glorious tradition that began with his father who, in the words of the Iron Sheik, was a world class jabroni, making a speech listened to by no one. The Commissioner then calling forth the winner of the Conn Smythe Trophy, in this case it being the Leaf netminder, Andrew 'Billy Goat' Cash. The fans at the Samsung-Blackberry Centre baa-aad long and loud for their man, a most deserving winner in the eyes of one and all. And then the Commissioner calling forth the Leaf captain, Logan Cash, shaking his hand in congratulations and handing over to him Lord Stanley's Cup, the photo op lasting a full minute. But then the moment we hockey fans always wait for: the lightly bearded captain - our Logan never was very hairy - wearing his freshly minted 'Toronto Maple Leafs: Stanley Cup Champions' ball-cap (made in China), hoisting the massive silverware into the air and commencing the happy skate around the rink. The Leaf faithful couldn't get enough of the celebration. Like bears emerging from an especially long winter, they were ravenously hungry for more and more and more. More skate arounds. More rinkside interviews. Ron McLean reminding Logan that he'd once interviewed him for Hockey Day in Canada in Halifax way back when Logan was a major midget.

'Do you remember that interview, Logan?' asked Ron.

'I sure do, Ron. We talked about the importance of teammates. And what I said then, more than twenty years ago, is just as appropriate now. It's nothing we all don't already know. Hockey's a team sport. You win as a team, you lose as a team. And without your teammates, you are nothing. You're a man alone. And we know how far that will getcha not only in a team sport but in life. And, well, no matter what, no matter how well or bad things are going, you just pull together, keep 'er goin'.'

'Well said, Logan. "Just keep 'er goin'". So, you waited almost an entire career to be part of a Stanley Cup Champion, is there anyone you'd like to mention as being central to your team? I mean other than the obvious: your Leaf teammates.'

'There are too many to mention, Ron, but if I have to single anybody out I'd have to start with my parents who've always been there for both me and my brother, and, really, for anybody who needed help or support of any kind.'

Logan began to look around, he was happy, but his commitment to this process was beginning to wane. Ron, ever the veteran reporter, picked up on it and simply said, 'Thanks for the time, Logan. Go and have some fun.' Logan said 'Thanks Ron', and as he skated away, Ron's words echoing in the loudspeakers scattered throughout the arena, the crowd clapped and cheered. Logan adjusted his ballcap and waved.

And so it went long into the night. The Leafs and their loved ones partied long and hard. The Cup was filled with champagne, emptied then filled again. Everything and everybody was covered in a lightly sticky boozy sheen as corks were popped and bubbly was sprayed and spilled in joyous celebration. The broadcasts had long ended, and the media long been sent away, by the time the players finally scattered and made their own separate ways to their homes and beds. None would get any sleep. They were too excited for that. But each eventually would lay there quietly to reflect on the year that was, the team that was, and the playoff that was. How it all added up just right. For once in a lifetime.

60.

Three weeks had passed since the Leaf victory. Life had more or less returned to normal, at least for me. The hospital was behind me, though a long rehab lay in front of me. That's where I was headed when my device rang. I was on the bus. The old biddy across the way, looked over at me like an old school teacher who'd just caught a pupil sticking their gum under their desk. Really, lady? I stared back at her. Cellphones had been ringing on buses for at least 30 years by now. Anyway, I listened to a bit of crackle on the line before I managed to say 'Hello?'

'Hello, Jack. It's me. Your wife, Mary Adams.'

Why she insisted on this sort of introduction every time she phoned me always puzzled me. Who else would be my wife? Was she practicing for when the senile dementia kicked in? 'Yes, dear. How are you?' I said.

'I'm great, Jack, really great.'

'Really, Mary Adams? What makes you so great, eh?' I teased.

'We have a breakthrough.'

'What? What sort of breakthrough? When are you coming home anyway?' I whined, only half faking it.

'In the peace process. Our folks here have signed an agreement. We're composing the press release right now.'

'To say what? That there's going to be "Peace in the Middle East"?' I let out a chortle which got old cranky pants' attention again. I stared her down forcing her back to her e-reader. What a loser, I thought. No one uses that crap anymore. Paper is where it's at.

'Yes, Jack. There will be peace in the Middle East. Don't you think that's fastastic?'

'What makes you so confident this time, anyway?' I asked. 'There's been a thousand of these agreements before. Half the bloody Nobel Peace Prize winners come from this part of the world. How do you know there will never be peace in a place? Someone there wins a Nobel Peace Prize, that's how.'

'No, no, no. You've got it all wrong. At least this time. It'll be different.'

'What gives you such hope.'

'The Leafs won the Stanley Cup didn't they?'

'Ya, and…?'

'Both the Arabs and the Israelis know that the day there'd be peace in the Middle East is the day the Toronto Maple Leafs won the Stanley Cup.'

'Hallelujah,' I said. 'Let's book a winter holiday to Tel Aviv.'

'See you in two days, my sweet.'

'It'll be good to have you home,' I said, and that was the understatement of the Century.

61.

It was Andrew's turn with the Cup. Traditionally each player on the winning team gets the Cup for a day. The doorbell rang. Maggie ran to answer it, violin and bow in hand. 'Hey, dad! Hey, dad! There's some guy here with white gloves and a big box,' she hollered. It was Kevin Shea, surely the oldest Cup minder in the history of the NHL.

'Good morning Mr. Cash, I'm here with your Stanley Cup,' said Kevin.

'Nice, thanks, come on in,' said Andrew. 'Have a seat. Cuppa tea?'

Andrew had given a lot of thought as to what he should do over the course of the day with 'his' Cup. The twins started things off in the henhouse, wheeling Lord Stanley's Mug down there in their little red wagon, collecting the morning's layings and placing them carefully in the Cup. They then wheeled the Cup back up to the house. 'Hey dad, look at all the eggs that can fit in the Cup!' they shouted. Next up, was the milking of the goats.

62.

Logan had given a great deal of thought to his career. Thirty-eight. A young man by most measures, except in professional sports where he was officially a dinosaur. And he felt stone-aged too. The Cup run had taken a great deal out of the old body. He ached everywhere. Getting out of bed in the morning was the hardest part. His Achilles was so stiff and tender that a half step was a whole lotta pain. The little table beside his bed looked like the back shelf at a pharmacy. He had hard-core painkillers prescribed by the team doctor. He also had a little marijuana baked into cookies which Wiener and Shakey swore by. Maybe this stuff worked, would get him over the hump, the oxycodone or oxycontin or whatever it was, but he didn't want to end up a junkie, addicted to the shit. And weed was never his thing either. Made him sleepy and hungry. The last thing he wanted to be was a fat slacker. A Stanley Cup Champion. No one could ever take that away from him. Perhaps the best thing to do was go out on top. Bjorn Borg style. The saddest thing to see is a celebrated athlete hang around and hang around, team management unwilling to pull the plug on some aging icon - like Willie Mays for example - but wishing the dude would see the light, smell the coffee, get on the bus and go home to do some fishing. Or hang around until you get hurt and end up in a wheelchair or worse, 'punchy' like some old fighter, swinging your fists whenever you hear the phone ring. Nope. Time to get out. Hang up the skates. Competitively anyway.

Logan had spent a lot of time over the last three weeks keeping Bella company. Yesterday was Logan's day with the Cup and he simply brought it over to the butcher shop and plopped it on a table over near the cash register right in front of the window. Mr. Dowhaniuk had placed a hastily composed and computer printed sign in the window, 'Stanley Cup Special: take picture with Cup and get 20% off your choice of meat'. Below the sign he had hand printed: 'Meet Mr Cash, Leaf Captin'. Logan spent the day chatting to thousands of people, having his picture taken, signing autographs and just hanging out. What with his sore Achilles and all, this seemed the most sensible thing to do: get a chair, put it near the Cup, sit and stand, sit and stand, hobble around a bit, excuse himself every once in a while to go in the back to take a pill or a bite of cookie.

The night of the Cup win, he had texted Bella: 'we won'. She texted back: 'I saw. Congratulations'. This was not quite the truth, but close enough. In Bella's view, how much of a hockey game did you need to watch anyway? A few minutes here or there it seemed to her was more than enough. He'd arranged to see her the following morning for coffee at her place in Caledon. He didn't want to risk an unannounced appearance in a public place without first getting the 'OK' from the higher ups. Management had arranged a formal media briefing for mid-afternoon.

Over at Bella's, the day after the Cup win, they had coffee and scones out on the veranda. The Airport Road traffic whizzed by almost non-stop some hundred, hundred and fifty, metres away. Logan was thankful for the gap, and for the presence of a number of fully grown blue spruce scattered around the property which soaked up both the CO_2 and the noise. He thought of how this house reminded him of his aunt and uncle's place in Irish Cove, which used to belong to Mary Adams' mom and dad, his grandparents. The big porch. The highway. The extensive property. 'The only thing missing is the Bras d'Or,' he said out loud.

'Excuse me?' Bella said.

'I was just thinking about how much this place reminds me of home. The Maritimes. Cape Breton. Minus the water, of course.' Logan thought this remark very funny, and laughed a bit.

'Do you miss the Maritimes?' She asked.

'Sometimes. Not often. I've lived away for so long. Besides, I go back every summer. Play golf, swim, fish. Visit my buddies.'

'Will you go back this summer?'

'Probably. I don't see why not. Maybe you'd like to come for a visit.' Logan perked at this idea, sat up out of his usual front porch slouch.

'That'd be very nice,' she said. 'I'd have to work it out with my mom, of course. She can't handle the catering on her own.' They each sipped at their coffees, nibbled at their cakes, remained quiet for a bit.

She had nothing to say about the hockey. About the "big victory". She did seem to register his limp, but said nothing about it. He loved this about her. Here is a person who lived life without hockey. And she was perfectly content. In the parochial world that is "all hockey all the time", such a person was surely a freak. But there was nothing freakish about Bella. Thirty-something Canadian business woman, obviously good at what she does, with lots of interests outside of the sports world, genial, attractive and intelligent. OK, the sense of humour he would have to work on, but otherwise, as far as Logan could tell, this was no "Fatal Attraction". Suddenly, Logan felt the deep bone ache of a body too often in motion, suddenly at rest, at peace, with nowhere to go and nothing to do. And, best of all, no giant Russian or Slovenian or Czech breathing down your neck ready to put you into the hospital should you turn one way rather than another. He lifted his mug, took a deep draught, felt the slight bitterness at the back of his throat. Offset it with a bite of scone sweetened with clotted cream and strawberry jam, all homemade. This, he thought, is my Stanley Cup party, right here.

'Do you like to hike?' Bella asked.

There was a short pause. Then Logan said, 'Sure... what?... now?'

This made Bella laugh. He laughed too, more for the pure pleasure of sitting out on a porch with good company, nowhere to go, and nothing else to do. Not wanting to do anything else.

'Not now silly,' she said.

'Good. I'm a bit sore still eh.' He placed his hands on the arms of the big yellow Adirondack chair, lifted himself up slightly, shifted position and groaned.

'Yes, I can see that.'

It was perhaps another five minutes before anybody said anything or made a move. They were simply happy in each other's company.

Logan thought a lot about his brief, but meaningful - so it seemed to him anyway - moments with Bella. He was not the sort of guy to make a snap judgement, a rash decision. But, well, 'the early bird gets the worm', his grandpa Charlie used to say. Which meant, in this case, that Logan would shop his idea for 'retirement' to Bella. Make no mistake, all of the attention from the Cup win was gratifying, he'd had a good year and a great playoff - a true captain's playoff - and now there was a lot of pressure on him to commit to another year. He'd been playing year by year now for a while, signing single-year contracts with the Leafs, happy to stay and play but wanting to be free to go if either he or they felt that to be the right thing to do. From the Leafs perspective, any player 35 years of age or over would only be offered a one-year contract. Hockey is a business, not a charity, or home for the aged. Fair enough, thought Logan. He'd make his formal announcement after he'd talked to Bella which, as he creaked around his kitchen, would be shortly after the drugs kicked in and he no longer resembled Frankenstein's Monster.

Over at Andrew's, the Cup, Bianca and the two older boys were being prepared for a day at Granite Ridge which was the Cash home course. Andrew was hosting a golf outing with his family and friends and for whichever teammates were still around and wanting to play a round under the public eye. Pressure from club management - both the Maple Leafs and Granite Ridge - ensured that there'd be more than the usual number of hangers on, local dignitaries and whatnot. Logan had said 'thanks, but no thanks', and Andrew knew that something was up. Rare is the occasion when Logan turns down a chance to golf with any of his extended family.

It was around 1030 in the morning by the time Logan felt confident enough to go out in public. He knew that the bulk of the media and other sorts of attention would be turned toward his brother and his day with the Cup. He would be under no particular scrutiny while accompanying Bella on her daily round of shopping. This meant a trip in to old Toronto and a gander around first St Lawrence Market and then through China Town. Logan offered to be the chauffeur.

'It's not too late to go to the markets is it?' asked Logan.

'No, a little late maybe, but not a tragedy,' said Bella. 'Maybe the best stuff is already gone, but as the day goes on the bargains begin to emerge.' She smiled a wry smile and winked at Logan, indicating that a new sort of game was about to begin.

'OK, then,' said Logan. 'Let the game begin!'

They had a lot of fun at each market where the dominant presence of ethnic and new immigrant communities meant that no one knew that Logan was front page news around the world. Captained by Logan Cash, the Little Engine that Could, aka the underdog Toronto Maple Leafs, had managed to finally lift a seven decade-old curse and emerge as kings of the professional hockey world. Ho hum. '$2.49 fo kilogram,' said the grocer. 'You must be kidding,' said Logan. 'No. You no like. You shop somewhere else.' Logan smirked, thought to himself, 'this is a game I could get to like.'

63.

Another day, another bus ride. And another phone call. I survey the blue heads that surround me and debate whether to answer my device thereby risking the wrath of the passengers on this geriatric express. 'Hello?' I say.

'He-ello, Jack?' There's a crackle on the phone. Long distance again.

'Yes. Who's this?'

'It's Ruth, in Maun.'

My old bruised ticker knocks out a bit of Phil Collins. 'Hi Ruth!' I say excitedly, and a bit too loudly. Dozing heads pop up around me, turn in my direction, but I don't care. 'Good to hear from you. How have you been?'

'Sandy's gone.'

'What? Where?'

'Dead. And gone,' she says with emphasis.

'How? What happened?'

'He'd been sick for a long time. Cancer. I mean, well, he is, er, was, 90.'

I tried picturing Sandy at 90. I hadn't seen them in twenty years. Back then he had skin like boot leather. He probably looked every inch the bushman at 90, like my old friend Roy Sesana.

'I'm sorry to hear that Ruth.'

'A croc took him.'

'What?'

'Ya. That's the way he wanted to go. Rather than endure the whole ordeal of chemo and all that. He said it was time to die. You know him. Anyway, the river's really high right now, so late last night he said "OK this is it", took a bottle of vodka and some dagga with him down to the water.'

'Wow,' was all I could muster.

'Ya, I know. His last words to me were "I love ya Ruthie. See ya in the next world".'

'So, how do you know a croc got him?'

'You know how it is here. For years there'd been a big croc coming back with the floods. We lost a lot of neighborhood dogs to that old guy. None of ours though. We had that big croc-proof gate, remember?'

I could remember. Their property fronted on the Thamalakane River, an outflow of the Okavango Delta. Sandy had built one structure after another over the years. In the end the place looked a bit like a mid-range safari camp, like Oddballs or something like that.

Mukwa Leaf Gardens was on the other side of the main house, up toward the road. I had a sudden pang of longing mixed with some kind of regret. This happens all the time when you're old. You're always missing this or that, wishing you had said goodbye to so and so, or gone and visited 'x' one last time. But you don't. Life gets in the way of itself. Ties you up in knots. Binds you to the here and now. And, in my case, with my 'dicky ticker', to a man bag full of blood thinners and who knows what other drugs, public transport, a bus pass and a date with old squeaky shoes at the hospital.

'Thanks for letting me know, Ruth. How's everyone else, by the way?'

'The family is great. Charlie's long taken over from Sandy, handed most things off to his son now. Lena's some big shot photographer in L.A. The New York Times called her "The Annie Liebowitz of her generation", whoever Annie Liebowitz is... or was.'

'And you?'

'Oh, you know me. I'm a Scot. I'm made of very stern stuff.'

'So was Sandy. It's a wonder a croc would take the old bird. Too tough to chew, I would have thought.' We had a brief chuckle, said our goodbyes, promised to talk again soon, but I knew that was unlikely to happen. There was that sudden pang again, but this time it felt like it was in my arm. I was starting to feel very uncomfortable on the bus. Rang the bell. Decided to walk for a bit. Thought that I should give Ged, Hutchie and Peach a ring while I was at it. My sister too.

64.

Logan announced his decision to retire just as he had planned. It surprised his dad, not so much his mom. Christine could see it in her son's eyes, that he'd had enough, that it was time for something else. Steve wondered at the passage of time, said to his wife, 'One down, one to go.' Pretty soon I'll be free and clear to start wearing my Guy Lafleur jersey again. Christine stared daggers at him from across the kitchen.

When the announcement came, Bianca and Andrew were out for a round of golf. They were on the 12th hole of the Ruby Course, a beautiful little par 3 with water all down the right side.

'What're you hittin'?' Andrew asked. They played off the tips together. Bianca carried a 4-handicap; Andrew was off of scratch.

'Eight iron,' she said.

'Really? From 162? What are you, part gorilla?' mocked Andrew.

'It's clean living, my boy, clean living.'

Logan had informed them ahead of time, said that he had new plans. Bianca said 'good for you'; said 'good for him' to his mom and dad. She had a theory about change, that change was the one constant in life and that we should embrace it, not fight it or run from it. She addressed the ball, settled herself, and let one fly.

65.

Following the press conference, Logan drove over to the butcher shop where Bella was holding down the fort. Mr. Dowhaniuk was out sick again and had rung Bella in the morning to see if she was able to come in.

The little bell ding-dinged as Logan walked in, smiled his shy smile.

'Hi,' he said.

'Hi. What's up?'

'Well, it's done. I'm straight from the press conference.'

'How do you feel about it?'

'Good, good. Yep,' he said, the last word uttered with a little intake of breath, like the Maritimer he was and would remain no matter where he went in life.

'So, what's next?'

'That's exactly what everybody was asking me, what everybody's been asking me. Mom and dad. Andrew.'

'Well, then?'

'Well,' said Logan, pausing to gather his thoughts, look at the meat in the display case. 'What I am thinking is this. I buy the butcher shop from Mr. Dowhaniuk. With you. Partners.'

'What? Really? Why?'

'Why not? I talked to the old guy last week and he said he's more than ready to sell and retire, move to Florida or Arizona. And you and me, well, I just have a good feeling about us. A really good feeling.'

'Do you really want to tie yourself to a butcher shop? You could do anything you want, the world is a big place, you know.'

'I know it's a big place. And I want a place in it. I want you in it with me. Teammates like. You and me, we make a good team.' Logan shrugged at the sappiness of his own self.

Bella blushed, looked away from Logan for just a second, then looked back at him. 'A butcher shop?'

'Not any butcher shop, or just a butcher shop!' Logan started to get excited, animated. 'We could expand, buy the bakery next door too, make this the face of your catering business. Our business. Bring your mom in on it for sure. Rebrand. "Wholesome Joe's", "Logan and Bella's Wheatgrass Emporium",' he chuckled. 'Or something. You get the picture,' said Logan nodding his head, encouraging Bella to nod hers too.

'Are you sure you want to stay here?' she asked, wrinkling her nose at him.

'Yes, why not? Anyway, this can be the start. This can be where I learn the ropes. You can teach me. You have been teaching me, anyway, every time we go down to the market. After we're successful we could open a branch in the Maritimes, in St Peter's or Big Pond. Big Bad Halifax even. Have a meat stand out on the highway in Irish Cove!' He laughed madly at the idea. 'Or we just stay here. Go slow. See what we see.'

Bella looked skeptical, but really she was just in a bit of shock. This proposal had taken her completely by surprise. 'A butcher shop?' she said again.

'You keep saying that. Yes, a butcher shop. And other things too. We can be as big or as small as we want. Pete's Frootique for the environmental-set; greens for the greens; green beef imported from Botswana!' Logan was totally into it, the ideas leaving him a bit tongue tied. He waved his arms around, shook his hands, smacked his lips, knitted his eyebrows together, trying to think of a way to help her see the vision he had for himself, and for them, that was so clear in his own head.

'Like Tim Hortons,' she said.

'What?' said Logan.

'Like Tim Hortons. He was a hockey player. Just like you. Though he never made "captain", she teased, swaying her shoulders and pursing her lips as if to say "Mr Big Shot".'

'Yes, yes. Go on,' said Logan.

'So Tim Horton started with one coffee shop and now look at him. A symbol of Canada. The place where the melting pot goes to meet. Where Christians and Muslims can both agree, the coffee is just OK, but that's the Canadian way.' She laughed at her own thought.

'Exactly! Old Timmie started with coffee. And I'll start with meat! I mean, we'll start with meat, and a bit of catering,' exclaimed Logan, 'and, your mom.' He went in behind the counter and grasped Bella's shoulders lightly with his big hands, stared into her eyes, gazed in earnest at her upturned face. She's so beautiful, he thought. 'So, whattaya say?' he asked.

'I say... OK!'

Logan picked Bella up in a big bear hug and kissed her on the lips, twirled her around as best as he could without bumping into anything. They were laughing and smiling, wondering at the possibilities of a life after hockey. The little bell dinged and an old woman shuffled in.

'May we help you?' they said in unison.

-The End-

ALTERNATIVE ENDING:
FOR LEAF HATERS AND THE HARD OF HEART

66.

With 45 seconds left to play, Logan stepped in to take the draw, this time to the left of Andrew along the far boards. In a pre-set play that they'd worked on day after day after day, Logan tied up Titov's stick, turned his big body into the Montreal player and kicked the puck back to Pronovost. Instead of retreating with the puck, Pronovost turned and fired a slap shot around back of his own net. PK2 hustled over to the near boards, blocking the puck from leaving the zone with his shinpads as he crashed sideways into the boards in front of the Leaf bench. The puck rebounded off his pads and as PK2 reached for it, Wiener beat him to it, chipping it off the glass and out. The crowd breathed a sigh of relief, but immediately became very animated. The puck landed on the Leaf side of centre and bounced once before being collected on his backhand by a hard driving Casher who, Mahovlich style, pushed off once with a powerful right leg, and swooped down toward the empty Montreal goal. PK1 and a passel of Russians gave mad chase. The crowd roared and stood as one.

Down at the Ryerson Centre the crowd also stood as one. Across the Leaf universe the people stood as one. In front of TV sets in family rooms and man caves, garages and back rooms, in bars and restaurants, in hospitals and old folks homes, in Tim Hortons everywhere they watched in seeming disbelief as their mighty captain, Logan Cash, caught from behind by the speeding train that is Bykovsky, lost the puck, slipped on the Habs' players stick blade and crashed hard into the boards.

'That can't be good,' said Hutchie just as pandemonium struck. The whistle blew. The crowd bayed for blood, for the head of the Russian on a stick. Logan writhed on the ice in pain, clutching at his ankle. The Leaf trainers were out on the ice before the whistle had even gone. Eventually a stretcher was brought out and Logan, never one to show weakness, was forced to submit to be carried off the ice. And even though the crowd clapped, they all knew that whatever the outcome of this particular game and this particular series, Logan Cash would play no further part in it.

Just as Bobby (call me 'Bob') Clarke's slash on Valery Kharlamov in the 1972 Summit Series sent the Soviet's for a spin, so too did the loss of Logan Cash badly impact the Leafs. On the ensuing faceoff, Tench went straight at Lopatou, cross checking the Montreal player hard across his right arm, before dropping his gloves and pounding the Hab into the ice, flooring him with a right cross, left hook combination. The Tench boys could really fight. But while the sentiment was right, the timing was badly wrong. When the dust had settled, the Leafs found themselves shorthanded for the rest of the game. The faceoff came back out to centre ice. And it was from there that the titanic collapse began.

Titov won the draw back to PK1 who fired across to PK2 who gained the centre line and fired the puck in. It was hunted down by Popovich who passed to Bykovsky who passed to Titov who scored. Yep, just like that. 2-2 with 35 seconds to play in regulation. Andrew's focus was off. His brother had just been carted off the ice on a stretcher. The boys were not twins, but they had been together for so long, and been through so much together that Andrew seemed to be suffering some sort of empathetic response. He began to ache all over. He barely made a move toward the puck before it went past him. He was suddenly listless, punchy, feeling sort of in another world, like an epileptic in a heightened state pre-seizure. Except there was no seizure. There was just this weird feeling that Andrew couldn't shake. The Leaf coach could see that something was wrong, called timeout, brought Andrew over to the bench.

'What is it Billy? You OK?' the coach asked Andrew.

'Whuh?'

The trainers were called in to have a look, said there was nothing obvious, but it was like he'd suffered a concussion. The symptoms were similar. What to do? What to do? What the coach did was sit Andrew down, put Sudsie into the game. Which was hardly fair on the back-up netminder, who'd seen no game action since the first round. But it didn't matter. The coach could have put anybody in net and it wouldn't have helped. The Leafs came apart like a house of cards. They fell like dominoes. First Logan, then Andrew, then the whole team followed. Oh, they put up a fight. Make no mistake. The game went into overtime. Long into overtime. Eighteen minutes and thirty five seconds to be exact. That was when Popovich scored the winning goal, a golden goal for Montreal but sudden-death for the Toronto Maple Leafs.

You can imagine the headlines the next day: Leafs Collapse - Everything Back To Normal. I also collapsed. On the steps up out of the place. Another major heart attack. I guess I should have figured that sitting so close to the ice would have its consequences. All those steps. Better the elevator up to the corporate box and then back down. I should have listened to Ged. And now I'm in an ambulance en route to the same damn hospital and Ms. Squeaky Shoes is going to see that I'm wearing some well-soaked depends. How embarrassing.

The Ryerson Centre was like a morgue where 25,000 specialists were now gathered to conduct a post mortem. My sister, the former nurse, just shook her head, felt the slightly ticklish trickle of hot tears down her dry cheeks. Over at the Samsung-Blackberry Centre, folks filed out stony faced, and like medieval gargoyles they looked down upon each other in utter silence.

67.

The day off didn't help. The entire team moped around like men on death row.

Over at Andrew's, the twins came in from the henhouse, their little baskets empty. -Dad! -Mom! The hens have stopped laying eggs! they shouted.

'Keep it down, kids,' said Bianca. 'Your father's got a very bad headache.'

In the same hospital as me, but over in a different ward, Logan received the news: ruptured Achilles; compound fracture of the ankle. With any luck, he'd be back on blades in time for his 40th birthday. 'Well, that's the end of my hockey career', he said to himself.

There's nothing like a Game 7 of the Stanley Cup Finals. This is it. The big show. And in Montreal. Hockey's mecca, where millions have travelled to worship at the shrine that is Les Habitants. Too bad for the Leafs. This is the one game they wanted to avoid. The Habs could smell blood. Andrew had not travelled with the team, been referred to a specialist down in Florida. Logan was in hospital. They were leaderless at the front;

rudderless at the back. A floundering ship about to be rent on the rocks that is the Bell Centre in Montreal.

The Leafs gave it their best shot, but it wasn't good enough. They were outskated, outplayed and outscored by a whirling, twirling dervish of a team. Let's be honest. It was a route. 6-0 Habs. Titov the Conn Smythe winner. The Montreal Canadiens the Stanley Cup Champions of 2036-37. Oh the pain of being a Maple Leaf supporter. To see all of that red and white skate around with Lord Stanley's Cup. Well, it was just too much for the Leaf faithful to take. As the score went up, TV sets had turned over to one reality show after another, first in the thousands, then in the hundred thousands, then worldwide in the millions. This was no feel good story. This was just a fact of life.

In the hospital, the phone rang. The big ugly landline phone. I picked it up, croaked out a 'he-e-llo'.

'Hello, Jack. This is Mary Adams, your wife. Mary Adams?'

'Yes, yes, yes,' I rasped with a great deal of impatience. 'What is it now?'

'I'm sorry to hear you are back in the hospital, Jack.'

'Ya, well...'

'I've got bad news.'

'More? What might it be this time?'

'We've got no peace deal. The Israelis walked out. The Arab League has declared war. Netanyahu says they'll use the bomb if they have to.'

I sighed. Hung up without saying goodbye.

That night, over in Georgetown, a fire had started in the bakery, spread to the butchery. The entire annex burned to the ground.

ANNEX
The 2036-37 Toronto Maple Leafs:

Coach: The Coach

The Forwards:

Donny Ellis (Ellie), Ian Keon (Wee Ian; Keener), Nazim Kadri Jr. (Naz, Kads) (the Kid Line)

Willy (Shakey) Walton, Logan Cash (Casher), Wayne (Wiener) Morris

Peyton Tench Jr. (PJ, Jammer), Frank Chan (FC, Channer), Chris Ireland (Buddy I)

John Pappin (Papps) - replaced by Keney Dramiuc (KD, Drams, Dramer), Donald Hutchison (Hutchie), The Big Swede

On Defence:

Rene Pronovost (Frenchie), Elliot Horton (Horts, the Yank) (no relation to Tim)

Richard Shaw (rikshaw), Sam Prince (Popper)

Guy Morgan (Gee, Morgs), Jack Kell (Keller)

In Goal:

Andrew Cash (Billy)

Wayne Sutherland IV (Sudsie)

ABOUT THE AUTHOR

Larry Swatuk was born in Riverside, Ontario, a small town swallowed up by Windsor in 1967. Like many Canadian boys of his generation, he dreamed of a career in the NHL. And, like most Canadians of all generations, that did not happen. Nevertheless, he has managed to play some version of hockey - be it ice or inline - in different leagues at different levels on three continents. And he has happily watched many of his friends make it to the big time, both in North America and Europe. He keeps a day job as an academic, plying his trade at the University of Waterloo, in Waterloo, Ontario. He is married to Dr. Corrine Cash and they live for most of the year in Kitchener/Waterloo, but spend large chunks of their time in Africa and Europe. In the late 1980s he was awarded the Joseph Howe Prize for Poetry at Dalhousie University. In the intervening 35 years he has written and published a great many things, but this book is his first work of fiction.

CONNECT WITH THE AUTHOR

The author can be reached in many different ways. He can be found at the following web-pages:

https://uwaterloo.ca/international-development/people-profiles/larry-swatuk

www.africaportal.org/person/larry-swatuk

www.balsillieschool.ca/people/larry-swatuk

His email is swatukinthebushes@yahoo.com

His skype address is larry.swatuk

Printed in Great Britain
by Amazon

26012960R00202